NETWORKING THE RULE OF LAW

Studies in Modern Law and Policy

Series Editor: Ralf Rogowski,
Professor of Law, University of Warwick

Also in the series

Social Systems Theory and Judicial Review
Taking Jurisprudence Seriously
Katayoun Baghai
ISBN: 978-1-4094-5402-1

The EU Economic and Social Model in the Global Crisis
Interdisciplinary Perspectives
Edited by Dagmar Schiek
ISBN: 978-1-4094-5731-2

Constitutional Evolution in Central and Eastern Europe
Expansion and Integration in the EU
Edited by Kyriaki Topidi and Alexander H.E. Morawa
ISBN: 978-1-4094-0327-2

Central and Eastern Europe After Transition
Towards a New Socio-legal Semantics
Edited by Alberto Febbrajo and Wojciech Sadurski
ISBN: 978-1-4094-0390-6

Democracy, Law and Governance
Jacques Lenoble and Marc Maesschalck
ISBN: 978-1-4094-0395-1

Judicial Accountabilities in New Europe
From Rule of Law to Quality of Justice
Daniela Piana
ISBN: 978-0-7546-7758-1

The European Social Model and Transitional Labour Markets
Law and Policy
Edited by Ralf Rogowski
ISBN: 978-0-7546-4958-8

Networking the Rule of Law
How Change Agents Reshape Judicial Governance in the EU

CRISTINA DALLARA
Italian National Research Council

and

DANIELA PIANA
University of Bologna, Italy and Associate Fellow at the Institut des Hautes Etudes sur la Justice in Paris, France

Routledge
Taylor & Francis Group
LONDON AND NEW YORK

First published 2015 by Ashgate Publishing

2 Park Square, Milton Park, Abingdon, Oxfordshire OX14 4RN
711 Third Avenue, New York, NY 10017

Routledge is an imprint of the Taylor & Francis Group, an informa business

First issued in paperback 2017

British Library Cataloguing in Publication Data
A catalogue record for this book is available from the British Library

The Library of Congress has cataloged the printed edition as follows:
Dallara, Cristina, author.
Networking the rule of law: how change agents reshape judicial governance in the EU / by Cristina Dallara and Daniela Piana.
pages cm. – (Studies in modern law and policy)
Includes bibliographical references and index.
ISBN 978-1-4094-3305-7 (hardback : alk. paper)
1. Rule of law—European Union countries. 2. Political questions and judicial power—European Union countries. 3. International and municipal law—European Union countries. I. Piana, Daniela, author. II. Title.
KJC4426.D35 2015
340'.11–dc23

2014049125

ISBN 978-1-4094-3305-7 (hbk)
ISBN 978-1-138-56414-5 (pbk)

To those who gently watch and move beyond the boundaries

Contents

List of Figures and Tables

Figures

Tables

List of Fiches and Boxes

Fiches

Boxes

Acknowledgments

The work we present here is the outcome of three research projects, conducted over the last six years, and in pursuit of two goals: to cast light on a new phenomenon—judicial networks—and to assess the effects this phenomenon might have for the administration of justice in Europe. Those projects focused on three different levels of analysis: individuals (judicial actors), organizations (judicial offices, judicial schools, and constitutional courts), and networks. The feasibility of integrating the results of these three projects and using them as three different streams of knowledge, putting under the spotlight what we call here "networking the rule of law" is possible due to the fact that the ideas and the practice of the research conducted by the two authors come from a long-lasting friendship and a common scientific background inspiring the entire scientific enterprise presented here.

As always in the case of a research-based publication, this volume would not have come to light without the constant and qualified support of all the institutions which are in one way or another involved in the policies of judicial cooperation mentioned herein. We express our sincere gratitude to the Commission for Democracy throughout Law, widely known as the Venice Commission, and to the CEPEJ, the CCJE, and the CCPE for the interest, encouraging dialogue and exchange they have offered us in our research during the years in which the different research projects whose results are reflected in this book were carried out. Especial thanks are warmly addressed to the President of the Venice Commission, Gianni Buquicchio, to Tatjiana Michelova (PR Office), professor Sergio Bartole and professor Neppi Modona (Italian members), and to Muriel Decot for CEPEJ.

Data collection and science vs institutions dialogue are just a part—and yet crucial of course—of such an undertaking. The preliminary work developed along the way has been discussed at a considerably large number of seminars, panels, and workshops, where we had the chance to meet great scholars, colleagues, and friends, all of whom made suggestions, and offered constructive criticism and constant fruitful interaction. It would be impossible to name all of them. We limit ourselves to those who are regularly part of our network and we list them in strict alphabetic order: Rosanna Amato, Simone Benvenuti, Tomas Berkmanas, Michal Bobek, Davide Carnevali, Daniela Cavallini, Ramona Ċoman, Francesco Contini, Harold Epineuse, Tatjana Evas, Marco Fabri, Antoine Garapon, Ole Hammerlsev, Philip Langbroek, Juan Mayoral, Otilia Pacurari, Karolina Podstawa, Michele Sapignoli, Peter Solomon, Rosanne Valvelde, Luca Verzelloni, and Mary Volkansek.

We are grateful to all the judges and prosecutors who agreed to offer us their time, who have been interviewed, in many cases twice, to double check the qualitative data we were collecting, and who have represented an irreplaceable source of ideas and inspiration for a deeper understanding of what it means to make the abstract principle of the rule of law into a rule of law in action, every day. For Chapters 2 and 3 we are grateful to the Global Governance Programme (GGP) at the European University Institute who provided funding, granting Cristina Dallara a Jean Monnet fellowship (2011–2012), the mapping on judicial networks and the focus on the Venice Commission. Within the GGP, Miguel Poiares Maduro and Antoine Vauchez in particular supported this project; for Chapter 4 we thank Domenico Airoma and the administrative staff of the Cosenza public prosecutor's office: Antonio Balsamo, Mario Barbuto, Elena Barca, Fabio Bartolomeo, Paolo Borgna, Edmondo Bruti Liberati, Claudio Castelli, Alessandra Cataldi, Bruno Di Marco, Frans Doelen, Barbara Fabbrini, Pasquale Liccardo, Lucia Lotti, Pia Marconi, Giovanni Melillo, Antonello Mura, Maria Eugenia Oggero, Jean Paul Jean, Alberto Perduca, Giuseppe Pignatone, Sandra Recchione, Maurizio Scalia, Mariano Sciacca, Francesco Scutellari, and Cuno Tarfusser.

We are indebted to Leonardo Morlino and Carlo Guarnieri for the countless ideas, remarks, and insights they have given us for such a long time that we would be unable to imagine how the work we have produced could ever have been possible without their scholarly support.

Finally, we wish to thank Alison Kirk and Ashgate. The idea of this book dates back to 2011. We were in the middle of our research at that time and we were in the deep waters of scientific enterprise, where you know there is something interesting to be discovered but the puzzle is not yet clear. Thanks go to Alison for your decision to wait and to support this project. We do believe that judicial networks are changing the way justice administration and rights enforcement is going to take place in the very near future. This change will be subtle, surely, but nonetheless significant for us as citizens, even more than for us as scholars. We do hope this book will represent a contribution to knowing a little bit more about this huge, subtle, and ongoing transformation of our times.

Introduction

Actors, Networking, and Rule of Law: A New Puzzle[1]

A Brand New Day in the Transnational Rule of Law

This volume is founded upon a compelling question: to what extent does promotion of the rule of law entail uneven and non-homogeneous legal and judicial orders? This promotion continues in its support of the judicial policies enacted in developing countries as well as by supporting the diffusion of best practices of justice administration in advanced democracies. This second stream aims to foster the modernization of the judicial sector by promoting the diffuse adoption of IT-based systems of case filing and case management, injecting into the court management tools inspired by a user-oriented approach, and more generally enhancing the managerial capacities of the judicial offices (Pauliat, 2007; Frydman, 2012). This comprehensive process of policy change stands as the most evident outcome of a new way of conceiving the rule of law, which one can word as an output-oriented approach as opposed to a rule-oriented one meant as a multi dimension "institutional ideal" combining output-oriented dimensions with rule-driven dimension. Otherwise said, the rule of law does not refer only to the rule-based behavior as opposed to the rule of men, it encompasses also behaviors and strategies aiming at ensuring the efficiency, the effectiveness, and the output legitimacy of those institutions that embody the rule of law principle.[2]

Despite the wide consensus this approach raises, this book tries to dig into the deeper consequences of the spectacular wave of international and transnational policies that this conception of the rule of law triggers. Moreover, as this process goes hand in hand with the rise of judicial networks, a key point of the research presented here is the following: actors have become involved in a comprehensive and cross-borders process of rule of law promotion and implementation. To what extent has this "method" turned out to be capable of provoking perverse or, at least, non-intentional negative effects? Authors are in fact asking a somehow key question, both for citizens and for institutions: *is it possible that the promotion of the rule of law jeopardizes the homogeneous enforcement of the fundamental rights of citizens and stakeholders, i.e. the right to an equal treatment before the judiciary*?

---

1 This chapter has been authored by Daniela Piana.

2 This is the reason with the expansion of the rule of law promotion in the EU that the rule of law is combined to the "quality of justice" (Piana, 2010, ch. 2).

This question is answered starting from a deep and multi-level analysis, whose conceptual and theoretical center is represented by agency. The core thesis of this book can be summed up as follows: actors are prominent and critical factors in the adoption as well as in the implementation of the rules promoted in the large variety of strategies and actions undertaken by international and transnational organizations to promote the rule of law and the quality of justice. The empirical validity of this statement increases in those organizational and institutional contexts where the mechanisms of hierarchical control—both political and professional—are weaker and where the judicial systems display a loose pattern of internal ties and intra-organizational links.

To state it differently, we put forth the hypothesis according to which *actors play a bigger role where institutions are weaker and the mechanisms of intra-organizational control are looser* (Weick, 1976; Sarat and Scheingold, 2005).

Moving from this general assumption, the authors approach a salient issue in contemporary politics: the role played by judicial networks in the overall process of rule of law implementation within the European area. This notwithstanding, this volume is not about networks *per se*. It focuses rather on the strategies, the instruments, and the resources that actors draw on, build, exchange, and expand through networks. This means that the subject of the volume is more accurately *networking*, i.e. the activities carried out through judicial networks. It is first and foremost for this reason that this volume firmly distances itself from the current analysis of judicial networks whereby networks are conceived as mere tools of socialization, whose significance in the transnational processes of policy making can be appreciated by observing the cultural change of judges and prosecutors that become members of these networks (Checkel, 2005). Some scholars hold that socialization triggers processes of change, which have an impact via culture on judicial behavior. We do not deny that, among other factors, to some extent socialization also takes place as a spill-over effect of networking activities. But we do not assume "socialization" to be the key mechanism by means of which transnational norms—hard and soft —impinge upon the behavior of judicial actors. This point is developed in depth in this chapter and the next. This book also steps back from a purely descriptive approach to judicial networks. Rather, the following pages trace a path toward an *explanatory framework*, which aims to disentangle those factors that, at different institutional levels, play as concomitant causes. These factors, combined, result in institutional changes, both formal and informal in their own nature. By this means, the combination of actors and new arenas—such as those represented by transnational institutions where networking activities are promoted and consolidated—facilitates the production and distribution of cognitive and political resources that can be used in the domestic context to promote changes. None of these causes are here conceived as *deterministic mechanisms* pushing or pulling judicial behavior. We always consider the context—comprising legacy, political and cognitive resources, organizational boundaries and opportunities— as an intermediating factor bridging macro and micro variables, namely, between structure and agency, norms and actors.

As already stated, the fundamental question this work wants to address is something of a paradox, i.e. the large number of non-intentional consequences originated by the bulk of activities carried out by IOs and NGOs to promote the rule of law and the quality of justice undermining the traditional pattern of rule of law.

Why does this create a paradox? There is a simple reason: the promotion of the rule of law, which is embodied in the multiple, differential, and polyhedral activities of the rule of law promoters, seems to create an extremely uneven, in some cases patchy, pattern of judicial governance. Rules, procedures, routines, practices, and policies are run differently, not only from country to country, but also from one sub-national area to the other and eventually from one court to the other or from court *y*, headed by the chief justice *x*, and the same court *y* headed, only few years later, by the chief justice *z*.

Therefore, both the promotion and the enhancement of the rule of law seem to be capable of triggering institutional changes without necessarily entailing the change of the formal rules that govern the judiciary. We might well observe a judicial system where the formal mechanisms of judicial appointment, promotion, and evaluation of judges and prosecutors remain untouched whereas, in the meantime, the practices of court management, of case filing, of users' communication, are so deeply and widely transformed to change from the "within" the judicial governance as it is put into motion (Piana, 2010, 2012).

This aspect is not the only critical point. A further point is worth recalling. Actors involved in the promotion and diffusion of norms and principles related to the rule of law seem to be protagonists on the forefront of an extremely variegated pattern of rule of law implementation. From t0 to t1, from one country to the other, from one institution to the other, the rise of agency as opposed to the rise of norms and structures seems to mark as a dominant feature the European area. With regard to this, a supplementary difficulty arises. We no longer live in a world where the same territorial and functional boundaries hold for the creation, the implementation, and the monitoring of laws (Priban, 2007, 2012). The strict link that once tied up a governed territory, a ruled society, and their legal authority has been thoroughly broken and from that breakthrough a multitude of plural and non-pre-ordered ensemble of norms has emerged, as if blasted from within the traditional modern order.

These considerations impact also on the manner in which *judicial governance* needs to be conceived.[3] In a state-centered order, where the judicial function is legitimated to the extent that it complies with the legal norms, the judicial

3 All institutional arrangements set up to ensure judicial and prosecutorial independence, for instance, belong to the broad empirical field referred to as the concept of "judicial governance": they include judicial appointment, career promotion schemes, judicial evaluation and mechanisms of disciplinary control, judicial ethics, and judicial training. On top of this, one should recall all rules incorporated into the civil and penal procedural codes, which draw the borders of the legitimate actions judges and prosecutors

governance can be designed to ensure the capability of the courts to enforce the rights of all members—but only those resident in the State—of society. The key point of such a system of governance is the impartiality of the judiciary. Legal certainty and predictability are pivotal. Judicial decision making, despite the differences that exist between the cases brought before courts, were required to comply with a uniform, homogeneous normative order (MacCormick, 2007; Palombella, 2009). Any point in the national territory, and, consequently, any individual living there, fell under the same rule and expected to be ruled in the same way as anywhere else, and therefore any other individual, living in the same State.

Judicial governance and the rule of law therefore are tied up in a strict and compelling relationship. It is because of the judicial governance that the rule of law is made possible. It is because of the rule of law that the authoritative allocation of values that any court is in the position to make is legitimized.

Two macro-scale phenomena have challenged this system (which has been established with the Enlightenment and has deeply marked modernity). The first is the fragmentation and the expansion of normative pluralism (Walker, 2002) featured in our contemporary world. Comparative political, and socio-legal scholars engaged in scientific research activities have already highlighted the multiplicity of possible institutional settings suitable from the point of view of the rule of law principle. The historical development of European States, to narrow our reasoning to a fairly homogeneous area, brought about a number of different models of judicial governance, spanning from a self-governed judiciary to a judiciary headed by the Ministry of Justice. Governance, in this context, takes on a broad meaning, covering several institutional and procedural dimensions, all of them connected with the rules, values, and normative inputs which provide a common framework whereby adjudication and prosecution are carried out.

The second phenomenon which is worth considering here as a macro-scale factor challenging the modern system is the outbreak of an international discourse appointing court administration and court management as pillars of the rule of law. Some scholars have labeled this process as the expansion of the performative approach into the law (Garapon, 2010; Priban, 2012; Piana, 2012). The thesis shared by these scholars is the shift from a procedure-oriented legitimacy featured by the judiciary (judicial decisions are legitimate to the extent they comply with the norms and result from the pure application of legal procedural codes) to a performance-oriented legitimacy (judicial decisions are legitimate to the extent they comply with standards of efficiency and effectiveness).

Without an efficient, transparent, and accountable management the rule of law would not be considered fully and properly implemented. Therefore the focus of policy makers has moved from the macro level—i.e. the national judicial system—to the level of the judicial offices, where the practices of court and

can undertake under certain conditions. See Voigt, 2005; Russell, 2001; Ginsburg, 2003; Kosar, 2010).

prosecutor administration come under the spotlight. In other and more synthetic terms, judicial governance today means a multi-level concept, ranging over the governance of the judicial system and the governance of the judicial offices.

Promotion of the rule of law incorporates this new facet by promoting highly developed blueprints designed to improve the organization of the judicial offices and drafting multiple checklists to guide judicial policy makers in their reform. Observation of this variety of court management schemes, IT tools, initiatives aiming to ensure that a good service is offered to citizens, human resources management, in-service training, etc. finally arrives at the following question: does the "networked rule of law" correspond to the primacy of the law as it is traditionally conceived? Does it correspond to an order ensuring the equality of citizens before the law regardless of their location within the European space? Is the networked rule of law an institutional order in the classical, traditional sense of the word? Or rather are we facing a new order which looks like a compound, and not necessarily even, order? It should be noticed at this point that the equality that is somehow entailed by a multi-dimensional rule of law, which encompasses both rule driven and output oriented approaches is itself compounded. It is not simply a matter of ensuring the equality of citizens before the rules – i.e. the laws – the equality should be also ensured in terms of equal response offered to citizens by those institutions that are vested with the task of making the rule of law into an institutional practice (among them, specially the judiciary).

Networking the Rule of Law

This volume engages in this debate by singling out the different components of this theoretical puzzle, and then tying them together again in the final chapter. We are going to focus on three components: the law; the rule; the network.

Our common sense is strongly influenced by the historically embedded idea according to which the rule of law, being related to the law, should be handled by legally binding mechanisms and institutions which have the legitimacy and the authority to make the law and enforce it in a stringent and compulsory manner. Therefore it is hard to see how the rule of law can be a suitable object for networking.

For this reason, "networking the rule of law" might well sound like an oxymoron to the reader. In fact, the rule of law is commonly meant as both an institutional ideal—therefore no need to make it work through a "net"—and a distinctive feature of constitutional democracies. Consequently, in order to refer properly to the process of "networking the rule of law" one needs to portray three faces of a complex and interdependent conundrum. The first face appears in the definition of the rule of law. Which kind of rule of law is networked, i.e. is conveyed by means of a non-hierarchical—or not necessarily hierarchical—structure of procedures, mechanisms of rule making and rule enforcement? In those territorial contexts where the law originates from a range of legal and pre-legal (i.e. cultural) sources, the definition of the rule of law as an object which can be carried across borders—for instance across national and institutional borders—is already in itself a political goal. The second face shows that the word networking is somehow misleading. When one thinks about the activity of networking one might have in mind the very fact of transmitting inputs in a system of governance where the relationships between the hubs of a vast net are located at different levels and are represented by individual (micro units) as well as by collective actors among whom no hierarchical order is pre-set. Third and last, but by no means least, is a new dimension of the rule of law, which consists of non-binding norms, mostly made of soft laws and standards.

These three points pose the puzzling questions raised by contemporary reality to the attentive view of a curious citizen. Are citizens who move across domestic borders equally protected under the rule of law of the European Member States (MSs)? What is the rule of law as minimum standard shared by all MSs? Is there any rule of law privileged promoter or are we in front of a multiplicity of rule of law promoters? And eventually if this is the case do mechanisms of mutual learning and policy transfer exist which ultimately ensure that future EU citizens will enjoy the benefits of a commonly built rule of law?

The claim we make in this introductory note is that in the European Union the rule of law is an umbrella under which a variety of policies coexists. There, policies are run according to a top-down as well as to a bottom-up pattern of rule making and rule enforcement. Actors involved at different stages and levels in this complex pattern of rule of law promotion within the European Union are predominantly acting through judicial networks. These, as the reader will be told in the second chapter, are transnational networks (TR-NTK). This differs from international settings since they do not necessarily originate from the inter-governmental agreements of States whose institutions are represented within the networks (see Chapter 2). What are judicial networks? European judicial networks did not exist when the Council of Europe and, slightly later, the European Economic Community were created. Otherwise judicial cooperation was not sought other than to create stable conditions for inter-governmental cooperation and thereby ensure peace and economic floridity. Since then the entire world picture has changed dramatically. The quest for fully fledged cooperation within the judicial field has become one of the pillars of the political agenda endorsed by European countries at the edge of the new millennium. Several events have marked this turning point: the enlargement of the European Union toward post-communist countries, these latter entering into a process of democratization and Europeanization; the end of the Cold War which was the drive behind creating completely new conditions for the EU to work and function, both inside and outside; the rise of new challenges for the international order, such as terrorism and the waves of migrations and crimes which were to take on an increasingly cross-national dimension. Inside the countries a process of de-structuring and re-structuring society pushed for a new quest for justice: cultural and social conflicts, which were to be settled by means of extra-judicial mechanisms—included social control—were now lodged, in the form of a case, at the courthouses. The overloading of judicial institutions started to be a topic debated not only by experts by also by the public, in the media, in politics.

Today, if a European citizen enters one of the rooms located in Strasbourg, on the other side of the road cutting across the European quarter between the European Court of Human Rights and the Council of Europe, she will observe a number of national representatives sitting around a large, semi-circular table discussing issues related to the rule of law, the quality of justice, presenting experiences or listening to experts and scholars in public administration, comparative law, sociology, and political science. National flags waving outside remind citizens and visitors that one day decisions made here need to be brought home and made into institutional and organizational practices.

All these empirical reasons contribute to the creation of a common understanding in the EU: justice is key to the well-being and the quality of life of EU citizens. Consequently the promotion of a reliable, homogeneous, and predictable legal environment where the primacy of the law is ensured gains a "top priority" position in the political agenda of the institutions. To be sure, Europe is not experience this phenomenon in a vacuum. For decades, the rule of law promoters have seemed to live in a fairly promising era. The echo of their policies expands across domestic borders and the legitimacy of their commitment to set up proper institutions pivoting on the constitutional principles in nascent democracies looks somehow undisputable. More realistically—and presumably less enthusiastically—the large spectrum of policies aiming to promote the rule of law worldwide—a heritage left over from the importance gained by international actors in anchoring new democratic regimes or in preventing potentially authoritarian regimes to take the road of the authoritarianism—brought new emphasis to the inquiry carried on ever since by political and legal theorists on the meaning of the rule of law. To radically simplify a much more complex story, the promotion of the rule of law might be conceived as an institutional experiment, which tests the empirical adequacy of our theories on institutional building and thereby helps understand better the deep nature of the concepts we use to grasp the core qualities of the institutions we want to describe when we refer to constitutional principles.

Who are rule of law promoters? And moreover which organizations, which configuration of the political and social power should we have in order to fit the core qualities of the rule of law?

In this book the focus of the analysis is put on actors and, more specifically, on "change agents." Change agents are those actors which are strongly committed to provoke and to steer processes of change. We draw inspiration from the use made of this concept in Morlino and Magen (2008), where the concept of the change agent (which comes from a earlier definition of Finnemore and Sikkink, 1998) features a highly intensive preference for change. From the point of view of the concept of operationalization, a change agent might be driven by a myriad of motivations (reasons) ranging from her expectations of professional upgrading to her idealistic engagement in a policy approach, comprising also office seeking and rent seeking motivations as well. Whether an agent fits one of these motivations is a question which should be answered on the basis of empirical research. The concept is abstract enough to cover different options of motivations and preferences. What is important in our analysis is the levels of governance and the institutions through which change agents act. In order to support her motivation to promote change and to steer the process of change accordingly a change agent needs resources, which can be of any kind: material (financial resources, for instance), cognitive resources (an experienced agent can be better situated than a non-experienced one), communicative resources (if a policy needs the support, the broad public communicative resources may play a crucial role in promoting it), and political resources (which stem from the position the agent has in connection with the political elite or any other type of elite).

Resources are not given—at least not necessarily. Change agents can gain resources via participation in different institutional actions and programs. This results in their empowerment. A footnote is worth adding here: empowerment is relevant to individuals and is considered as a transformation process that affects individual capacities to act. A hidden premise stands at the base of this way of reasoning. Change processes are costly; they need time, legitimacy, capacity, ideas, connections. And once they are launched, they demand again time, legitimacy, capacity, ideas, and connections to make sure that they will reach the promised goals. Finally, this never actually happens. Change processes are open processes by their very nature. Therefore, the expected goals are always different from the goals actually reached. This is a strong point in favor of a number of accountability mechanisms which force change agents to be responsive and responsible for what they do, in particular when they need to adapt their strategies or to redefine their goals. This aspect will be highlighted in the concluding chapter.

To go back to the levels of governance and the institutions which represent different context where change agents can play, we need to depict this reflection in more detail.

As we will explain in the first chapter, in a traditional institutional setting, such as the one featured in a modern State, change agents are located at the apex of the public institutions, at the interface between politics and administration. They play as brokers of new ideas and solutions which, once agreed by the political elite, are consequently applied with hierarchical mechanisms of rule enforcement. The lowest level of the bureaucracy is not allowed to play as change agent. In this model inputs for change come from the highest level of the pyramid, which is politically—electorally, in a democratic State—accountable.

Contemporary politics performs in a radically different way. Inputs to change organizational practices adopted in the public sector come from a variety of sources, located at different levels of the systems of governance and displaying different rationalities (public or private ones).

In the judicial sector things are made even more complex by the coexistence of two different types of input: legal and non-legal ones. Legal norms descend from the legal system, which nowadays features a highly marked transnational dimension. In the case of the European Union, the primacy of EU law within the Member States triggers an unpredictable, revolutionary, and still under-explored process of change in the national jurisdictions. The flow of legal arguments, norms, jurisprudential interpretations across the national borders of European countries in strict relationship with the activity of judicial networks is not the core subject of this volume (but see Bobek, 2013; Claes, 2006; Groppi and Ponthoreau, 2013 for a critical approach to this phenomenon). A slightly different, but related phenomenon will be better addressed and developed in the third chapter of this volume, where we debate the case of the transnational evaluation of the judicial review mechanisms adopted in EU Member States (especially in new members).

However, what should be mentioned here is the intertwining of national and supranational jurisdictions as one of the drives for legal and judicial change. This entails that rather than the legislative being the unique source of legal changes, in a post modern setting the judiciary eventually becomes the crucial source of legal and judicial changes, first of all by means of the jurisprudential developments.

Changes observed and explained in this volume do not exclusively concern the legal norms. It also entails a shift from a purely domestic law-centered approach in the judicial training, and in some cases in the career promotion scheme, to a more Europeanized approach. Such a shift varies in intensity and in durability from one domestic system to the other. However, overall one can safely argue that judges and prosecutors are nowadays referring to a legal system which covers transnational norms as well as foreign (from other domestic jurisdictions) norms: "the supremacy principle which establishes the primacy of EU law throughout the whole of the EU, even overruling domestic law, has represented for more than three decades a formidable power pushing through the integration of radically different legal systems (Piana and Guarnieri, 2012, p. 139; see for a broader analysis Arnull, 1994; Dehousse, 1998).

Not only does the process of transnationalization of the law entail an increasing transnationalization of the processes of law-making and a profound transformation of the process of law enforcement (Garapon, 2010). It also triggers processes of change due to the high salience of domestic systems to external inputs and, consequently, to the capacity of domestic judicial offices to enter into a communication with other similar organizational units (courts and public prosecutor offices situated in different, but still European jurisdictions). Among the many aspects of these phenomena of radical change experienced by judicial institutions, dialogue among courts has proved to be one of the most effective mechanisms of institutional change put into motion (Alter, 2000; Goodwin-Gill and Lambert, 2010).

Horizontal interactions among which the dialogue among courts (Slaughter, Stone and Weiler, 1998), the transfer of legal practices and reasoning (Scott and Trubek, 2002), and the networking activities bridging domestic institutions once upon a time enclosed in their domestic borders seem to trigger further processes of change. Nowadays more than twenty judicial networks are active within the European area, either because they relate to the political action of the European Union or because they have been created within the framework of the Council of Europe. Each of them involves the participation of at least 28 national representatives[4]—if not 47 when we consider the Council of Europe's judicial networks.

A spectacular growth of networking activities has been left almost completely unexplored. Why? Because judicial networks are a slippery terrain to move on, with empirical research design in mind. They do not enjoy in most cases any legally binding power, their positions and policy statements are most of the time differentiated if not divergent in some—not fully insignificant —cases. They do not have any body awarded with enforcing competences.

Therefore, judicial networks need to rely on the enforcing will and capacity of States. And finally, what is the product of these networking activities? Recommendation, blueprint, checklists, policy guidelines—are we simply referring to these? Or is it the case that judicial networks enter into the complex and multiple causal chain connecting transnational levels to sub-national levels of the judicial governance in a significant way? And if this is so, which mechanisms of change are at work?

In short, here, we will summarize what this volume is going to present in precise detail; judicial networks are instruments, institutional tools, created to respond to a functional need shared by some—not all—domestic judicial institutions and more likely some representatives of them: there is a need to create new arenas where fresh sources of legitimacy are available to judiciaries. Such a legitimacy can be instantiated in several ways, such as: 1) gaining the approval of a transnational—i.e. apolitical from the domestic point of view—epistemic community in cases of contested judicial reforms; 2) referring to transnational standards to strengthen the domestic representation of the judiciary; 3) referring to a transnational source of norms when the European Commission is in need of asking an EU Member State to reshape its judicial reforms or to respect the European directives in the field of civil and penal judicial cooperation (Leaf and Alegre, 2004; Jimeno-Bulnes, 2010; Guild and Geyer, 2008).

Hence, the rise of judicial networks connects directly with the reshape of the balance of power between the EU and domestic judicial systems as well as with the rebalancing of the power and competences within the national judicial governance. More precisely we will disclose how and why change processes can take place within some judicial offices and, in doing so, they can more or less intentionally reshape the capacity of the center—either the High Judicial Council or the Ministry of Justice—to set down the standards of quality of justice within the domestic legal space of the EU members.

The pages that follow show the reader that judicial networks perform as multi-functional bodies:

4 Most of them have been created during the enlargement toward the CEECs. They will be composed of 28 members (in the case of EU networks) because of the entrance of Croatia to the EU on July 1, 2013.

- they create an arena to discuss domestic judicial policies;
- they develop a transnational policy discourse on judicial policies;
- they set up standards of quality of justice;
- they award recognition of highly performing country or badly performing country and accordingly allocate moral costs; and
- they empower national representatives that participate in the meetings and seminars organized by judicial networks.

The reader can conclude from this list that this book, which considers the judicial networks and investigates the process of networking the rule of law as a complex, multi-layered process whereby actors have the opportunity to adopt, promote, diffuse and learn rules related to justice administration, is about judicial politics and, at a fundamental level, a book about power.

Research Design: Hypotheses, Cases, Data

The research question addressed in this work can be phrased as follows: "Have the policies of rule of law and quality of justice promotion ended up with a convergent pattern of justice administration? Which forces are driving the processes of change triggered by these policies?"

We deem the European Union as a profitable and promising terrain for answering these questions. Several reasons explain this choice. First of all, the European Member States share a common framework of fundamental rights and are all subject to the jurisdiction of the transnational courts, especially the European Court of Human Rights. Second, in the last two decades, the European Union has made an unprecedented effort to promote the rule of law in incoming members—in the Central and Eastern part of the continent and in the Balkans—and to support the quality of justice in all members, included the old Member States. Of all the different examples of regionally integrated systems we can observe today in the world, none can witness such a highly intensive and massive commitment in the justice sector. Third, and most importantly, the European Member States display different national legal cultures and feature different models of judicial governance. This means, in a nutshell, that they have followed different paths in bridging the institutional ideal of the rule of law and what we can call "rule of law in action." Therefore, the institutional and organizational differences that do exist among the States are variables that should be taken into account by a comparative design aiming to test if the rule of law and quality of justice promotion leads to a pattern of convergence.

Therefore, the *explanandum* considered here is the rule of law in action. By saying this, we refer to the well-known distinction made between law in books and law in action. The latter can also be defined as the assemblage of all organizational and institutional norms, practices and routines, aiming, altogether, to ensure an impersonal and an impartial application of the law for EU citizens. This is what happens in practice. If a European citizen travels across the EU and, for the sake of our argument, interacts with at least one judicial office in each EU Member State, she will sense several differences which depend not only on the differences displayed by civil and penal procedures, but also on the different strategies of division of labor, human resources management, training, communication with the public, etc. that have been adopted punctually in European judicial offices. A myriad of local practices, partially institutionalized and partially at the early stage of experimental attempt, mostly aiming to improve the administration of justice with a user-oriented approach, are now vibrant and living organizational material existing all across the EU without any homogeneous shape if observed at the systemic, i.e. macro, level. At the same time, the policies promoted in the incoming members, designed on the basis of a "European conception" of rule of law, have been implemented with a context-sensitive approach. Not only can a citizen easily detect the differences in the capacity of the courts to enforce her fundamental rights dependent on where the court is located but also the same citizen can sense the difference between the judicial governance adopted before the country joined the EU and after membership has been obtained.

Therefore, the *rule of law in action* does not refer to the formal setting of legal systems nor does it refer to the formal definition of competences, as it comes from the constitutional and the legislative texts adopted in the EU Member States. We are here speaking of the rule of law in action as it comes out of the judicial governance put into motion in the daily activity of the courts and the public prosecutors across the domestic borders of the EU. Of course, this would refer to a broad and multiple phenomenon, which covers almost all policy sectors as long as each of them impinges upon the enforcement of fundamental rights. In order to narrow down our empirical field and analyze it in more depth the choice made joins a flourishing research agenda, i.e. the study of the judicial policies and the transformations undergone by the judicial institutions in the contemporary age. The rule of law in action is therefore what results from the rule of law as an institutional idea once it is put into motion through the vast range of institutions among which the judiciary play a key and crucial role. Observing the rule of law in action means observing the output of the long and complex process by means of which the rule of law is put into motion. For if the rule of law is nowadays deemed multi-dimensional, scholars and policy makers cannot any longer consider only the rule-driven rule of law, but need to observe also the output oriented rule of law. Accordingly this volume is concerned specifically by the rule of law to the extent and in the way it refers strictly to the judicial sector and the justice administration.

The process we are going to reconstruct is the "rule of law networking." This phenomenon started in the EU in the late nineties, triggered by two distinct, but progressively interrelated vectors. The first consisted in the promotion of legal and judicial guarantees of judicial independence as the most viable solution to entrench the rule of law in action into incoming Member States. A whole range of policies, ranging from the design and implementation of the constitutional courts to the rewriting or the replacement of civil and penal procedural codes, has been adopted under the auspices of the European institutions. With the passing of time, once the institutional guarantees of judicial independence were considered to be in place and the fundamental rights to a fair trial ensured by proper rules included within the legal codes were deemed to be sufficiently protected, the concern of the rule of law promoters—namely of the EU and the Council of Europe—moved away from the grand politique and started to incorporate into the policy focus the court administration and all the conditions that will have made the judiciary work efficiently. In most cases, the support provided by international and transnational actors was instantiated by the creation of a wide range of financial incentives which made the option of the judicial reforms profitable for the domestic elites. The financial programs and the so-called financial conditionality thus joined the membership conditionality and created a set of incentives for all domestic actors who wanted to seize the opportunity offered by an external actor to reform and to change the court system. Surely the system itself—by supporting financially the transfer of best practices from old Member States to incoming members as well as by supporting the learning by imitation and the circulation of ideas—the EU and the Council of Europe set up favorable conditions for the socialization—or rather the re-socialization—of the domestic judicial actors and the legal experts. However, as we are going to show, this socialization did not happen homogeneously. Rather it took effect later when the transfer of ideas and the internationalization of new frames and ways of doing things in the judiciary fit with the domestic context. None of the judicial actors picked up new ideas from the external environment—which is to say also through the judicial networks—if these ideas did not help them to gain reputational benefits or professional advantages at home.

The dynamic of the process as a comprehensive phenomenon arising from the combination of strategies adopted by actors at different levels of governance is fairly complex. Several consequences have been originated thereby. What is "networking"? "Networking" is considered to be a complex process whose components can be measured and analyzed once they are singled out and broken down into problem framing, rule making, policy diffusion, and monitoring. Problem framing, rule making, policy diffusion, and monitoring are four sub-processes connected with a not-homogeneous, uneven, complex, and somehow patchy change of the pattern of rule of law (as the rule of law is implemented) across the EU.

Here it is promising to introduce a further distinction. The strategies adopted by actors did not aim to intervene in the judicial system with the same goal in mind. Policy objectives appear to be differential and consequently to entail a different logic of action.

In most cases, actors tried to adopt new rules, including the concept of both hard and soft law. The rule adoption is a strategy governed by a logic of action where external pressure plays a key role. Despite the differential reaction of incoming Member States to the conditionality exercised by the EU and the Council of Europe, one can say that under the effect of external pressure the acceding countries adopted new rules fitting with the general principles and standards supported internationally and transnationally. However, rule adoption alone does not cover the entire spectrum of the process of networking the rule of law. A further step should be considered, which is rule implementation. Here the role played by domestic judicial actors emerges as critical and in most cases almost dominant. Without the will of domestic judicial actors to put into motion the rules adopted, none of these rules has become a permanent part of the judicial governance. Finally the rules implemented in only a few cases have been transformed into part of the frames accepted and endorsed by judicial actors to regulate their own behaviors. The transformation of explicit rules into implicit regulative behavioral principles needs the intervention of processes of training and cultural reinforcement that in similar cases took place across borders, between domestic arenas and transnational ones.

Networks enter into this broad phenomenon as *arenas* to begin with, even though in those cases where judicial networks are recognized by external institutions—such as the European Commission—they act as if they were unitary actors. This "as if" is of the utmost importance. It means that once the recognition of an external actor ends, the judicial network will not necessarily act as a unitary actor. The nature of a unitary actor is, consequently, not intrinsically of the network. It can emerge under certain conditions (see Chapter 3 in this volume).

To develop a comprehensive framework and to single out the explanatory factors we need to refer to two different, and still related, strands of research. The first, which dates back to comparative political studies of the seventies and eighties carried out on Latin American and Southern European democratization processes, tries to disentangle the relative weight of domestic and international factors in shaping the patterns of change featured in democratizing countries. Here the main point concerns the way domestic and international factors intervene and trigger the process of change: what causal role do they play? Are they concomitant factors or rather is the domestic dimension dominant whereas the international influence comes in only to the extent it makes sense for national players? Some scholars have argued the opposite, that international pressure, also created by means of comprehensive processes of institutional imitation and isomorphism, drove national institutional changes and somehow created opportunities for these latter to converge. Some others have rather been inclined to support a different view where national policy makers and elites managed to exploit and take benefit from international resources, such as financial programs, legitimate norms and values, and ended up by being influenced by international conditionality only to the extent that this latter impacted upon the expected pay-off of the different options and strategies they had at hand to undertake the national reforms.

Here comes a very important point in our analysis. What is a change agent? Change agents or "norm entrepreneurs" (Finnemore and Sikkink, 1998) could be defined as "domestic actors that mobilize to pressure decision-makers to adopt … rules; they also engage domestic decision-makers in processes of persuasion and social-learning to redefine their interests and identities" (Magen and Morlino, 2009). This broad definition should be narrowed in order to fit with the empirical field analyzed herein. This can be done by referring to the following empirical observation: transnational non-legally binding norms are often transferred into the organizational unit by individuals (Piana, 2007a; Radaelli, 2005) who play the role of normative entrepreneurs, i.e. catalysts of organizational and cultural changes (Kelley, 2004; Finnemore and Sikkink, 1998). They often bridge between exogenously originated norms and their own working place, their own organization (Piana, 2009). These actors are located at the micro level, i.e. within the judicial offices, either the courts or public prosecutor offices. Most of the time they are the chief justice or the chief public prosecutor, but this is not necessarily always the case.

From this point of view judicial networks work first of all by mean of participative actions carried on in transnational arenas with which change agents can be connected. Exchange of expertise and knowledge is also part of the activities carried out by judicial network members. Therefore judicial networks are instrumental to communication, which is a key mechanism in getting national public officials involved in a common activity, to help them share common views, ideas, and frames. Moreover, judicial network actors can undertake other types of activities in which norms and values are spread out, shared and transmitted: most are training activities. Training may take place in transnational arenas, such as ERA (Legal Academy of Trier) or EIPA (European Institute Public Administration) or may be offered at the national level by means of programs that incorporate transnational standards and policy guidelines. Also deontological codes, which are nowadays widely adopted and taught to young public officials through initial and in-service training, may reflect norms set down by actors through judicial networks.

Previous research has showed that change agents are not necessarily members of judicial networks. They may be inspired by the frames, the norms, the policies, and the routines shared by representatives of judicial institutions through the communicative activities running through the judicial networks. This inspiration can come in direct or indirect ways. Direct, because in order to legitimate an initiative entailing organizational changes a change actor should refer to a not contended and not contestable source of norms. Indirect, because in some cases external sources of norms etc. are used as sources of legitimacy by experts appointed as leaders in projects aiming at promoting organizational innovations—fitting with transnational inputs—or appointed by external agencies which run projects of organizational innovations under the financial programs set up by the European Union.

This debate, which is now enriched by scholarship developed around the European Union and the EU conditionality, is helpful for our purpose since it offers an insight into phrasing the first few competitive hypotheses:

HP1: Domestic changes are determined by external factors; if external factors change, domestic policy frames, norms, policies, and routines change accordingly. Alongside this view, we should expect a fairly homogeneous change in the judicial governance at the national level once transnational frame, norms, policies, and routines of rule of law are changed as well.

HP2: Domestic changes are determined endogenously; if external factors change, domestic policy frames, norms, policies, and routines change only if change agents are in the position to take benefit from a compliant strategy of reform. Alongside this view, we should expect that in different countries and in different times, but within the same country, a differential pressure from the external environment does not produce a change. To check this hypothesis we need to see whether in cases of equal expected pay-off and equal external inputs, domestic players behave differently.

The second debate which provides a sort of reference point for our analytical reasoning is the debate comparing the empirical adequacy of culture-based versus agency-based explanation. Here we touch upon a classic puzzle in social research. Is the social actor determined by culture? Or is she ultimately free to act and therefore the reasons to act are causal factors explaining social processes?

In the context of our empirical research, this very abstract puzzle can be phrased as follows. We have two competing hypotheses:

HP3: Changes are due to the degree of fitness in terms of legal and judicial culture between the transnational discourse and the domestic one. Therefore, in cases of highly fitting countries we should expect more intensive and diffuse changes following the guidelines produced by means of the communicative, cognitive, and deliberative activities run within the judicial networks (as arenas).

HP4: Changes are due to the capacity of change agents regardless of the degree of fitness featured by the cultural environment where they are located. A high misfit can create a barrier, a reason to resist, but it is not, on its own, a sufficient reason to explain changes undertaken within the judicial governance. Therefore if this hypothesis holds true we should expect that the existence of powerful and capable change agents triggers a process of change which might be eventually similar in its pattern across different countries.

A third scholarly debate we consider here is the one that stems from an epistemological dichotomy agency versus structure. What is the driving force of change? To what extent does agency become pivotal in highly institutionalized contexts, as the judicial contexts are?

In order to frame our research in this debate we have considered a two-level research design, taking first into consideration a system where the center is weak, i.e. Italy. We then took into consideration two big organizations which have two similar cases and to assess whether agency becomes a leading drive of change regardless of the territorial location, the function of the organization (one is a court, the other is a public prosecutor office). The second step of our analysis is to compare a weakly regulated system – Italy before 2012 – and France to assess the relative impact of the variable "governmental capacity of the centre" in the implementation process of the policies stemming from quality of justice standards.

To test these explaining and interpretative hypotheses, we designed a three comparative project, which check the above mentioned hypotheses in three different contexts.

External Conditionality Contest

Here we are going to test by comparative analysis the process of networking the rule of law in the context of the Venice Commission's screening of the constitutional reforms adopted and implemented in Hungary and in Romania at two different moments. In Table I.1 we offer a synthetic view of the comparative design. As is shown, we consider two countries, both concerned by the pre-accession strategy and afterwards by the institutional adaptation which is specifically asked of new incoming Member States.

Table I.1 External conditionality in Hungary and in Romania: the impact of the Venice Commission

Country / Timing	Before accession	After accession
Hungary	High fitness with EU standards	Rule of law reversal
Romania	Low fitness with EU standards	Rule of law reversal

However, the two countries differ from the point of view of their legacies and their relationship with the external actors. In fact Hungary has been considered, during the pre-accession period, as a leader country. The constitutional law-making process which took place there was observed as a positive example, a successful story, mostly because of the path-breaking role played by the constitutional court. Romania, on the opposite side, has been always seen as a country lagging behind, featuring not only a less prominent constitutional culture—less than Hungary, Poland, and Czech Republic for instance—but also with a higher degree of misfit with EU standards. The interest in a Hungary/Romania comparison lies in the apparently similarly institutional behavior adopted after accession. In both countries we observe a rule of law reversal without any formal prerogative of the European Union to prevent or to stop such a process.

Judicial Training Contest

Since the late nineties, judicial training has gained a central position in European rule of law promotion. Better trained judges and prosecutors are deemed to be more inclined to properly apply EU laws and eventually enforce the fundamental rights of EU citizens. Better training meant, for the first time, better informed, and richer, in terms of offer, courses and programs on legal matters. With the passing of time the European approach to judicial training experienced a shift. Whereas during the pre-accession strategy the judicial training promoted in candidate countries was mostly concerned with EU law training programs and the need to accustom judges and prosecutors to the rule of law in order to strengthen their independence, after accession and during the first decade of the twenty-first century the quality of judicial training started to be measured in terms of its capacity to enhance not only the legal competence, but also the communicative and managerial skills of the judicial staff as well as of the administrative staff appointed by judicial institutions. This is mirrored in the guidelines and in the standards set up in the field of judicial training. Here our analysis will aim to disclose to what extent legal and judicial culture can explain the changes undergone within different countries through programs of judicial training. We have selected countries with a similar culture (Italy and France; Poland and Czech Republic) and put them into two pairs which share a relationship with the external factor. Therefore for both sets of countries (Italy and France; Poland and Czech Republic) we can argue that the external factor is a parameter. Then we have selected a third pair of countries featuring a differential relationship with the external factor and a differential culture (Table I.2).

Table I.2 Comparative design for the analysis of judicial training programs' changes

Country / Target	Judicial school created because of external pressure	Adaptation of training programs to EU standards
Italy	No	Partial
France	No	Agenda in progress
Poland	Yes (coming later)	Partial
Czech Republic	Yes	Partial
Macedonia	Yes	Complete
Turkey	Yes	Partial

Sources: https://www.academic-projects.eu/menuforjustice/default.aspx

Organizational Innovation Contest

This third facet of our analysis tries to address the following questions: to what extent do common transnational standards, searched persistently by policy makers and international experts, fall short in accounting for the actual path followed by judicial organizations—courts and public prosecutor offices—in improving the quality of justice? Ultimately, are the standards good and acceptable proxies of what can be considered as an objectively described practice of quality of justice? To what extent can we rather observe the localization of standards and best practices? Again, here we deal with the key question whether actors and norms, judges and prosecutors, together with standards, are parts of a matrix whose variables are always determined according to the same logic of action. Can we use standards as a predictor of judicial behaviors (Miller,1990)? To try a new avenue in answering those critical questions this article covers three case studies, both marked by the introduction of innovations in terms of division of labor, organizational practices, and management. We consider two countries, with a similar formal setting of judicial appointment, promotion, and evaluation, as well as having a similar legal culture: Italy and France. They differ though in two different ways. First, they do not display the same level of territorialization of the public sector (Italy is less homogeneous than France, for historical reasons). Second, Italy has the benefit of European structural funds allocated on a sub-topic related to the justice administration, something that France has not experienced at all. However, both countries needed to comply with the overall European discourse on quality of justice, of justice de proximité, for users and citizens.

The three cases are analyzed with a qualitative approach, which provides a comprehensive narrative of middle range variables (organizational culture, patterns of human interaction) and individual variables (such as the professional profile of the leader, which in these cases is represented by the chief and the deputy chief prosecutor). Our focus is oriented toward two courts of first instance, located in Milan, and one public prosecutor's office, located in Naples (in the south of Italy). The data and the evidence used to support the arguments come from two in-depth field studies, both conducted by the author between 2009 and 2013. Therefore, we are offering here very new and fresh data. To check the relative weight of the domestic context, we added one more case which shares with Italy the same system of judicial governance (notably with the High Judicial Council competent to appoint and promote judges and prosecutors), that of France. We want, in this way, to check if the national variables, such as the degree of centralization of the decision-making processes, explain the different pattern of change undergone by the judicial policy making (Table I.3).

Table I.3 Comparative design for the analysis of organizational changes introduced within the judicial offices

Country	Level of change	Territorial location	Units of analysis
Italy	Judicial office	Northern Italy	Milan court of first instance
		Southern Italy	Naples public prosecutor's office
France	Court system	N/A	Judiciary

The purpose of the analysis is hopefully meaningful for both judicial and organizational studies. Despite being under the influence of homogeneously worded inputs—such as the "European" conception of the rule of law—these offices exhibit a pattern of organizational change that, despite being strongly inspired by that conception, differs considerably in the process of innovation and in the output of the reform process. Our point will be then to spot how change agents worked out a successful/ not successful process of organizational innovation. If our argument holds and delivers a truthful message, organizational innovation is rarely successful when approached on the sole basis of transnational standards and quantitative indicators. The role played by actors is highlighted by the Italian cases. This seems to support empirically our initial assumption, according to which the process of rule of law networking is led by actors in more prominent ways, the weaker the domestic institutions or the less capable they are of leading a process of policy change. As we will stress, however, this cannot be easily labeled as a bottom-up method of judicial policy making. Actors promoting a quality of justice approach anchor their actions and their strategies to a European discourse—which provides them with legitimacy. On the other hand, once the European material resources are supplied, the role of agency comes out as triggering mechanisms of change to the extent that actors can decide not to take the opportunity offered them to improve the judicial office. This room for maneuver might turn out to be a factor jeopardizing the homogeneity of the services offered to citizens and parties in trials.

The analysis unfolded in this volume relies on a large data set, covering both quantitative and qualitative data. These have been drawn from official sources—such as constitutional and legislative texts, European laws and case laws, and all documents formally adopted by the judicial networks considered in the three levels of analysis: the Venice Commission, the European Network of Judicial Training, and the European Commission for the Evaluation of the Efficiency of the Judiciary—and from primary sources—semi-structured and in-depth interviews with qualified actors at the three levels of governance considered: transnational, national, and sub-national. The analysis covers a time span which runs from 1997 to 2013. The sources used to treat these cases range from semi-structured interviews, to international court reports drafted by the judicial networks (such as CEPEJ), to official documents adopted by the judicial offices analyzed.

Why Should we Care about Networks?

Being confronted with the issue of how and to what extent European court systems have been changing over the last two decades leads the researcher to deal with a complex phenomenon which on the surface looks as follows: the raising of normative frameworks at the supranational level singling out the multiple dimensions of the rule of law and the quality of justice; a constant effort to apply this framework at the domestic level by means of a relentless process of (re)adaptation; the reshaping thereby of the supranational frameworks by means of a process of monitoring and updating the domestic court systems. Rules are made up, then authoritatively affirmed and stated, and transferred to domestic systems. Afterwards, from the domestic court systems inputs and inspirations come to be uploaded onto the agenda of transnational judicial arenas.

The transnational judicial networks analyzed in depth in the pages to come are numerous and for the most part date back to the late nineties and to the first decade of the twenty-first century. They have been created either by the spontaneous initiative of national judicial institutions (such as the European network of judicial councils) or by the authoritative impulse of the European Union (such as the European civil network), or by the authoritative impulse of the Council of Europe (such as the Consultative Committee of European Judges, among many others).

The nature of the phenomenon investigated by this work is fairly new in two senses: institutionally, as long as the networks seem to have a way to exercise some influence upon one of the most traditional and reluctantly changing institutions, i.e. the judiciary; scientifically, as far as the networks act as a whole and as a range of bridges built between single actors located in single judicial offices. Judicial networks are composed of representatives of domestic judicial institutions: individuals who serve both as judges or prosecutors in their own countries, and as members of a judicial network at the transnational level, in Brussels or in Strasbourg. The macro–micro combination that comes from this double-faced professional profile of judicial network membership is what makes the phenomenon analyzed in this book challenging and compelling.

To what extent is it a salient phenomenon? A glimpse at newspapers and official documents issued in all European countries would easily convince a non-European reader that something dramatically important is going on within the justice sector in the EU. To provide just a taste of this: over the last decade more than the half of the European States adopted reforms whose aim was to target the court system. A comparative analysis of the policy discourse developed at the national level, when policy makers and practitioners come to talk about the justice system, reveals the absolute priority given to making courts more efficient and more transparent, namely more accessible for citizens and users. If a researcher then steps into a courthouse anywhere in an EU State she will find an on-going process of innovation, either impinging upon human resource management, or communications policies with the public, or the intense implementation of IT-based systems of knowledge management and e-filing: these could include participative practices of quality of justice assessment in Finland, financial claim systems in England in petty cases, the creation of front desks for e-filing and document delivering in Spain and Italy, not to mention the relentless process of reform and readjustment that has been taking place in new European Member States since their accession.

Therefore, one may safely argue that this is a very prominent phenomenon that represents a compelling reason to go further into the scientific investigation of its engines. Of course, these changes take place at different paces and with different outcomes in different countries. But it is beyond any reasonable doubt that European court systems are now on the way to experiencing a comprehensive process of (re)adaptation. But, (re)adaptation to what?

By observing the entire process, both at the domestic level and within each judicial office, one may disentangle at least two factors that seem to pull the court systems into a process of institutional and organizational adaptation. To be sure, here we are not referring to legal reform, which introduces procedural or substantial innovations to the civil and criminal procedural codes or to the civil and penal code. One can detect at least the following forces exercising an influence on domestic judiciaries. The first comes from inside the national political system. Judicial functions have been experiencing a deep transformation within most EU countries. From being a function whose main aim was ensuring the equal application of the laws to the national territory, it has become a function whose performance needs to encompass a much bigger number of tasks, among which the legal ones are just one part, albeit an important part. Judges (and also prosecutors in countries such as France, Italy, and Spain, where judges and prosecutors share the same career path) are asked to perform efficiently from a managerial point of view; they are supposed to cope with media exposition; they are in the position of acting as bridges between the supranational level of legal and judicial cultures and the domestic systems.

The second factor is exogenous—if we consider the court system as a national structure. The exogenous nature comes from the fact that nowadays the judicial function is a matter monitored, assessed, and debated within institutionalized judicial networks. State actors and supranational institutions reached such a large scale that it would be myopic to analyze today a system of judicial governance without considering as co-participating forces both state and non-state actors, and both domestic and supranational authorities (Charnovitz, 2006). Courts are not an exception to this claim. Despite being a locus traditionally devoted to the enforcement of domestic legal rules, courts are nowadays involved in multi-level and multi-layered systems of collective action where they perform their function amidst a multi-voiced set of norms and values much more complex than the one they were confronted with in the past (Kappen-Risse, 1995; Benda-Beckmann, 2002).

Most important of all, supranational institutions, which in principle are not entrusted with any competence in the field of judicial governance, in the early nineties of the twentieth century started to set up a wide and comprehensive process of reflective policy making (Rogowski, 2007), targeting the models of judicial governance, the practices of judicial administration, and the mechanisms by means of which courts interact with the external environment—such as media and citizens (Voermans, 2007). Standards of rule of law and quality of justice have been set down by networks whose membership ensures a systematic link between supranational and domestic policy arenas, since these judicial networks are composed by judges and prosecutors, representatives of domestic judicial institutions (Piana, 2010).

Despite being set within the formal jurisdiction of sovereign States, courts have turned out to be a promising and fertile terrain on which, under specific conditions, standards set abroad have been implemented at home. In other words, non-legally binding norms (standards), shaped by representatives of domestic judicial institutions throughout a regular process of reflexive policy making enacted at the supranational level, influenced—to a different extent, depending on the context the standards encountered within each country—the ways courts are organized and work. The simplest example is represented by the introduction of the court manager in those countries that did not yet have such a role. Finally, but not less importantly, all courts have been facing an increasing demand of justice featuring increasing complexity and fragmentation. In a way, the judicial function has been asked to perform much more heavy tasks in a highly demanding context, where prompt, transparent, homogenous, and fair responses are expected.

To sum up, as we will argue in the concluding chapter, this book has a two-fold goal. On the one hand, it is going to check the empirical adequacy of competing hypotheses concerning the role of external/internal factors and the role of culture/agency in triggering processes of change affecting the judicial governance of EU Member States and thereby influencing the implementation of the rule of law principle. On the other hand, it is going to engage in a critical discussion of three aspects featured by the EU rule of law promotion: 1) the quantitative measurement of judicial governance and of the rule of law; 2) the gap between expected outcomes and actual results reached by the EU rule of law promotion; 3) the lack of proper and effective mechanisms of accountability which are necessary if our thesis is confirmed, namely if change agents are the real drivers of the changes which take place within judicial governance.

Chapter 1

Rule of Law Between States and Networks[1]

The Rule of Law and the State: A Puzzle of Modernity[2]

When modernity established itself as the backbone of Western culture, the dominant view of the social order balanced on three principles. The first is the *centrality of the individual*, conceived as a compact, self-sufficient, and stable entity featuring moral responsibility and ontologically forced to choose, to take decisions, as a free being (Lyotard, 1979; Dahrendorf, 1980; Boudon, 1993; Giddens, 1991; Burchell et al, 1991; Habermas, 1998). Any kind of collective action stemming from this presupposition is destined to conflict with the need to accommodate morally autonomous and free individuals into a stable and predictable collective order (Smith, 1796; Simmel, 1920; Hayek, 1978). The second principle, accordingly, fitted into the rationalist view of the social order, as it resulted from the regulated combination of individual actions aiming to set up common rules either by means of a social contract or by means of an incrementally developed adaptive order. Having left behind forever the ideal of an order made possible and guaranteed by a transcendental authority, modern thinkers engaged in a comprehensive and path-breaking reflection on the creation of an *order made by men* and, this notwithstanding, capable of ruling men, despite their riots, their resistances, their dissents, their differences. An impersonal set of rules, ruling types of actions and not types of men, can be rightly deemed as one of the most significant legacies of modernity. The third principle refers directly to the need to shape this abstract order, as a set of general rules, into an actual order, a working system of governance. How can we expect to have an impersonal order put in place and maintained if it is handled by humans? Is not this an underhand way of retrieving what has already been discarded, namely the discretionary power of decision makers?

Given these premises, a crucial position is held by the judiciary, whose fate it is to have two functions: that of guardian—holding all rulers accountable to the

1 Daniela Piana has authored the sections on "The rule of law and the State: a puzzle of modernity" and "Beyond the modern tradition. The rule of law at the present time." Cristina Dallara authored the section "From Judicial dialogue to networked judicial governance".

2 This paragraph relies on the definition "rule of law" in the International Encyclopedia of Political Science. See D. Piana, (2011) 'Rule of law,' in B. Badie, D. Berg-Schlosser, and L. Morlino (eds), *International Encyclopedia of Political Science.* Thousand Oaks, CA: SAGE Publications, pp. 2336–47.

law—and that of governed —being held accountable to the law itself (Cappelletti, 1988; Dahl, 1969; Matteucci, 1961).

Therefore, in a modern world, autonomous and rational individuals create a social order which binds all of them by means of impartial and impersonal enforcement mechanisms. The instantiation of this is the building of the judicial function into the constitutional political system as the best reflex of the abstract institutional ideal named rule of law.

One should remember that the rule of law, which is definitively recognized as a pillar of the modern State, was not in itself created during modern times. As early as the Middle Ages, deep and comprehensive analyses of the primacy of the law were apparent, even though the law was then considered an epiphenomenon of the existence of God. Going even further back in time, Roman legal culture supported the idea of an order ruled by laws as a pivotal feature of the empire. What makes the difference between pre-modern and modern conceptions of the rule of law is undoubtedly the nature of the law, which becomes—with a qualitative leap from the Renaissance to the Enlightenment—the *law made by men* to govern their lives and to pave the way for their future .

For these reasons, which provide a radically simplified but not subverted view of the tight connection between the rule of law and modernity, the judicial function is a fundamental component of any system of governance. In fact, the judicial function plays a critical role in putting the rule of law into action.

History teaches us that the institutional configurations adopted to implement the principle of the rule of law can vary according to the cultural and political context, although all these configurations tend to vouch for the legality and legitimacy of political power. For this reason it is possible to identify a common thread among the different exemplifications of the concept of rule of law, a thread that refers to the way in which the *form of government ensures that rules (laws) do not become a mere instrument of domination*. It is in this vein that, as noted, the history of liberal constitutionalism gives flesh to an institutional ideal (Palombella, 2010), the rule of law, whose meaning is determined in relation to the nature (source, form, content) of government rules. The organizational form of power—the form of government that substantiates an architecture where powers are separate or are mutually accountable—cannot but operate by virtue of the institutional ideal of the rule of law, never being the rule of law itself.

Without doubt, in different countries and at different times several different institutional solutions have been proposed in the quest for a system of governance capable of making a system of impersonal rules into a sociopolitical order based on impartially applied rules and procedures. In this respect the governance of the judiciary is of utmost importance. In fact, the judicial function, despite not being a prerogative exclusively granted to the State, performs within a State the critical role of a system whose *rules made by men are applied equally by men* whose independence and integrity are so embedded and protected that all may assume that judicial decision making will be impersonal and thereby fair and legitimate. This holds in civil justice as well as in penal justice (Damaška, 2003).

In continental Europe, where the civil law tradition has been and still is dominant, these very abstract and general aspects took a specific and culturally determined shape. In a bureaucratic judicial system, legal and bureaucratic logic—which prescribe that decisions should be based on legal norms and be at the same time respectful of the legal doctrine set down by senior judges and prosecutors (usually sitting in a Supreme Court)—co-participate to produce a distinctive pattern of judicial governance, in which the independence of the single judge is substantially subordinated to the independence of the magistracy as a system (Guarnieri and Pederzoli, 2001; Bell, 2006).

The rationale behind this goes in the same direction as the principle of public administration autonomy from political institutions. As Max Weber correctly pointed out, judges who work in bureaucratic settings benefit from a very particular type of guarantee, such as their independence and their professional status. Once recruited by means of a general, standardized procedure, which resembles very much the procedure adopted to recruit civil servants and bureaucrats, they are inserted into a machine in which they will spend their entire career. Each judge is expected to behave in way that is respectful of several different rules and standards. Her behavior should be lawful, should respect the organizational values that constitute and shape the identity of the judicial system in which she works, should respect the professional ethics of the legal professions, should respect a standard of effectiveness and efficiency in the use of organizational resources, and should respect the rights of the citizen, ultimate holder of democratic sovereignty. "This complex picture figures out a situation where judges expect costs and negative rewards if their behavior does not respect a set of several different standards. Some of them are weaker and informally enforced, while some of them are harder and legally binding" (Piana 2009, p. 4). One may safely say that the bureaucratic judge (a judge who is working in a highly bureaucratic judicial system) is held accountable by means of a vertical chain of rule enforcement, whose effectiveness depends on the internal cohesiveness of the judicial hierarchy.[3]

What ensures the legitimacy of a judicial decision is the balanced combination of a procedurally correct process of decision making on the case (evidence taking, hearing of witnesses, etc.) and the cohesiveness of the judicial decisions taken along the years/decades and among different courts belonging to the same system.

3 A bureaucratic logic of action goes about the application of general norms in a neutral way. Ideally a bureaucratically oriented agency does not perform its role other than by classifying a case as an instantiation of a general norm and deductively reasoning this case on the basis of the specific obligation the norm contains. Creativity, discretionary comprehension of the case and extra normative arguments do not have any salience in this picture. Legality sticks to this view if it is intended to be a formal principle, which stands on a meta level vis-à-vis the ordinary application of legal norms. What makes the adjudication legitimate is the belief and the common expectation that a judicial actor will apply a legal norm along a pattern of reasoning that is strictly procedurally correct.

The consistency of the judicial hierarchy and the respect for legal procedures both aim to ensure the impartiality and the imperturbability of the bench vis-à-vis possible influences coming from the external environment, either politics, or the market, or other foreign legal systems.

This picture no longer corresponds to the real state of affairs in which contemporary adjudication takes place. First and foremost judges are now placed amidst a global, complex, multi-layered and multi-centered system that spans legal cultures that are many miles away, and which generates norms that should generally be accommodated case by case, rather on the basis of deductive and intra-systemic reasoning. Ordinary judges are allowed to be attentive to the normative creations of foreign courts and, accordingly, to pass over or to overrule in some cases, the doctrine endorsed by the senior judges who are responsible for their career promotion. In issuing a sentence judges are no longer only interested in their domestic reputation, but can become particularly sensitive to the international fame in academic or judicial networks and entourages. Not only does the legal procedure start to engage with "heteronomic" inputs (i.e. inputs coming from different "nomos," different normative orders), but also the judicial hierarchy is put under pressure by an increasingly important interaction with colleagues placed beyond the formalized borders of the bureaucracy in which the hierarchy is embodied.

Non-democratic judicial systems fit into this picture with some nuances and under specific conditions. It should be remembered for example that in authoritarian regimes judges are usually not subjected to any particular form of politicization, whereas the scope of their action is mostly and considerably reduced by limiting the number and the types of cases on which ordinary courts adjudicate. In this respect, the development of a hierarchical judicial organization is less important for authoritarian rulers, because they do not aim by any means to influence society through the adjudication. Sensitive cases and politically delicate issues are treated outside the ordinary courts in special judicial bodies (military courts are a fairly common example of that). Unlike authoritarian regimes, totalitarian regimes desperately need the support of the bench in applying the law in line with the dominant (and unique) ideology. Therefore, courts adjudicating under totalitarian rule are asked to become part of the system rather than being left outside of it (Sólyom, 2003; Sajo, 2006).

Accordingly judicial behaviors are inclined to become over-proceduralized in order to cover with the sacred value of procedure (impersonal by definition) the authoritative allocation of values (Easton, 1953) (from the point of view of citizens) of their decisions. Moreover, judicial hierarchy is vital to achieve an effective transformation of the courts into the arm of the regime. The more cohesive the hierarchy, the more values injected into the system from the top of the hierarchy, namely at the level of high judges, are likely to be enforced through all levels of the judicial system, from the supreme court to the ordinary courts. Strong socialization to ideology is distinctive in this system (Bihari, 1986; Lane, 1996). Whereas high ranked judges are appointed by political bodies, ordinary and low ranked judges are influenced by means of their socialization with senior colleagues and hopes for career promotion (decided by senior judges). Central and Eastern European countries are very representative of this second model. This is however only a theory. With the passing of time, socialist States were rapidly experiencing a collapse of authority and of cohesiveness. Organizational units, in principle belonging to the same State, were in reality under the influence of external interests and unable to stick to a common, organization-based set of values, because of the lack of a fully-fledged impersonal approach. Therefore, in post-communist societies bureaucracies are in a very uneasy position. On the one hand, they are a vital instrument for the processes of institutional change and institutional re-building necessary to democratize the State. On the other hand, they are the scope of reform, the largest part of which aims at sweeping away authoritarian attitudes from public sectors. Beside the problem of the inner contradiction between the fact that public institutions have been both instrument and target of reforms during the post-communist period, post-communist bureaucracies are also faced with a problem of capacity building. In fact, in these societies the legacy of the non-democratic regimes mainly consisted of a largely politicized State, which had undergone in the last decade of communism a process of de-legitimization. At the sunset of communism, States turned out to be captured by a political elite intertwined with the dominant party and masked behind heavy proceduralization and a comprehensive formal legalism. Beyond the *façade* of a compact structure, local elites were intertwined with public officials and civil servants, whose loyalty had been turned against the central hierarchy and had instead addressed themselves and been devoted to local networks, clubs of influential persons working between politics and bureaucracies. The coherence and the cohesiveness of the State in the moment of the decline of communism were both very low. The lack of hierarchical coherence, the legacy of a regime that had dismantled any capacity to undertake individual enterprises matched the bureaucratization of the whole public sector. The 'socialist rule of law' was the label used to refer to a State that was organized according to the law, and performing according to hierarchical rules—to which a deductive systems of legal sources corresponded—and was respectful of the legal correctness of procedures. However, behind this mask, to varying degrees, all Central and Eastern European countries experienced at the end of the communist era a weak State, wrapped in a blanket of procedural splendor (Ajani, 1996).

The specific features of the non-democratic States are of appreciable relevance for our argument because a considerable part of the European rule of law promotion targeted the CEECs for more than a decade and still is targeting the Balkans (Marčeta, 2010). Therefore, the judicial governance which results from the combination of domestic institutions and external inputs conveyed by key policy makers and change agents also carries on in some way the specific aspects inherited from the past (Costa Pinto and Morlino, 2013).

Beyond the Modern Tradition; The Rule of Law at the Present Time

Whatever difficulties scholars confront in assessing the impact of the European integration process on domestic courts, it would perhaps not be controversial to claim that over recent decades in almost all European democracies judicial institutions have gained considerable weight. There are plenty of reasons for this state of affairs: courts have been targeted by an increasing number of claims suited by individuals and collective actors; the number of claims that goes through the parliamentary arenas has dropped (Putnam and Pharr, 2000); the complexity of normative sources in which judges and prosecutors frame their decisions has increased enormously; the vagueness and the indeterminacy of the set of norms leaves a window open to wide interpretations, also in countries in which the judicial culture pivoting on the principle of the judge as "bouche de la loi" dominated for centuries—and definitely during the modern age.

If judicial decisions have been affected both in their content and their genesis, the processes of law making and law enforcement have also undergone an institutional turmoil: the matrices of the national States, which ensured straightforward implementation of political decisions and respect of the rule of law, have been influenced by processes of law and soft-law making, as comprehensive as they are fragmented, which stemmed from supranational rather than national bodies (Slaughter, 2004; Peters, 2005). For legal accountability had been if not undermined, at best fragmented and puzzled by new actors and new layers of governance (Stone Sweet et al., 2001) all of them involved in the making of laws and the mixing of hard laws with soft laws.

One way to phrase this complex process of change, which entailed, among other consequences, the loading of huge pressure on judicial institutions, includes the following: de-nationalization and fragmentation of law making, together with the weakening of the link courts to legislative arenas (Russell and O Brian, 2001; Stone Sweet, 2000), and reshaping *the mechanisms by means of which courts as organizational entities are held accountable to the law and reallocate judicial institutions' capacity to hold judges and prosecutors accountable and answerable.* At best one might safely say that judicial actors are nowadays responsive to many different sources of norms, among which some do not stem from domestic institutions' exercise of power.

European courts experienced these phenomena in a distinctive way, as the domestic processes of re-adaptation to a new social and economic landscape went hand in hand with the withdrawal of domestic competences by European institutions and the involvement of ordinary courts in supranational law making. Mechanisms of cross-national coordination—such as, for instance, under the previously called Third Pillar—have been enhanced to breaking point through the architecture of the States and have unbound the borders of domestic legal systems (Börzel and Cichowski, 2003; Falkner, 2011; Chalmers, 2000; Wallace and Wallace, 2000). Both internal and external forces of change affected the way judicial institutions are held accountable to citizens and redistributed the mechanisms of checks and balances that work across the layers of European governance (Stone Sweet, 2000; Dehousse and Magnette, 2006; Bellamy, 2005).

A glimpse at the newspapers and official documents issued in all European countries would easily convince a non-European reader of the fact that something dramatically important is going on within the justice sector in the EU. Just to provide a taste of this: over the last decade more than half of the European States adopted reforms whose aim was to target the court system. A comparative analysis of the policy discourse developed at the national level when policy makers and practitioners come to talk about the justice system reveals the absolute priority given to make courts more efficient and more transparent, namely more accessible for citizens and users.

Despite being within the formal jurisdiction of sovereign States, courts have turned out to be a promising and fertile terrain on which, under specific conditions, standards set abroad have been implemented at home. In other words, non-legally binding norms (standards), shaped by representatives of domestic judicial institutions throughout a regular process of reflexive policy-making enacted at the supranational level, have influenced—to a different extent depending on the context the standards encountered within each country—the ways courts are organized and work. The simplest example is represented by the introduction of the court manager in those countries that did not yet have such a role.

Therefore, to sum up, judicial governance, which is considered as the pivot of rule of law implementation, is the result of the intertwining of several vectors, which impinge upon different dimensions of governance itself. Partly formal rules—laws, regulations, and procedures—are affected by the transnationalization of the law. In this respect, as the reader will see in the next paragraph, European judicial networks represent new arenas where the mechanism of legal harmonization—where possible—and legal coordination—most of the time—are enacted. Furthermore, non-legal dimensions of judicial governance are targeted as well. For instance, the composition of the high judicial council, the institutional status of the judicial school, the way courts and public prosecutor offices are organized, etc.

In Table 1.1 we present an overview of the dimensions of judicial governance which are under the spotlight in European institutions. For the sake of clarity it should be emphasized that these dimensions are not targeted through the same mechanisms and by means of the same policy instruments (Table 1.2).

The processes of change triggered by these mechanisms are complex and non-linear. However, one can detect, as a common trend, the transnationalization of law making as well as of legal and judicial cultures. This does entail per se the existence of a pattern of convergence (Piana, 2010). As a matter of fact, over recent decades scholars have increasingly contested the monopoly of national States in creating and enforcing legal norms (Zürn, 2000; Börzel and Risse, 2005). Indeed, they showed that national States are embedded in a multi-level system of legal norms, procedures, and routines that have completely transformed international and domestic law making (Abbott and Snidal, 2000; Youngs, 2001). Due to this fact,

Table 1.1 Dimensions of judicial governance and instruments of influence in the EU rule of law promotion

Formal rules	Institutional settings	Organizational setting	Professionalism	Public perception and trust
Law making (EC law); ECJ case law	Judicial Networks; DG Justice and Home Affairs; Council of Ministers of Justice; Parliamentary Committee of JHA	Benchmarking; standard setting; Regulative Impact Assessment	Professional ethics; identity	Identity; social values; rights
Funding of legal experts (TAIEX, PHARE)	Mutual agreement; Treaties; Monitoring of policy; conditionality for candidates; structured implementation	OMC; networking; audit (Court of Audit; DG on sector-based projects)	Training; socialization; international communication	Training; socialization; networking; embedding in platforms and committees

Table 1.2 Mechanisms and instruments of EU influence

	Law making	Standards	Training	Communication	Twinning and legal advice
Legal harmonization	x		x		x
Judicial cooperation	x		x	x	x
Judicial dialogue		x			x
Standard setting		x		x	
Monitoring		x			x

legal actors are forced to deal with a multi-centered set of sources of legal norms and values (De Sousa Santos, 2005). (It may be worth noting for our purposes that the multi-layered feature of politics goes beyond the phenomenon labeled as "normative transfer" or "legal transfer." While the transfer of legal norms occurs by establishing a bilateral relationship between two institutions, a multi-centered system of normative inputs are exchanged horizontally and vertically).

Therefore, the multi-level organization of political actors and the multi-level interaction of legal experts seem to be, so to say, two faces of the same coin. This general statement also holds in the case of European integration (Stone Sweet et al., 2001, p. 14); an extensive effect might arguably be expected as for the transmission of the legal knowledge. In fact, instead of being exposed to a flux of inputs coming from her national legal system, any judge is exposed to the legal knowledge (by the concept of "legal knowledge" we are referring not only to the knowledge of the law, but also to the knowledge of the legal doctrine and the ideologies more or less explicitly incorporated into it) that comes from several sources, none of them clearly ranged in a clear and stable hierarchical order in which domestic law occupies a clear position (Mokrà, 2007; Zemanek, 2003; Dezalay, 2007; Teubner, 2005).

The effect this has on the adjudication should not be underestimated. Beside the burden of adjudicating on a case any ordinary judge is called nowadays to make many other choices, some of which consist of providing a reasoned, acceptable, but still contingent and bond to evolve the order of norms taken from different sources, sometimes offered by scholars of different nationalities or embedded in different legal cultures. Furthermore, an increasing number of cases feature a supranational nature: they emerge from disputes involving actors based in different countries or they require the intervention of several judicial institutions, not all of them located under the same domestic rule of law.

The impact of legal ideologies is, as a consequence (Allard and Garapon, 2005; Priban, 2007), basically grounded on the State's monopoly of law production. In different terms, systems that have exhibited a firm preference for a *Rechtstaat* model and a positivist approach are eventually subjected to steady pressure, as they should somehow distance themselves from a conception of legitimate adjudication simply based on the knowledge of the domestic legal norms. This impact is arguably stronger in countries whose legal culture is centered on the legal doctrine of scholars. This happens for several reasons. Not only is the domestic character of legal knowledge questioned and finally puzzled out by the globalization and fragmentation of law (De Sousa Santos, 2005), but also the merely legal character of norms used to shape the arguments provided in adjudicating a case is somehow less sharp and clear than it was before. Norms come from quasi legal systems. In some cases, they incorporate non-legal norms, such as managerial principles and performance–based standards (Langer, 2004). Constitutional principles that remain unwritten have a fairly high importance in leading judicial interpretation, and standards of trial timeframe in adjudicating a case, as is the case in Europe (Albers, 2008; Frydman, 2007) where the European Court of Justice, adjudicating on *Sciortino vs Italy* supported its argument also on the base of the infringement Italy had committed against European standards of trial timeframe (Fabri, 2005; Langbroek, 2005). Lastly, legal scholars and professors of law are the frontrunners in opening up national systems as they are more inclined than other institutional actors to get in touch with colleagues who work abroad (van Caenegem, 1987). The more important their voice, the more one can expect external inputs in terms of legal doctrine to be facilitated to enter the domestic system (even though the latter remains at the stage of an interpretative hypothesis that should be tested on an empirical basis).

The consequence of this manifold change is that supranational judicial epistemic communities (Haas, 1992) come out as very influential arenas, where knowledge and ideas are exchanged among their participants. Among these participants we find most of the change agents, i.e. actors who played the role of gate-keepers (Piana, 2007a), because they exploited at the domestic level the cognitive skills and the expertise provided by the supranational institutions (Börzel and Risse, 2005; Lundvall and Tomlinson, 2002).

Within the European Union this process of transnationalization has been speeded up coincidentally alongside the enlargement process which took place between 1993 and 2007. Particularly during the period of pre-accession, one of the concerns of the European Union was precisely the capacity of new Member States to receive and execute judicial decisions taken by any other European court. Furthermore, the capacity of judicial offices to exchange data and evidence concerning controversial cases has represented for years one of the most challenging objectives pursued through the pre-accession strategy (Grabbe, 2002; Piana, 2006). By taking part in the meetings, seminars, and conferences organized by these communities and by being involved in the communicative actions that these communities encourage, judicial actors are enabled to construct capacities (not only cognitive capacities, but also capacities to interact, get in touch with international organizations and supranational arenas) and gain a stock of knowledge that they may use at home. International communication empowers actors (Morlino and Magen, 2008; Risse and Sikkink, 1999; Slaughter, 2004) by providing them with information about other judicial systems and connections to colleagues. The considerations deployed above are of the utmost importance for a better understanding of the impact the promotion of the rule of law enacted by the European Union in post-communist countries had on the structure of trials in these countries. Even if a final assessment can't yet be provided, some points may still be raised. During the pre-accession period, the European Union exercised its influence in CEECs in different ways (Kochenov, 2004; Kubicek, 2003). It casts several mechanisms to strengthen the capacities of judicial actors (European Commission, 1998, 1999 and 2006). These actors have been strongly encouraged to enter as members in epistemic communities or networks (Piana, 2007a and 2009). To do so, the EU used four kinds of policy instruments: monitoring; training; communication; twinning. First of all, the European Commission regularly monitored the judicial reforms adopted in the candidate countries and established a dialogue between judicial actors, representative of judicial institutions, and the experts who work with the European Commission. Second, the European Commission introduced *twinning* (European Commission, 1997).

Twinning relies on the appointment of experts within public administrations. These experts introduce experiences and patterns of problem-solving successfully adopted in other public administrative agencies. Twinning projects are intentionally addressed to support a *transfer of best practices* from the old member to the prospective new member (Papadimitriou and Phinnemore, 2004; Piana, 2006). Therefore, the twinning projects have represented a model for exporting patterns of behaviors, procedures, and rules. Thirdly, judicial training has been put on the political agenda of the European Union, since it has been considered as key-leverage in the construction of the European legal space (European Commission, 2006). Not only has training been promoted by financing training programs (ENJT, 2007 and 2006), but also by financing the creation of Judicial Schools in the new Member States. Last, but not least, together with the Council of Europe, the European Commission has encouraged the creation of judicial networks. (As this chapter shows, the Council of Europe champions the rule of law promotion. This is also due to the formal mandate of the Council of Europe. Since its institutional status is equivalent to an international organization, the legitimacy of its policies relies upon the mandate of the Member States. See Council of Europe, 2005.)

From Judicial Dialogue to Networked Judicial Governance[4]

It is the 2010 EU Stockholm Program and the process creating the EU Area of Justice that, in some way, "institutionalized" judicial networks as a key feature of the EU RoL networking. However, the emergence of the networks structure in judicial and security matters has its roots much earlier, specifically, in the effects produced by the globalization of threats and crimes and in some specific developments related to EU governance.

The networking model has been primarily considered as a key feature of world order in the twenty-first century. Slaughter (2004) in her pioneering work described the emergent global governance as increasingly founded on the coordinated activity carried out by networks of national officials, which exchange information, best practices, experiences in addressing common problems on a global scale. This is because "networked threats [and challenges] require a networked response" (Slaughter, 2004).

Thus, as Amato (2014) suggests, a first rationale for the remarkable diffusion of this form of collaboration lies in the effects produced by globalization on law and institutions and, in particular, on the emergence of more sophisticated forms of crime that cannot be efficiently faced through a purely national pre-emptive or repressive response. Indeed, the latter are carried out through flexible and

4 A first version of this paragraph was originally developed by Amato in the paper Amato and Dallara (2012) Judicial and legal expert networks. New actors for a EU area of justice?. Paper presented in the conference National courts vis-a-vis EU law: new issues, theories & methods, 29–30 November 2012, European University Institute (Fiesole).

networked organizations, which operate at a transnational level in order to take advantage of both the benefits normally allowed to legal economic activities but also of the existing differences between national legal and judicial systems. As a consequence of the "*securitation ethos*"[5], after 9/11, governments' attention was increasingly focused on cooperation by networks. These arrangements contribute to building trust among participants, by offering technical assistance and professional socialization; furthermore, it can combine soft power instruments, such as persuasion and the sharing of information, with hard power instruments, such as the action carried out by national authorities to enforce law (Amato, 2014).

These arrangements further proliferated with the introduction of the Schengen Agreement, since, with the focus on free circulation of individuals, all the issues concerning justice and security gained relevance. Amato (2014) describes, as early as the seventies, "the need to manage new challenges as terrorism urged member states to put in place intergovernmental *ad hoc* inter-state arrangements to coordinate national policies. Among them, the better-known was TREVI group, aimed at identifying better solutions to fight terrorism and other forms of organised crime" (Amato, 2014, p. 52). Moreover, "Even if at that time the nature of such collaboration was fundamentally political and focused on a macro level, working groups operating at the third level of TREVI's architecture can be considered, *in nuce*, as a first example of modern networking, since membership was composed of public servants and law enforcement officers and the main operating method used was based on the informal exchange of experiences and information" (Amato and Dallara 2012, p. 5).

Since the middle of the nineties, cooperation between national judicial authorities has gradually become one of the *leitmotifs* of judicial cooperation in criminal matters. The rationale for this new trend was the need expressed by European judges and prosecutors to confront each other on new cross-border challenges and the claim for more efficient means of cooperation, especially the effective implementation of certain rules concerning procedures of mutual legal assistance provided by the Application of Schengen Agreement.

More specifically, it has to be emphasized that the first moves for the creation of the judicial networks analyzed in this book could be found in the practices of judicial dialogue that courts put in place autonomously all around the world, starting in the 1990s (De Vergottini, 2010).

Judicial Dialogue

In very general terms, "judicial dialogue" and "courts dialogue" refer to the "judicial conversation" that unites judges around the world in a sort of "common enterprise of judging" (Slaughter, 2004). Indeed, the term "dialogue" is mainly used to characterize the judicial practice of reading and applying the logics of

5 See Wouters J. and Naerts F. (2004), 909–35.

foreign and international judges in their own interpretative approach, or in their academic writings, as well as quoting the relevant precedents.

Overall, this form of conversation enables judges to benefit from judgments issued by other courts; as a matter of principle, it may be considered a valid source of inspiration for the judge, especially when the relevant national law is unclear, contradictory or out-of-date; furthermore, it can exercise a sort of "persuasive authority" on the decision issued by the judge (McCrudden, 2000). Of course, the ways in which judicial dialogue is performed can vary; it can be realized through informal methods of interaction and/or via the establishment of network-based cooperative bodies. Traditionally, dialogue has occurred in the form of cross-citation of judgments. This phenomenon was favored by the use of information technologies, most notably, common databases or e-newsletters. These instruments, generally designed to cover specific areas of law, can be used to limit linguistic barriers since a translation service (into English) is often foreseen. Amato (2014) underlines also that cross-references are more frequent among national systems belonging to the same legal family or that are more homogeneous from a linguistic and cultural point of view. The more systems differ, the harder the comparability. In this light, another limit of traditional cross-citation can be identified in the fact that this method allows national judges to have a good knowledge of foreign law and its application in the foreign national contexts; nevertheless, it does not allow judges to be well aware of important non-legal factors that have to be taken into account (Baudenbacher, 2003).

In this context, judicial networks could be considered *fora* where the transnational judicial dialogue has become routinized. For national authorities they represent a privileged way to directly confront each other on legal problems raised within the domestic jurisdiction, to learn from foreign experience and to coordinate the interpretation of shared supranational legal texts and the implementation of international and supranational law within the domestic order (Cassese, 2007). As already stated, the latter plays a pivotal role for cooperation, since it can foster mutual understanding and confidence between national authorities and can favor the adoption of convergent approaches among different judicial systems. Several judicial networks operating at EU level are provided by IT architectures and tools, which allow each member to actively cooperate or to exchange confidential information. Information technologies are applied not only to allow judicial authorities to use common databases, but also to avoid communication barriers from hindering operational cooperation.

Thus, it is possible to state that the shift from the informal dialogue between national courts to the establishment of structured and formalized networks of national judicial authorities is remarkable; through these more advanced arrangements judges from different jurisdictions are formally engaged in a transnational conversation that could contribute not only to filling the gap eventually identified in national legislation, but that could facilitate the development of shared legal values and principles, fostering judicial operational cooperation.

Towards Networked Judicial Governance?

It was with the beginning of the new millennium that the EU settled new strategic programs devoted to justice and security. Meanwhile, European Institutions have witnessed an ever-growing interest in networking between judicial authorities as a way to effectively realize its action in the field of judicial cooperation in criminal matters. In 1998, Joint Action 98/428/JHA established the European Judicial Network, namely the first polycentric structure of contact points, whose task is to act as intermediaries, providing legal and operational support to judicial authorities of Member States.

In 1999 the European Council set a new political agenda and prioritized the construction of a European space of Freedom, Security and Justice. The anticipated goal of a truly European judicial space (de Vervaele, 2004) put cooperation among judicial systems of Member (and candidate) States, transparency and predictability of judicial decisions and policies at the top of European political priorities, before making them principled ideas. In doing that, the EU in a way joined the Council of Europe, which has been committed, itself, since the date of its creation to the establishment of mechanisms of judicial cooperation within the European space.

A brief mention of the ties between the EU and CoE in the judicial cooperation field is essential for an understanding of how the practice of judicial networking became so widespread in Europe.

A first important step in establishing these ties was represented by the first moves of the enlargement towards Central and Eastern Europe. The European rule of law promotion has been tailored on the basis of two distinctive goals: reshaping the judicial organization of the candidate countries before they entered the EU and at the same time establishing instruments of coordination among the judicial civil and criminal policies of Member States (Dallara, 2010; Piana, 2010). It is worth mentioning that this EU strategy of rule of law promotion was largely constructed together with other international organizations already working on the rule of law, above all the CoE. In the RoL promotion field, the Council of Europe could be really considered a "partner for prestige" (Piana 2010) of the EU in identifying standards and criteria related to judicial cooperation, anti-corruption and fighting organized crime, especially for the Eastern Europe countries. This continuity and complementarity is also extremely relevant in the field of fighting organized crime in which the CoE is pursing some specific targets, although using mainly soft-law instruments and tools. The combination of CoE and EU conditionality, as well as the combination of the enlargement policy and the judicial cooperation policy, has surely created a multiplying effect with positive consequences.

Over the last two decades, European institutions have developed a wide array of policy instruments (Hood, 2007) that ranges from standards used in the assessment of domestic judicial reforms to norms enforced in order to coordinate domestic courts, from financial programs supporting projects of organizational reforms to specific mechanisms encouraging domestic institutions to enter into a regular process of transnational communication with foreign courts and judges.

The essential meaning of such an activity may escape one at first sight, as it does not show any systematic character or any overall logic of action. The European Union has never been granted full competence in the judicial sector. Even in those sub-sectors where the European Union enhanced the coordination of domestic criminal policies and the fight against trans-border crimes—such as human trafficking, terrorism, money laundering—the competence remains partially in the hands of Member States. The EU can only adopt legal norms which impact upon the civil and the criminal procedures of Member States, can promote exchanges and communications between courts and can set specific instruments, such as the European Arrest Warrant, that could facilitate the solution of cross-border crimes and cases, but it cannot lead the latter to converge toward a common model of adjudicating and prosecuting crimes or to train judges and prosecutors or even to appoint judicial staff (Delmas Marty, 2002).

Thus, in the view of fostering harmonization and effective judicial cooperation, both the CoE and the EU converged toward the creation of new arenas of networking and socialization, composed of judges and prosecutors from the higher courts, as representatives of the main judicial institutions. These networks are arenas through which national judicial institutions are asked to coordinate their policies in civil, commercial and criminal fields. They have been created merely with the purpose of providing national judiciaries with a common "space" in which they can exchange information and straighten their mutual trust. Unlike the EU, the Council of Europe promoted and expanded the agenda of networks whose activities consist mainly in the setting of standards or monitoring the compliance of national legislation and policies with international standards, especially in relation to anti-corruption and money laundering. Within the 2010 Stockholm Programme, envisaging the creation of a truly open and secure Europe, more specific lines of close cooperation and joint actions between the EU and CoE have been proposed with reference to those sectors in which the CoE was able to create powerful instruments, groups or legal frameworks.

The Stockholm Programme has created direct contact between national senior officials in areas covered by Justice and Home Affairs among the key mechanisms to foster mutual trust and affirmed that these should be further promoted. In addition, it has been stated that, where appropriate, such networks should be able to take part in the development of the relevant strategic tools. Along the same lines, the Lisbon Treaty has promoted the use of ever more intense forms of collaboration between national judicial systems.

The Area of Freedom, Security and Justice is, in fact, conceived as "common space" balanced between the need for pluralism on one side and the purpose of consolidating EU competencies in areas covered by TFEU on the other side; it appears as a system based on low-sacrifice standards for jurisdictional sovereignty of Member States, whose load-bearing axis is the principle of mutual recognition of judgments and judicial decisions (Amato, 2014).

As a consequence, the functioning of this area is strongly dependent on a higher degree of mutual confidence between the members involved. In this light, transnational networks represent as defined by Toniatti and Magrassi (2011) a "sustainable operational tool"[6] which can meet these basic needs. Nowadays, judges are, in fact, required to decide on an increasing number of cases involving issues of international and foreign law; moreover, they are routinely involved in the regulation of transnational activity. A growing number of decisions, practices and judicial doctrines, produced by courts of different levels and nature, are flanking traditional law-making mechanisms. As Amato (2014) argues, judicial activity is changing and courts seem to serve an integrative function and national judges seem to play a sort of problem-solver role, adapting law to a multifaceted and ever complex legal landscape.[7] In particular, within the EU, this is where the unity of the legal order depends not only on a "vertical coherence" between European Court of Justice and national courts, but also on a "horizontal coherence" between national judicial authorities and other actors involved in justice and security fields.[8]

6 Toniatti, R., Magrassi, M. (eds) (2011), p. 10.

7 See Cassese, S. (2009). See also Shany, Y. (2007), pp. 109–10.

8 See Poiares Maduro, M. (2003), p. 519, 527 and ff. On the same topic see also Littlepage, K. (2011), p. 1 and ff.

Chapter 2

Judicial Networks and their Instruments[1]

The European Union has of course pioneered the governance by networks, creating networks of ministry officials, legislators, experts and professionals to govern many sectors of the EU polity and economy (Slaughter, 2004). In line with this trend, over the past decade networks of judges, prosecutors and legal professions have also spread increasingly across Europe. From a wide-ranging perspective, judicial networks can be described as groups, conferences, commissions or organizations of legal experts, judges and academics (coming from different countries) established at a transnational level in an autonomous way or under the wing of international organizations.[2]

In this respect, Anne-Marie Slaughter's description of global judicial governance as most emblematic of a "new world order" has opened a new research avenue. As she puts it, "judges around the world are talking to one another: exchanging opinions, meeting face to face in seminars and judicial organizations, and even negotiating with one another over the outcome of specific cases" (Slaughter 2004: 66). They mostly participate in information and enforcement networks, thus contributing to a gradual construction of a global legal system.

There is now a whole stream of research from political science, law and sociology investigating this emerging phenomenon (Allard and Garapon, 2005). In addition to Slaughter's pioneering work, other sociologists and political scientists have developed further interesting studies on the topic. Ferrarese (2010), in an inclusive study on law and governance, defines "judicial governance" as one of the main expressions of Global Governance. Judicial governance, acting mainly through soft-law instruments, is one of the new institutional settings producing a new form of global law in many varied fields. Networks of constitutional, supreme and lower courts, panels and forums of judges and prosecutors, conferences and meetings of judges and legal experts all are expressions of judicial governance.

---

1 Cristina Dallara has authored this chapter.

2 This chapter is largely based on the working paper "Judicial and legal expert networks. New actors for a EU area of justice?" written by Amato and Dallara. The Paper was presented in the conference "National courts vis-a-vis EU law: new issues, theories & methods," 29–30 November 2012, European University Institute (Fiesole). The author of this chapter was responsible for defining the structure of the working paper, the titles of each paragraph and the content. Nonetheless, the analysis and the description of the networks established within the EU legislation was done by Rosanna Amato in the context of her PhD thesis titled "La cooperazione giudiziaria in rete nello spazio di liberta`, sicurezza e giustizia." Unpublished PhD thesis in European Law, University of Bologna.

Furthermore, Vauchez (2008), focusing on the European legal space, emphasizes that lawyers and legal experts, thanks to multiple networks acting around the European institutions, contribute to the construction and the legitimization of a specific political order. Operating in legal and political arenas of mediation at the European level, they actively contribute to the creation and to the functioning of a new European legal field. From a legal perspective, Claes and De Visser (2012) elaborated a good mapping of the existing judicial networks in Europe evidencing their potential for judicial dialogue among national courts.

As Magrassi (2011) pointed out, the difficulty for the States to agree on harmonizing the legislation, also in the field of judicial procedures, has been balanced, at least in part, by the role of judicial networking. Judicial networks affect the institutional balance between European organs, the powers of Member States and also the national system of the separation of powers. The role of national judiciary is not merely that of passive safeguard of the legal system. In the context of the pending Area of Freedom, Security and Justice, national judiciary promotes European integration but pursues its own institutional interests, through the instruments and institutions created by the Treaties or through self-organized bodies. According to the author, the analysis of judicial networking shows that the attitude of national judiciary is all but passive; the EU Area of Justice appears to be an additional arena in which national judiciary may pursue its own "political agenda."[3]

In spite of this salience, as Vauchez (2008) has pointed out, so far the majority of legal and political science scholarship has essentially focused on "effects" and "outcomes" in terms of jurisprudence and judicial Decision-making, with a particular interest in cross-referencing between national Supreme Courts. There is a general lack of knowledge in regard to who engages in these networks and what happens within these transnational arenas. This lack of knowledge contributes to the misunderstanding of what is actually "at stake" in these scenes. What circulates among these networks is not just references to judicial decisions (the so-called "cross-fertilization" or "judicial comitology"), but more generally opinions, best practices and reports related to shared values and elements of rhetoric, judicial procedural standards and models of professional excellence, etc. Moreover, many of these soft-law documents deal with crucial aspects of the judicial system organization and functioning such as the judge status and role or the guarantees of judicial independence. In addition, within the EU framework, judicial authorities that are engaged in transnational networks operate as active intermediaries, supporting the proper application of supranational provisions or smoothing the operations of judicial cooperation procedures.

3 Magrassi (2011) specifies that this is a voluntary over-simplification in order to promote the debate.

Mapping Judicial Networks

The number and the varieties of such networks are increasingly growing across Europe, and especially within the EU; for this reason, different approaches can be adopted in order to describe this ever expanding phenomenon. For instance, from an organizational perspective it is possible to distinguish between two main groups, namely "institutional networks" and "networks of individual national contact points." The former are mainly composed of national institutions, while the latter are composed of single national representatives of Member States (Amato, 2014). In Magrassi's view "the metaphor of network can describe cooperative relationships between judicial authorities in the exercise of judicial functions (judicial networks, or networks of jurisdictions); on the other hand, it is commonly applied also to the organizations operating in the training and cultural exchange between judicial professionals (networks of judicial professionals or networks of judicial institutions)" (Magrassi, 2011: 10).

Amato (2014) describes how a further classification of those networks could be made from a chronological perspective. Within the European space, the emergence of networks as organizational forms followed mainly a two-step path (Canepa, 2010). Each step corresponds to the structural evolution of such arrangements and has led to the creation of different generations of networks, which match the aforementioned groups. As a matter of fact, during the first phase, which started around the end of the nineties, networks working as national contact points were created; in this case national representatives were appointed by reason of their specialization, in order to answer the growing need for the sharing and exchange of technical or operational information between States' administrations. By contrast, the so-called institutional networks—which have flourished since 2004—were aimed at promoting the development of shared rules and practices, above all with regard to policy fields where a supranational or international action could not be sufficiently incisive.

Finally, it is also possible to hypothesize a further transversal categorization among networks on the basis of the main function they perform. This classification allows to subdivide networks into four main subgroups: a) networks established in order to promote training, cultural exchange and lobby activities aimed at fostering the autonomy and the independence of the judiciary; b) networks aimed at promoting meetings and forums for discussion devoted to inform and to bring other members up to date as regards domestic experiences; c) liaison networks devoted to deepening specific topics by means of studies and research; d) technical networks: namely groups of experts in charge of promoting techniques and operating methods among Member States and in charge of building databases (Amato and Dallara, 2012). The latter type, generally put in place by EU institutions, aims at acquiring and sharing technical and operative information concerning the action carried out by national administrations in specific fields. Their main aim is to favor the exchange of information in order to promote the most efficient application of certain practices at a national level.

In this chapter, in order to provide an accurate overview of transnational networks operating in Europe in the fields of justice and security, we propose a different way to depict this phenomenon, by distinguishing European judicial networks on the basis of the type of institutional process[4] through which they were created. Indeed, some networks have been established as a result of a top-down process by means of supranational legal acts, while some others rise from a bottom-up process originating from the spontaneous dialogue between judiciaries themselves. A third group of networks results from a hybrid process of institutionalization, such as those established under the aegis of the Council of Europe, since its origins are rooted in the institutional dialogue between European States, and its setting up has been formalized under international legal acts. Therefore, this classification allows us to identify three different groups of networks: a) networks established under EU law by means of EU secondary legislation; b) spontaneous networks established thanks to the initiatives of their own members; and c) Council of Europe networks.

Networks Established under EU Law by Means of EU Secondary Legislation[5]

All networks set up by the European legislature are contact-point networks, aiming at improving the coordination among national legal and judicial systems of EU Member States and to increase mutual trust, which is an essential condition for systems of mutual recognition to work (for a partial mapping see Table 2.1). They are mainly formed by one or more national contact points, appointed by Member States from the central authorities responsible for international judicial cooperation, as well as the judicial and prosecuting authorities working in this field. These contact points operate actively in the chain of judicial cooperation, through the exchange of information and informal contacts.

Among the networks established under EU legislature the best known is the European Judicial Network (EJN), which was the first mechanism of judicial cooperation to become fully operational. Having demonstrated its usefulness in the facilitation of judicial cooperation in criminal matters, in 2008 its legal basis was changed and Joint Action 98/428/JHA was repealed by Decision 2008/976/JHA. This change lay mainly in the wide implementation of the decentralization process of mutual legal assistance, as foreseen in Article 6 of the Convention on Mutual Assistance in Criminal Matters[6] and in the gradual application of the legal

4 Here the reference to "institutional process" means that, adopting an historical institutionalism approach (Pierson 2000), we will focus on the generative phase of the networks and the related acts throughout which they were created.

5 This paragraph was originally developed by Rosanna Amato for the paper "Judicial and legal expert networks. New actors for a EU area of justice?" See note 2 above.

6 Council Act of 29 May 2000 establishing in accordance with Article 34 of the Treaty on European Union the Convention on Mutual Assistance in Criminal Matters between the Member States of the European Union (2000/C 197/01). Art. 6.1 of the Convention states as follows: "Such requests shall be made directly between judicial authorities with

instruments based on the principle of mutual recognition of judicial decisions. These tools have confirmed the principle of direct contact between national judicial authorities and have further accelerated the procedures at issue making them entirely judicial.[7]

In more than 15 years of existence, EJN can be considered as a leading actor in the field of judicial cooperation, not only by reason of the impressive work realized, but also because it has become a model for other judicial networks within and outside Europe (Serzysko, 2011). The rationale behind such success can be found in the human factor, namely in the personification of a network's nodes. Beyond legal ties interlocking with contact points, members of the network constitute a genuine community of judges, prosecutors and officials from the national central authorities, strongly committed to making their experiences available for the benefit of judicial cooperation.

The same aim and structure also belong to the European Judicial Network in civil and commercial matters (EJN-civil), which brings together national authorities responsible for assisting local courts and for facilitating judicial and legal cooperation between Member States. Its main objective is to help people involved in civil and commercial disputes with a cross-border dimension, which is where more than one Member State is involved. The EJN-civil is composed of contact points, central bodies and central authorities provided for European and International legal acts, liaison magistrates where they have responsibilities in this field of law, legal professions and any other appropriate judicial or administrative authorities with responsibilities for judicial cooperation in civil and commercial matters (Amato and Dallara, 2012). The key role is played by the contact points, who assist judges when they need assistance/support in their contacts with foreign courts, local judicial authorities and other Network members. They reply to questions about European regulations, cooperation procedures, other Member States' laws, and authorities providing legal instruments relating to judicial cooperation in civil and commercial matters (such as national central authorities dealing with cases of parental responsibility or child abduction). Although this type of network can be considered to be "first generation," it is used to a very great extent to encourage cooperation, above all concerning security matters, since it represents a suitable method to favor the application of the principle of availability. By way of example, one can bear in mind Council Decision 2007/845/JHA, which requires Member States to put in place a network of Asset Recovery Offices, acting as national contact points, to facilitate EU-wide tracing of assets derived from crime, by exchanging information and best practices, both upon request and spontaneously (Arts. 3 and 4 of Council Decision 2007/845/JHA),

---

territorial competence for initiating and executing them, and shall be returned through the same channels unless otherwise specified in this Article."

7 Every year more than 1,000 cases of judicial cooperation in criminal matters have involved the assistance of the EJN. See "Report on the operation on European Judicial Network," 24 December 2008–24 December 2010.

regardless of their status (that is, administrative, law enforcement or judicial authority). The same approach has been adopted by the Commission in the so-called Strategy in Action,[8] which foresees the setting up of network-based arrangements composed by specialized contact points in order to handle a wide range of issues.

Council of Europe Networks

The networks established/instituted within the CoE are generally established throughout international agreements in the framework of the CoE. Although created outside EU legislation, they could be defined as institutionalized bodies acting in cooperation with EU institutions in the building of the EU Area of Justice. Formally, they have the status of "advisory body" of the CoE and they are primarily involved in standard-setting activities in the domain of judges' status, judicial organization and, more generally, rule of law promotion. The reason to look specifically at the CoE Networks is twofold: first, these networks have until now been studied less in respect to other networks; second, the CoE is becoming more and more the key advisory partner of the EU in connection with legal cooperation and other matters.

Piana (2010) defines the CoE a "partner for prestige" of the European Commission in the domain of legal and judicial cooperation, highlighting how the CoE, with the enlargement towards Central and Eastern Europe, was vested of a leading role in standards-setting (throughout its Networks) in the justice field. Today, the CoE is increasingly applying its empowered agenda in the justice field towards other countries and towards current EU Member States as well. This can also be regarded in light of the conclusions of the Juncker Report (2006)[9] on the relationship between the Council of Europe and the European Commission that suggests: "to move forward on the path to this pan-European legal and judicial area, the EU and the Council of Europe should also set up a joint platform to assess the feasibility of the EU's taking over Council standards, and vice-versa, each in accordance with its own responsibilities."

Many expert networks are working under the aegis of the Council of Europe in its three main domains of activity (Human Rights, Democracy and Rule of Law), but the most active and directly involved in judicial politics are the CCJE (Consultative Committee of European Judges), the CCPE (Consultative Committee

8 Communication from the Commission to the European Parliament and the Council, "The EU Internal Security Strategy in Action: Five steps towards a more secure Europe." Brussels, 22.11.2010 COM(2010) 673 final.

9 Juncker J.C., "Council of Europe – European Union: 'A Sole Ambition for the European Continent'" (Report by Jean-Claude Juncker, Prime Minister of the Grand Duchy of Luxembourg, to the attention of the Heads of State or Government of the Member States of the Council of Europe) 11 April 2006 http://assembly.coe.int/Sessions/2006/speeches/20060411_report_JCJuncker_EN.pdf

of European Prosecutors) and the CEPEJ (European Commission for the Efficiency of Justice). Among these it is also worth considering the European Commission for Democracy through Law (better-known as the Venice Commission), which is a sort of "leading actor" in terms of prestige and links with European Union institutions. Some judges and prosecutors also work within the GRECO network (Group of States against Corruption) or the Committee of Experts on the Evaluation of Anti-Money Laundering Measures and the Financing of Terrorism (MONEYVAL). Membership of these CoE networks is nationally based, meaning that the members are judges and prosecutors (but also law professors and officials from the Ministry of Justice in the cases of the Venice Commission or the CEPEJ) who are appointed from national political institutions to represent the country that is a member of the network. The political institutions appointing the network members can vary from country to country. In the majority of cases national governments (upon consultation with judicial institutions) appoint the individuals that will represent the country within the various CoE networks.

Spontaneous Networks Established at the Initiative of their own Members (Bottom-up Networks)

Within the European landscape, since 2004 a striking number of networks has been established at the initiative of national institutions or individual judicial authorities, which actively created relations with their counterparts in other Member States. Overall, these networks can be conceived as a tool for a voluntary horizontal collaboration, irrespective of national boundaries; they represent a sort of "agreement" *inter partes*, who serve similar functions in their own Member States.

These networks are usually created by representatives of specific judicial institutions (Supreme Courts, Constitutional Courts, Councils for the Judiciary, Training schools of the magistracy, etc.) that, by their own initiative, decide to establish an association or networks in order to have their own supranational body of reference. Among the most widely known networks falling into this group there are: the European Networks of the Council for the Judiciary (ENCJ), the European Judicial Training Network (ENJT) and the Network of the Presidents of the Supreme Judicial Courts of the European Union. Some of these networks are also supported by the European Commission, which also provides them with partial funding.

In this type of network the membership is generally nationally based, meaning that the members are judicial institutions of a specific State (for example, the Supreme Court of a country), and then two (or more) judges or prosecutors are appointed to represent the judicial institution member of the network.

A sort of sub-group of this type of network is composed of the international association of specialized judges such as the Association of European Administrative Judges (AEAJ) or the Association of European Competition Law Judges (AECLJ). These are supranational apex associations, and national associations of judges from countries of the European Union and the Council of Europe can become members. These international associations are primarily involved in organizing conferences, seminars and events to exchange ideas, to present common problems and to offer tools and solutions for the judges' activities.

Nowadays, the number of networks falling into this group is remarkable. Like EU networks, the main aim of bottom-up networks is also to foster judicial cooperation by performing an informative mission; nonetheless, the type of information that is shared, as well as the grounds for the sharing of such information, are different. EU contact points' networks can be considered as a tool to foster the effective application of legal instruments put in place by European Institutions to handle transnational challenges that cannot be addressed through a purely national response. As a result, information is mainly exchanged to solve practical problems resulting from judicial cooperation. Otherwise, within spontaneous networks, information is shared to favor the mutual knowledge and understanding of legal and judicial systems of each node and ultimately to identify opportunities for cooperation. The piece of information exchanged is instrumental to the creation of a common informative background and of a common legal and judicial culture. As already stated, the latter are of utmost importance within the EU framework, since a shared way of thinking contributes to building trust among Member States and can make the effective application of certain EU provisions based on mutual recognition acceptable and less traumatic. In substance, they could be considered as the expression of a soft strategy aiming at achieving long-term objectives, which relies on the socialization of its own members.

Table 2.1 Summary of the three groups of judicial networks operating in the EU space of justice

Network (or Commission)	Founding Act	Structure and Membership
Group 1: networks established under EU law by means of EU secondary legislation		
European Judicial Network (EJN)	Council Decision 2008/976/JHA	Central authorities responsible for international judicial cooperation; judicial or other competent authorities; liaison with magistrates (where appropriate); Commission's contact-point.
European Judicial Network in civil and commercial matters (EJN-civil)	Council Decision 2001/470/EC	Central bodies and authorities; liaison with magistrates (where appropriate); other appropriate judicial or administrative authorities; professional associations representing legal practitioners

Network (or Commission)	Founding Act	Structure and Membership
European Crime Prevention Network (ECPN)	Decision 2001/427/JHA, repealed by Council Decision 2009/902/JHA of November 30, 2009	National authorities competent in crime prevention; specialized researchers and academics; other actors in crime prevention; Commission representative.
European network of c.p. in respect of persons responsible for genocide	Council Decision 2002/494/JHA	National authorities (police or justice departments) in charge of investigation of genocide, crimes against humanity and war crimes
European Network for the protection of public figures	Council Decision 2002/956/JHA (amended by Decision 2009/796/JHA)	National police services and other services responsible for the protection of public figures (Candidate countries and Europol can participate)
Information network for combating high-tech crime	Council Recommendation 2001/C 187/02	Law enforcement networks combating IT-related crime
Immigration liaison officers network	Council Regulation 377/2004, amended by Regulation (EU) 493/2011	Representative of Member States, posted abroad by the immigration service or other competent authorities.
Group 2: Council of Europe networks		
European Commission for Democracy through Law – the Venice Commission	Resolution (90) 6 on a Partial Agreement establishing the European Commission for Democracy through Law	Judges or academics representing the Member States.
Consultative Committee of European Judges (CCJE)	…	Ordinary judges
Consultative Committee of European Prosecutors (CCPE)	Decision of the Ministers' Deputies on July 13, 2005	Ordinary prosecutors
European Committee on Legal Co-operation (CDCJ)	…	Representatives of all the CoE member states, principally from the ministries of justice.
European Commission for the Efficiency of Justice (CEPEJ)	Resolution Res(2002)12 of the Committee of Ministers of the Council of Europe	Judges and judicial experts

continued

Table 2.1 *concluded*

Network (or Commission)	Founding Act	Structure and Membership
Group 3: Spontaneous networks established at the initiatives of their own members (bottom-up networks)		
Conference of European Constitutional Courts (CECC)	…	Constitutional Courts
Network of the Presidents of the Supreme Courts (NPSC)	Constituent Assembly 10/3/2004 - (financial support AGIS program).	Supreme Courts
European Networks of the Council for the Judiciary (ENJC)	ENCJ Constituency assembly – Rome, May 20–21, 2004	High Judicial Council
European Judicial Training Network (EJTN)	…	National judicial training institutions
Association of the Councils of State and Supr. Administ. Jurisd.	Institution agreement -16th colloquium (Stockholm) from 14 to 17 June 1998	Councils of State; Supreme Administrative Courts; Court of Justice of the European Union
Association of European Administrative Judges (AEAJ)	Founded on March 24, 2000 in Trier	National associations of administrative judges from Member States of the European Union and the Council of Europe
Association of European Competition Law Judges (AECLJ)	Created in Luxembourg in September 2002	Groups national judges working in the area of European competition law
The European Judges and Prosecutors Association (EJPA)	…	Judges and prosecutors from nine different European countries (F, ES, IT, PT, D, NE, Cz, HU, RO).

Judicial Networks Instruments

In the light of the proposed categorization, our aim is to identify different instruments through which each different type of network contributes to RoL promotion across and beyond Member States' territories. In this way we would like to go beyond a general description of judicial networks as functional in judicial dialogue and informal judicial cooperation, aiming at evidencing the differences among the multitude of judicial networks and, in particular, the different formal and informal mechanisms of diffusing and implementing EU law principles.

Networks Established under EU Law[10]

Overall, the tasks performed by EU networks can be mainly related to a fundamental activity of exchange of information as well as technical and specialist support or, to a lesser degree, coordination activities. The final aim is clearly to foster the effectiveness of the system as a whole; for this reason, generally, networks' contact points have to give assistance to the national and local authorities of their own Member State and have also to be available to support contact points, local judicial authorities and other competent authorities in other Member States. This goal can be achieved through different operating methods, for instance by putting in place mediation mechanisms through which it is possible to provide for an efficient circulation of data and information, as well as deepening specific topics and problems through studies based on common examinations and meetings aimed at sharing methodologies used at a national level.

Active intermediation in mutual recognition procedures and mutual assistance instruments

Networks falling within this category are inspired by an idea of "mutual assistance" and, in certain cases, by forms of "spontaneous assistance"; accordingly, competent national authorities can lend mutual support, even in absence of a formal request for collaboration. This type of assistance is carried out to encourage the circulation of useful information. One good example is the aforementioned ARO's Decision, which provides for spontaneous exchange of information, within the limits of applicable national law.

Another good example can be found in the European Network of Contact Points in respect of persons responsible for genocide, crimes against humanity and war crimes; thus, art. 2.1 states "within the limits of the applicable national law, contact points may exchange information without a request to that effect." This network was established in 2002, in the immediate aftermath of the entry into force of the Rome Statute setting up the International Criminal Court (ICC), with a view to foster cooperation in combating genocide, crimes against humanity and war crimes. The European Union is deeply committed to cooperating with the ICC in order to put an end to perpetrators committing such crimes with impunity; it expressly advanced universal support for the effective and efficient functioning of the international Court and the implementation of the principle

10 This paragraph was originally developed by Rosanna Amato for the paper "Judicial and legal expert networks. New actors for a EU area of justice?" See note 2 above.

of complementarity. In the light of the latter principle, the investigation and prosecution of genocide, crimes against humanity and war crimes continue to be the responsibility of national authorities. Therefore, in order to ensure that these crimes can be combated successfully, Member States are called to show closer cooperation between the competent national authorities and are asked to designate a contact point for the exchange of any available information that may be relevant in the context of such investigations. Nowadays, the EU Network represents the most significant progress made within the EU's JHA policy in relation to accountability for serious international crimes. By reason of the growing horizontal operational cooperation, the Network evolved from a "paper body to a real tool of practical relevance to prosecutors, police investigators and ministries of justice alike", allowing national authorities to send and answer mutual requests for cooperation, avoiding recourse to traditional procedures of mutual assistance. Since its entry into force, the Network has successfully supported the prosecution of several cases in the national courts, also ensuring close cooperation with the national authorities of third states, the International Criminal Court, and other international tribunals and civil society.

Concerning the European Judicial Network (criminal), the main operational method used by the Network consists in a sort of mediation mechanism aimed at facilitating judicial cooperation between Member States, particularly concerning actions to combat forms of serious crime. In this context, contact points have to operate as "active intermediaries." Such an activity covers a variety of actions, which can be divided into two main types. As to the first type, contact points are asked to provide information concerning the national law of the "requested" Member State; data can be demanded by contact points of other Member States as well as by national or foreign local authorities in order to have a knowledge of a broad variety of topics; by way of example, many requests concern the features of the national legal or judicial systems or the application of local law. The second type of activity is more heterogeneous, since it is aimed at ensuring support during the preparation, execution or delays of execution of a request for judicial cooperation, especially in respect of the classic mutual legal assistance procedures—as envisaged in the Convention of 29 May 2000 and its Protocol, agreed in 2001—and to the application of mutual recognition instruments.

In the light of the evaluation Report issued in 2010, almost half of the requests for assistance addressed to contact points (coming from both national and foreign authorities) concern the mutual assistance procedure; other types of intervention are less common, with the exception of requests concerning the EAW, which represent a significant percentage of the total amount.

Periodic meetings to address common problems and to adopt common positions

One of the main operating methods used by these networks consists in the organization of meetings focused on specific topics. For instance, the Network of Contact Points in respect of persons responsible for genocide, crimes against humanity and war crimes organizes periodic meetings devoted to investigations and prosecutions of suspects in relation to a certain conflict as well as identification and access to witnesses abroad, witness and victim protection or the international framework for international cooperation and cooperation with the ad hoc tribunals, the ICC and NGOs. With a view to make investigations and prosecutions more effectively national, contact points do not limit their contributions to the sharing of information, but they try to identify common needs that could be addressed jointly, possibly via action of the EU Network and with the support of the European Commission. Particularly important are the sections of these meetings open only to judicial authorities, where the exchange of confidential information is allowed.

The EJN (criminal) also uses this operating method, with a view to sharing practical experiences and creating living documents aiming at developing and fostering the Network's work. In particular, it organizes plenary meetings devoted to the creation of internal rules of functioning; for instance, during the 33rd plenary meeting, attention was paid to the vision of the EJN Secretariat and the structure of the Network in the aftermath of the entry into force of both the EJN Decision and Eurojust Decision. Other important meetings are those organized, at least once a year, by national correspondents to discuss administrative and budgetary matters mainly. This mechanism is also a good tool for fostering more effective cooperation between the EJN and third parties, for instance with Eurojust, ECLAN, CoE or other regional judicial networks such as IberRed.

Updating of IT tools supporting judicial cooperation

It has to be stressed that the effective functioning of such a mediation mechanism is strongly tied to the development of different modern IT tools aimed at ensuring informative support. For example, in compliance with art. 3 (c) and art. 8.1 of Decision 2008/976/JHA, the EJN is committed to regularly providing a certain amount of up-to-date background information, in particular by means of an appropriate telecommunications network. These pieces of information have to be available on a website which is constantly updated by the EJN Secretariat and must also be diffused by means of appropriate telecommunications tools in the fight against transnational crime. Nonetheless, several problems affect operational/strategic cooperation activity, above all the attitude of national judicial authorities who are not very keen on supranational coordination. In addition, although formally conceived as an "agency," Eurojust performs some of its functions in a similar way to other networks operating in this field; it has to be evidenced that certain functions can be overlapped in networks' activities, above all those carried out by the EJN. In this light, the full exercise of a coordination role in respect to transnational investigation seems to be a partially dormant potentiality. Similar observations could be driven also in respect to Europol, is the European Union's multi-disciplinary criminal intelligence agency operating in the field of police cooperation. Although Europol's competencies were expanded and it was assigned both a quasi-operational function and an advisory function, the main tasks performed consist in the collection, storage, processing, analysis and exchange of information and intelligence by means of liaison officials.

To summarize, networks established under EU legislature perform their informative mission with a view to fostering the effectiveness of the system of judicial cooperation created within the AFSJ (Area of freedom, security and justice). These are human networks providing updated information concerning national systems as well as technical and specialist support through two main channels. The first is participation in periodic meetings, which can also constitute an opportunity for the adoption of common positions and for the elaboration of reports addressed either to EU institutions or to Member States. As to the second, it consists in mediation mechanisms put in place by the contact points, through which practical support can be granted to national judicial authorities in the fight against crime.

Thus, the activities of these networks could be described as practical support exercised by judicial actors (national contact points) which, by performing their judicial functions, contribute to the concrete cooperation among national judiciaries in relation to supranational judicial cases. The impact of this first group of networks on EU law diffusion and implementation is direct and easy to describe as they contribute to the effective functioning of EU judicial cooperation in civil and criminal matters and in the application of mutual recognition instruments, such as the European Arrest Warrant (2002/584/JHA), Freezing Orders (2003/577/JHA), Financial Penalties (2005/214/JHA) and Confiscation orders (2006/783/JHA).

Council of Europe Networks

Standard-setting activity on the basis of EU fundamental rights

As already mentioned, the work of the CoE networks is mainly focused on standard setting based on the production of recommendations, opinions and best practices. These types of document are commonly defined as "soft-law" instruments, meaning that they are non-binding in their nature. Within these documents, "minimum standards" of democracy and rule of law are proposed. Opinions, recommendations and best practices could be requested by the individual country members of the networks (concerning specific draft law or amendments or specific problems) or by other European bodies. In the case of the CoE networks, the CoE Parliamentary Assembly, the Committee of Ministers and Secretary General and also the European Union (namely the European Parliament or the European Commission) request opinions as legal adviser activity. The CoE networks activity is mainly focused on the functioning and on the organization of judicial systems, with specific attention paid to the guarantees related to judges' status. Here the point is that, although in the EU the organization and the rules concerning judicial systems remain a matter of each state's sovereignty, it seems that judicial networks are proposing, in a more or less nuanced way, institutional models for the organization of judicial systems and judicial institutions, especially for countries within the EU. This activity is also supported by EU institutions and is functional in the "institutional and legal harmonization" of judicial systems that is one of the preconditions of the EU Area of Justice.

Regarding the Opinions of the CCJE (Consultative Committee of European Judges) and the CCPE (Consultative Committee of European Prosecutors), it is interesting to focus our attention on the topics they deal with. They range from "Standards, concerning the independence of the judiciary and the irremovability of judges," "Training for judges," "Council for the Judiciary in the service of society," to "Relations between Judges and Prosecutors in a democratic society".[11] All of them are topics related to the organization of the judicial system and, concerning their content, they propose "best solutions or practices" to organize judicial institutions. For example, an opinion issued by one the networks listed above (CCJE) suggests the creation of High Councils of the Judiciary as the best way "to safeguard the independence of the judiciary and the rule of law". As for the Opinions of the CCPE (Consultative Committee of European Prosecutors), the type of suggestions they propose is very similar to those of the CCJE.

The documents elaborated by the CEPEJ (European Commission for the Efficiency of Justice) are, instead, less focused on the institutional role of the judiciary or on the guarantees of judicial independence and more tailored on the efficient functioning of justice. Thus, they also elaborate more practical tools to be applied in the concrete courts management, such as a handbook for court satisfaction surveys, a compendium of "best practices" on time management of judicial proceedings, a time management checklist and a checklist for promoting the quality of justice and the courts.

Finally, there is the multitude of Opinions elaborated by the Venice Commission (VC), perhaps the most widely known CoE Commission. Concerning the VC, it is worth mentioning that this network is not only formed by judges or prosecutors but, instead, by members who are primarily academics, supreme or constitutional court judges or members of national parliaments. In truth, many of the academics appointed by the national government at the VC are—or were—judges in Constitutional or Supreme courts. Moreover, although the original mission of the VC was specifically related to the "Constitutional assistance" (as it is the CoE advisory body on constitutional matters), during the last 10 years the number and the type of activities performed by the network has significantly increased, going beyond its original function of advisor on constitutional matters: the Commission has played an increasingly global role in producing knowledge, documents, opinions and guidelines on various governance issues. Within the multitude of the topics dealt with, many topics of judicial policy have also found a place.

In effect, the VC has produced many Opinions on specific country laws related to the judicial system, judicial appointment, judges' status, etc. These Opinions were requested either by individual countries or by CoE bodies. Recently the VC has further enlarged its production by elaborating Opinions not only concerning specific

11 Opinion no.10 (2007) of the Consultative Council of European Judges (CCJE) to the attention of the Committee of Ministers of the Council of Europe on the Council for the Judiciary at the service of society. This Opinion was adopted by the CCJE at its eighth meeting (Strasbourg, 21–23 November 2007).

country law, but also concerning European Standards of judicial independence, European Standards of the Prosecution Service and judicial appointment. At the basis of all these standards and best practices there is the diffusion of EU principles of law respecting the EU's fundamental principles and values.

The right to an independent and impartial court was laid down clearly in Article 6 of the European Convention on Human Rights and, by way of the Article of the EU Treaty, it is also inserted among the EU fundamental rights. The work of the CCJE, the CCPE and the CEPEJ is set in the context of the implementation of this right, with the aim of strengthening the rule of law and the effective protection of human rights in democratic States.

Thus, from a general point of view, the opinions elaborated by the CoE networks have been primarily useful for CoE Member States for the purposes of drafting national regulations and legislations concerning the functioning and the administration of justice, for the organization of the work of legal professions and for judges and judicial service commissions. This is the first type of mechanism through which these networks contribute to the diffusion and application of EU law principles. Sometimes the suggestions elaborated by the networks were, and are, spontaneously adopted by countries as a way of international legitimization of national reforms.

Formal request for technical assistance by EU institutions

In the light of the aforementioned increasing cooperation between the CoE and EU institutions in the field of justice, EU bodies are starting to request official collaboration and technical assistance from CoE judicial networks in order to define important aspects of EU judicial policy. In 2013, for example, the CEPEJ Bureau accepted the request from the European Commission to prepare a report on the impact of the functioning of judicial systems on the economy of the EU Member States, based on the CEPEJ methodology for evaluating judicial systems and justice administrations.

Elaboration of binding criteria and standards for EU enlargement policy

Going into more detail, it is worth mentioning that documents elaborated by the networks and commissions of the CoE were, in many cases, behind judicial reforms adopted in Central and Eastern European countries during the EU pre-accession stage, as the European Commission made explicit use of these standards in preparing the yearly Action Plan for each candidate country with a list of reforms and legislative changes they had to introduce in order to advance towards EU membership. Several studies concerning cooperation between the European Commission and the CoE networks are available in the context of the EU enlargement policy, all evidencing how the standard-setting activity of these networks was absolutely critical to the EU proposing to candidate countries specific criteria and solutions for reforming their judicial systems and other public administration bodies. For this reason, CoE networks were frequently cited as terms of reference within the multitude of EC Annual Reports prepared to monitor the progress of all countries involved in the EU enlargement policy. These are still the terms of reference for the Balkan countries with a status of candidate or potential candidate for EU membership.

Recently the CoE judicial networks have been working officially as partners of the European Commission, not only in relation to the rule of law criteria, but also in the context of the EU Neighborhood Policy that is a specific policy-action to establish political and commercial relations with countries outside the geopolitical borders without a membership perspective.

Cooperation with the EU institution in monitoring EU law application

In the last few years, formal ties have significantly increased between the CoE networks and EU institutions in relation to aspects of judicial politics. The Venice Commission, for example, is progressively becoming a sort of leading advisory body not only for the CoE but also for EU institutions. An interesting case of cooperation between the VC and EU institutions is related to the high-pitched debate on the Hungarian Constitution that will be analyzed in the next chapter.

The increasing interest of EU institutions towards the work of the Venice Commission is also witnessed by a recent request from the European Commission. Within the framework of the EU and Bosnia and Herzegovina's Structured Dialogue on the work of the judiciary, in October 2011, for the first time, the Venice Commission was formally asked to elaborate an opinion concerning "how the judicial framework, the division of powers and the existing co-ordination mechanisms affect legal certainty and the independence of the judiciary in Bosnia and Herzegovina." The opinion, issued on June 2012, was an important point of reference during the third meeting of the "Structured Dialogue on Justice between the European Union and Bosnia and Herzegovina." In its Recommendations, the European Commission expressly stated that "it expects that all competent authorities will take stock of the detailed expert assessment provided on several key areas throughout the opinion."

Sources and terms of reference for ECHR rulings

VC Opinions and Recommendations, together with the documents of other CoE Networks, were also frequently used as "Other relevant sources" in the ECHR rulings. The documents elaborated by CoE networks are cited as "minimum standards" courts have to guarantee, especially regarding the right of a fair trial as stated in Article 6 of the European Convention on Human Rights. To give an example of this practice, we use the ECHR ruling on "Bulanov and Kupchik vs Ukraine" issued in March 2011. This was the case of two Ukrainian citizens (their applications were joined due to a common legal background) who complained that their cases had not obtained access to appeal due to an apparent conflict of jurisdiction between the Higher Administrative Court and the Supreme Court.

Here the ECHR, after having cited all the relevant Ukrainian laws for the topic, lists as "Relevant Council of Europe material" the Opinion of the Venice Commission on the Law on the Judicial System in Ukraine. The Court further cited that the observations of the Venice Commission and the Council of Europe Directorates were particularly relevant in determining the competence of the Supreme Court and its duties to accept such cases. Thus the Court concluded that there was a violation of Article 6.1 of the Convention and the right access to court had not been secured.

The relevance of the Venice Commission Opinion relies on the fact that it was cited as the standard to follow in order to establish Supreme Court competences. In this way the VC Recommendation acquires a different status in respect of the non-legally binding document it was supposed to be. CEPEJ documents are also frequently cited in Judgments of the European Court of Human Rights as a source for determining the rights of a fair trial. Here, the tie with EU law application is strong and clearly stated by the already mentioned inclusion of the fundamental rights as guaranteed by the European Convention in Article 6 of the Treaty on the European Union.

Bottom-up Networks and Judges' Associations

Networks of judicial institutions and professionals affect the diffusion and the implementation of EU law by way of a multitude of tools and instruments, such as conferences, training courses, collaborative projects and collective reflections on problems linked to judges' work.

As highlighted in the study of Claes and De Visser (2012) the specific aims of these networks are the improvement of the knowledge of other legal systems to share practical experiences and the promotion of the exchange of ideas establishing best practices or a common legal culture. Finally, and in particular for judges' associations, their aim is to advance the interests of their members at the national and/or European level.

Activity of socialization and diffusion of EU law principles

Among the European bottom-up networks of institutions, one of the most active and well known is the European Network of the Council for the Judiciaries (ENCJ); it was established in 2004 with a view to consolidate the relationship that spontaneously developed between the national Councils and the Judiciary of EU Member States, especially for want of an Italian one. In response to the developments affecting the EU, and consequently the role of national judges, the Network was conceived as a tool to get acquainted with each other's systems and organizations, to exchange information, to learn about each other's accomplishments and mistakes and to assess the possibilities for cooperation in various fields. Nowadays, the ENCJ is an institutional network representing, at EU level, all the Councils for the Judiciary or other national institutions which are independent of the executive and legislature (or which are autonomous), and which are responsible for the support of the Judiciary in the independent delivery of justice. Although this Network was set up out of the EU legal framework, the role it plays, clearly, is strongly tied to the strengthening of the AFSJ and, in a certain way it is possible to say that the ENCJ serves EU objectives. Its Statute expressly highlights these ties.

In compliance with the network's internal rules, ENCJ mainly performs its functions by means of working groups created to deal with specific topics. Members of each team realize a close examination on particular aspects related to the function of the judiciary in EU Member States, with a view to developing common actions aimed at fostering and approximating practices at a European level.

In addition, the European Judicial Training Network (EJTN) is a very important bottom-up network. It was founded by the schools of judges and other institutions specifically responsible for the training of the professional judiciary of all EU Member States, in order to develop among them a genuine cooperation. Within this network, participant institutions can coordinate their actions, share best practices and develop common curricula for judges and prosecutors. Moreover, the EJTN has been given exclusive responsibility by the EU institutions for implementing the Exchange Program for judicial authorities. In the view of the DG Justice "Training of judges and prosecutors on European law and on national legal systems and its cooperation at European level are more advanced than for other professions thanks to the creation of the European Judicial Training Network (EJTN) in 2000, which has the monopoly of coordinating at European level the activities of the national judicial training schools and structures of the EU member States, and thanks to the involvement of its members in the EJTN's activities."

Participation in consultation with EC stakeholders

Some of the bottom-up networks were also actively engaged in the consultation procedure issued by the European Commission. As is widely known, the EU sometimes faces criticism for the lack of clarity or for the poor quality of its legislation, and for this reason the need for better law making has been recognized at the highest political level and has been realized through an ever expanding activity of consultation performed by the Commission. Opinions and reports concerning different fields of law can be proposed to EU institutions spontaneously or by request of the Commission. The ENCJ, for example, elaborates recommendations or opinions in response to the consultation of stakeholders by the European Commission. The ENCJ was also asked to elaborate a form, written in all the languages of the Countries concerned, to enforce a payment order for uncontested pecuniary claims in civil and commercial matters across the European Union. More recently, ENCJ participated in a broad consultation of all stakeholders in judicial training matter launched by the Commission with a view to define core activities and priorities in such a field. Apart from the ENCJ, many other European networks were also asked to take part in this consultation, inter alia the European Judicial Training Network (EJTN) and its members.

Know-how and collective interests representation

Concerning the specific logic of action of judges' associations, they are primarily involved in organizing conferences, seminars and events to exchange ideas, to present common problems and to offer tools and solutions for judges' activities (such as the Association of the Councils of State and Supreme Administrative Jurisdictions of the European Union), the NPSJC (Network of the Presidents of the Supreme Judicial Courts), the EJPA (European Judges and Prosecutors Association) and the AECLJ (Association of European Competition Law Judges).

The AEAJ is currently one of the most active networks, encouraging improvements in the availability of legal redress vis-à-vis public authorities and it promotes the legality of administrative acts, while respecting the legal cultures in the various national legal systems. The main activity of this network is the dissemination of information on legal redress in administrative matters by means of an extensive exchange of pertinent case law and legislation. It also provides its members with practical know-how concerning exercising their national mandate, with special attention to matters concerning European law. As described by Claes and De Visser (2012), in 2010, for example, the Association of the Councils of State and Supreme Administrative Jurisdictions of the European Union organized a working visit of two weeks for 12 judges to a court of another Member State. The invited judges participated fully in the daily activities of the host institution: they attended hearings, deliberated on the verdict and assisted in the writing of the final judgment. At the end of the training, the participating judges wrote a report about their visit.

Finally, as already mentioned, these networks aim to advance the interests of their members at the national and European level. Thus, the AEAJ is not only involved in improving the knowledge of other legal systems, but another of its objectives, as written in its Statute, is to "promote the professional interests of administrative judges at national and European level vis-à-vis the institutions of the European Union and the Council of Europe." The description of the bottom-up networks' activities and logics of action allow us to affirm that these networks are performing more and more as real stakeholders in the EU policy building the Area of Justice.

Inclusion as main actors and stakeholders in EU judicial policy actions and programs

In line with the aforementioned statements, recent documents, issued by the European Commission on the creation of the EU Area of Justice, also stressed the relevance of judicial networks for EU judicial policy.

On 13 September 2011, the European Commission adopted the Communication "Building trust in EU-wide justice: a new dimension to European judicial training." Here it is explained as "The Commission is encouraging national and European level networks, professional organizations and training structures to work together, exchange best practices on training methods, build consortia and set up trans-sectorial training activities." Then, in the Proposal for a Regulation of the European Parliament and of the Council on the Justice Programme COM(2011) 759, this Specific action is described as: "support for main actors, ... support for key European level networks whose activities are linked to the implementation of the objectives of the Programme; networking among specialized bodies and organizations, ... ; funding of experts' networks; ... ." Finally, the EC Justice Programme 2014–2020, with a budget of €416 million, aims at the creation of a European Area of Justice by promoting judicial cooperation in civil and criminal matters. Specific action to be supported in the program will be: "Strengthening EU cooperation on justice and rights issues through networks of legal practitioners, non-governmental organizations and policy-makers."

Furthermore, it seems that the European Commission is starting to involve judicial networks in a more official way in some specific areas such as judicial training. In fact, recently, the DG Justice has launched a tender for a study on judicial training in Europe, stating that one of the specific aims of the project that will be financed has to be the "Promotion of cooperation between judicial stakeholders concerned by European judicial training" and in particular "the cooperation between the European Judicial Training Network and its members with judicial training providers and with the European level judicial organisations such as the European Network of the Councils for the Judiciary, the Network of the Presidents of the Supreme Judicial Courts, the Association of the Councils of State and Supreme Administrative Jurisdictions and the Network of the General Prosecutors of the Supreme Judicial Courts of the EU."

The DG Justice will also aim at having an overview of the "state of play" of the respective roles of the European Judicial Training Network together with its relevant partners and networks at European level and to sign a "Roadmap" for the cooperation among them in order to improve the training of judges and prosecutors in national legal systems and traditions, as well as in European Union law and judicial cooperation procedures.

Conclusion

Judicial networks in Europe are numerous and heterogeneous in their composition. With the aim of mapping the field with a wide-ranging perspective, we apply a broader definition of judicial networks including all the groups, conferences, commissions or organizations of legal experts and judges that: 1) are coming from different countries; 2) are established at a transnational level; and 3) are involved in the exchange of ideas and practices, in the production of recommendations, opinions and best practices concerning different fields of law and the functioning of the judicial system, and in the organization of seminars, conferences and training of judges and legal experts. Within this broad category we define three main groups of networks on the basis of the institutional process through which they were created. In this way we found a first group of networks established under EU secondary legislation and primarily involved in the concrete operative functioning of judicial cooperation in cross-border cases. Then we considered as a specific group all the networks and commissions established within the framework of the Council of Europe and actively engaged in judicial standard-setting activity functional in EU institutions. Finally, we analyzed the networks created by representatives of specific judicial institutions (Supreme Courts, Constitutional Courts, Councils for the Judiciary, training schools for the magistracy, etc.) or by group of specialized judges, that by their own initiative decide to establish an association or a network in order to have their own supranational body of reference (Table 2.2). Having in mind these mechanisms, one of the next steps in the research on judicial networks could be focused on the deeper analysis of how the judicial networks activity differently impacts on the following three levels: on the definitions of national laws (coherent with the EU law principles); on the applications of EU rights and policies by national courts; on EU policy and law making (also by mean of the possible future major integrations between the ECHR system of fundamental rights protection and that of the EU).

Table 2.2 An overview of the main networks' instruments

Type of judicial network	Instruments
EU Law Networks	Active intermediation supporting mutual assistance procedures and mutual recognition instruments Organization of meetings to address common problems and to adopt common positions
Council of Europe Networks	Standard-setting activity on the basis of EU fundamental rights Formal requests for technical assistance by EU institutions Elaboration of binding criteria and standards for EU enlargement policy Cooperation with the EU institution in monitoring EU law application Sources and terms of reference for ECHR rulings
Bottom-up Networks	Networks as recognized arenas of socialization and diffusion of EU law principles Participation in EC stakeholder consultations Inclusion as main actors and stakeholders in EU judicial policy actions and programs Know-how and collective interests representation

Chapter 3

The Role of the Venice Commission in Two RoL Reversal Cases: Hungary and Romania[1]

Introduction

As already pointed out in the previous chapters, we consider RoL networking to be a process through which actors, located at different levels of governance, create, diffuse, enforce, and dismantle procedures, routines, policies and standards of RoL and quality of justice.

Different instruments, which range over a wide spectrum, from advising to standard setting to training, are used and put in place by each of the judicial networks to promote and, in some way, to protect the RoL.

In this respect, our hypothesis focuses precisely on (the determinacy of) the external mechanisms of influence. Is the mechanism of influence—a structural variable—the causal factor that could explain the adaptation to RoL policies being externally driven? In what way, and under which conditions, could some TR-NTKs act as "external agents of change"?

As already described, the EU is currently engaged in an unprecedented process of building a common and reliable Area of Justice based on cooperation and trust among Member States and national judicial institutions. In doing this, the EU (namely the EC) together with the CoE, is actively engaged in a process of externally promoting harmonization and cooperation among national judiciaries (Piana, 2012). The existence and the enforcement of common RoL standards and principles is a pre-condition to foster these goals. The EU is founded on the "rule of law." The expression appears in the preamble to the EU Treaty and then again in Article 2 TEU as one of the Union's key values together with democracy, freedom and respect for human dignity.[2] This is the reason why respect for the RoL is one

---

1 Cristina Dallara has authored this chapter.

2 As Pech (2009) reminds us, the 2007 Lisbon Treaty, which entered into force on December 1, 2009, merely reproduced the provision previously contained in the Constitutional Treaty, which means that the Treaty on European Union (TEU) now contains a provision known as Article 2 TEU and which provides that: "The Union is founded on the values of respect for human dignity, freedom, democracy, equality, the rule of law and respect for human rights, including the rights of persons belonging to minorities. These values are common to the Member States in a society in which pluralism, non-discrimination, tolerance, justice, solidarity and equality between women and men prevail."

of the fundamental criteria candidates have to fulfill to join the EU and which each Member State has to guarantee.

In this context, our aim is to focus on the mechanism of external influence to depict how it could explain changes and convergence in national judicial policies. Specifically, we would like to describe how some judicial networks act and intervene in this two-level game reinforcing and, somehow, replacing the external influence exerted by the European international organizations.

With reference to the candidate countries for EU membership, some scholars (Parau, 2013) have argued that translational legal and judicial communities exert a sort of "extra-conditionality" on candidates in the field of judicial governance.[3]

In this chapter our aim is to analyze a peculiar judicial network, the Venice Commission, in acting as an RoL promoter and its increasing "supplementary role" in protecting EU funding values. The focus on this transnational Commission will allow us to reflect on the determinacy of the external influence model and, on the other side, to assess how, under specific circumstances, judicial networks could become external change-agents able to introduce and maintain internationally driven changes on national judicial policies.

The Venice Commission: In Between the CoE and the EU

The Council of Europe Venice Commission, formally named European Commission for Democracy through Law, is defined as the Council of Europe's advisory body on constitutional matters.[4] By statute, "the role of the Venice Commission is to provide legal advice to its member states and, in particular, to help states wishing to bring their legal and institutional structures into line with European standards and international experience in the fields of democracy, human rights and the rule of law." Moreover, "it also helps to ensure the dissemination and consolidation of a common constitutional heritage, playing a unique role in conflict management" and provides "emergency constitutional aid" to states in transition. Countries' representative members (of the various countries) are "university professors of public and international law, supreme and constitutional court judges, members of national parliaments and a number of civil servants."[5]

Its permanent secretariat is located in Strasbourg, France, at the headquarters of the Council of Europe. Its plenary sessions are held in Venice, Italy, at the

3 See Chapter 1 in this Book.

4 The analysis of this case is largely based on findings of the research project conducted by Cristina Dallara with the Jean Monnet fellowship (2011–2012) in the Global Governance Programme at the European University Institute of Fiesole, under the mentorship of Miguel Poiares Maduro. I would like to thank Antoine Vauchez (CNRS-Sorbonne) for his suggestions on the topic.

5 See the official website http://www.venice.coe.int/WebForms/pages/?p=01_Presentation.

Scuola Grande di San Giovanni Evangelista, four times a year (March, June, October and December).

We are faced with a peculiar type of transnational network for several reasons:[6] first of all for its composition, since it mixes high court judges, legal experts and some parliamentary members. Second, although formally placed under the edge of the CoE, the VC, starting from its creation in 1990, had an independent and peculiar organizational development that will be described in detail later on. Third, among the members are included not only CoE Member States, but also a good number of North-African and Latin American countries. Moreover, the OSCE (Organization for Security and Co-operation in Europe) and the EU are official members of the VC and, as with other members, they are entitled to ask the VC to intervene on specific matters. On this last point, it has to be kept in mind that, in the majority of the cases, the VC intervenes upon request of national institutions (be they governments, Constitutional Courts or other institutions) or upon request of the CoE Secretary General or Committee of Ministers. This specific role of true "advisory body upon request," mainly differentiates this transnational network from those others mentioned in previous chapters. This point will be recalled later on, evidencing and highlighting the increasing connection between the VC and the EU (namely the EC and the EU Parliament) and in particular describing cases in which EU institutions "officially" call for VC intervention and advice.

Foundation and Institutionalization of the VC

The Venice Commission was created in 1990 and since its establishment it has played a crucial role in disseminating European fundamental legal values and providing Constitutional first-aid to individual states. In effect, it was initially conceived as a tool for emergency constitutional engineering, as a partial agreement of 18 Member States of the CoE. A focus on this generative momentum is crucial for a deep understanding of the peculiarity of this Commission.

La Pergola was the founding father and the key-actor of the entire VC project. Fiche 3.1 summarizes the main biographical information on La Pergola, which is particularly relevant/useful to understanding his role in the foundation and development of the VC.

As described in Fiche 3.1, La Pergola was the Italian Minister for the Community policies from 1987 to 1989, thus participating in the CoE Committee of Ministers. In this context he proposed the creation of a specific group of constitutional experts within the CoE with the aim of maintaining close relations with other constitutional judges and experts in Latin America and in the Communist area.

6 The majority of Venice Commission members that the author of this chapter interviewed in 2012–2013, did not agree on defining the VC as a transnational network. They stressed its peculiar role and composition which make it more similar to an international organization in the broad sense.

Fiche 3.1 Biographical information on La Pergola

Antonio La Pergola* (1931–2007) was professor of constitutional and public law at Padua University, and subsequently at the University of Bologna and Rome. He was also visiting professor and honorary professor at several foreign universities.

La Pergola was a member of the Italian Supreme Council of the Judiciary (1976–1978), judge at the Constitutional Court, acting as rapporteur for significant judgments in the field of relations between Community law and domestic law (1978–1986), then President of that Court (1986–1987) and Minister for coordinating Community policies (1987–1989). During this appointment he sponsored the law on fulfillment of the obligations resulting from Italy's membership of the European Communities (1986–1989). Then he held important positions at EU level: firstly, Member of the European Parliament and Chairman of the Committees on scientific research and culture and of the Committee on Energy, Research and Technology (1989–1994) and then Advocate-General and judge of the European Court of Justice (1994–2006). In the EP he was appointed for the Socialist Italian Party and during his whole mandate he also acted as Delegate in relations with the countries of Central America and with Mexico. He was a member of a number of international expert bodies for constitutional and legal matters. Within the Council of Europe, he founded and chaired the Venice Commission from 1990 to 2007, year of his death.

* Information and data gathered by different public websites, in particular the European Parliament website, the Academy of Europe website, the Enciclopedia Treccani. These were confirmed in an interview the author had with Gianni Buquicchio (President of the VC), La Pergola collaborator and successor.

Source: Fiche compiled using data from the website of the Venice Commission <http://www.venice.coe.int/webforms/events/?id=684 >.

This proposal was rejected two times, as the dominant idea at that time considered constitutional justice to be the "sancta-sanctorum" of national sovereignty.[7]

In 1989 however, he created an independent international group of constitutional experts that only had the patronage of the CoE. Then in 1990 an historical critical juncture (Pierson, 2000) turned in favor of La Pergola's idea. With the fall of the Berlin Wall the CoE understood the need for an official body able to monitor and dialogue with jurists, legal experts and political actors from Eastern Europe and then agreed on the creation of the VC. This was the "policy window" (Kingdon, 1995) allowing the European international organizations (OSCE, CoE and EU) to play their game and to start with the massive international influence that political science research had extensively analyzed and described. The VC was officially constituted in January 1990 on the occasion of the second *ad hoc* international conference held in Venice, organized by the Italian government

7 Interview with Gianni Buquicchio (President of the VC) La Pergola collaborator and successor.

with the participation of CoE Member States. Later, the CoE Committee of the Ministers formally recognized it with a partial agreement[8] in May 1990 among the 18 Member States (Bode-Kirchhoff, 2014). During the 1990s the VC was actively engaged in assistance and advice to the Eastern European countries in transition and in particular, in the introduction—or in the reforms—of the constitutional review principle within these states. In order to understand how the VC gradually developed in this first phase of its activity it is important to keep in mind the roles that La Pergola was undertaking at the EU level. This connection confirmed the idea of an international community of lawyers and legal experts that was flourishing in the EU space starting from the beginning of the 1900s (Vauchez and De Witte, 2013).

Although the original mission of the VC was specifically related to the "Constitutional assistance" and "emergency constitutional aid" of the states in transition, during the last 10 years, the number and the types of activities performed by the network have been significantly increased, beyond its original function of advisor on constitutional matters. In effect, it is playing an increasingly global role in producing knowledge, documents, opinions and guidelines on various judicial governance issues (Dallara, 2012).

In this respect, another critical juncture for the VC development could be seen in 2002 when, after the accession to the CoE by many other countries, among which are included almost all the post-communist countries and Russia, the Statute was modified and the VC was recognized as an enlarged agreement among all CoE Member States, also allowing the participation of some non-CoE Member States. This was the definitive confirmation and institutionalization of the relevance of the VC for the CoE and more generally for the EU international space.

Subject areas covered by the Venice Commission today are categorized in three official areas: 1) democratic institutions and fundamental rights; 2) constitutional justice and ordinary justice; and 3) elections, referendums and political parties. Its primary task remains that of helping states which wish their legal and institutional structures to be consistent with European standards and international experience in the fields of democracy, human rights and the rule of law. As already mentioned, individual members are primarily academics, professors of public and international law, supreme or constitutional court judges or members of national parliaments (and sometimes civil servants). In truth, many of the academics appointed by the national government were also judges in the Constitutional or Supreme courts. They are appointed for four years by Member States, but act in their individual capacity. Thus, its first distinctive feature is this mixed-composition that includes legal experts, higher judges and parliamentary representatives. Today, 59 Member States are members of the Commission: the 47 Council of Europe Member States, plus 12 other countries (Algeria, Brazil, Chile, Israel, Kazakhstan, the Republic of Korea, Kyrgyzstan, Morocco, Mexico, Peru, Tunisia and the USA).

8 Resolution (90) 6, On a partial agreement establishing the European Commission for Democracy through Law, adopted by the Committee of Ministers at its 85th session.

Since February 2002, the Commission has allowed non-European states to become full members. The European Commission, OSCE and ODIHR (Office for Democratic Institutions and Human Rights) participate in the plenary sessions of the Commission. The CoE's liaison office to the EU in Brussels facilitates and promotes working relations between the EU and the Venice Commission. A representative of the European Commission's Legal Service regularly participates in the Venice Commission's Plenary Sessions. Since March 2012 he/she has been accompanied in the Plenary Sessions by a representative of the newly established European External Action Service, which is among the closer contacts of the Venice Commission within the EU framework, the others being the Directorate General for Enlargement and the EU missions in the field. As regards the Venice Commission, contacts depend on the substantial questions in the case at hand.

Since 2009, Gianni Buquicchio has been President of the Commission and successor to La Pergola. He is the other founding father of the VC, as he collaborated with La Pergola once the idea of the VC had emerged. For this actor also, the biographical information is relevant to understanding how much professional and personal background matter in these transnational arenas (Fiche 3.2).

Fiche 3.2 Biographical information on Buquicchio

Gianni Buquicchio (1944–) is an Italian jurist.

From the mid-1970s, he worked within the Directorate of Legal Affairs, Council of Europe, then he became Head of Section and was Responsible for a number of intergovernmental experts' committees dealing with administrative law, international law, the free movement of persons, data protection, etc. From 1981 to 1994 he was responsible for the Conferences of European Ministers of Justice. From 1990 to 1996, he was responsible for the opinions requested by the Committee of Ministers, the Parliamentary Assembly and the Secretary General.

He acted as Secretary of the Venice Commission from 1990 to 2009 when he officially retired from the Council of Europe and was elected President of the Venice Commission (re-elected in 2011).

Source: Fiche compiled using data from the website of the Venice Commission <http://www.venice.coe.int>.

The Source of its Prestige and its Method of Working

The description of the institutionalization process of the VC and the focus on its founding fathers and members help to explain why this Commission is considered so relevant and prestigious for the EU international community. We can say that the process through which the VC was created and subsequently institutionalized marked it as a neutral and independent body influencing positively its legitimacy. The fact that it originated spontaneously from a group of jurists and legal experts and that it gradually acquired the imprimatur of the CoE and the status of international commission, contributed to its reception as an autonomous body without specific political goals. It is worth noting that, especially in the first decade, the VC was rarely mentioned and included in activities promoted by the EU. Thus the institutionalization process took place quite independently from any other politically sensitive organization. The idea of a group of experts that could assist countries on constitutional issues and problems was welcomed and supported by many of the national governments that later on asked to be part of the VC. In institutional theory, legitimacy is critical for organizational survival and development. Legitimacy refers to the extent to which actors exist or act in accordance with the norms and the social expectations of stakeholders in its organizational fields (DiMaggio and Powell, 1983; Meyer and Rowan, 1977; Tolbert and Zucker, 1983).

Another distinctive feature in this respect is the method of working, which could also explain the ability to influence RoL reforms within third party countries. Here the link is within the broad literature on procedural justice (Tyler, 2003) or on procedural legitimacy (Majone, 1999) and credibility of procedure with reference to independent agencies and expert bodies (Majone, 2000; May, 2007).

In terms of inputs to the process of issuing Opinions, these could be requested either by individual countries, or by the CoE bodies. Table 3.1 summarizes the three main groups of institutions that can request Opinions from the VC.

Table 3.1 Bodies and institutions entitled to request VC Opinions

Member States	Council of Europe	International organizations
• Parliaments • Governments • Heads of state	• Secretary General • Committee of Ministers • Parliamentary Assembly • Congress of Local and Regional Authorities	• European Union • OSCE/ODIHR • Other international organizations involved in the Commission's work

Source: Table compiled using data from the website of the Venice Commission <http://www.venice.coe.int>.

The VC, at the request of a Constitutional Court or the European Court of Human Rights, may also provide *amicus curiae opinions*, not on the constitutionality of the act concerned, but on comparative constitutional and international law issues. The Commission also co-operates with ombudsmen through *amicus ombudsman opinions* mainly concerning the legislation related to their work (Table 3.2).

Table 3.2 Bodies and institutions entitled to request VC *amicus curiae opinions*

National Constitutional Courts	ECHR	National Ombudsmen
Can ask for *amicus curiae opinions* on the compatibility of a specific act with comparative and international law issues	Can ask for *amicus curiae opinions* on the compatibility of a specific act with comparative and international law issues	*amicus ombudsman opinions* mainly concerning the legislation that governs their work.

Source: Table compiled using data from the website of the Venice Commission <http://www.venice.coe.int>.

The method through which Opinions are prepared and delivered is based on an accurate choice of the *rapporteurs* made by the Secretariat on the basis of the necessary expertise to assess a specific topic on the cultural proximity and language skills required to read official documents from the country under assessment and to dialogue with the national authorities. Then, obviously, *rapporteurs* are chosen on the basis of their availability for work in order to be included in the working group.

One of the key steps for the preparation of the Opinion is the official visit of the *rapporteurs* within the country to meet, first of all, official political authorities and then some non-governmental organizations or local expert groups. According to members of the VC, this visit and permanence within the country is an important element that contributes to the legitimization by the national authorities of the whole process. The contact and dialogue with the national actors is always accomplished before the final Opinion is prepared (Table 3.3).

This working method has been maintained over the years and is appreciated and fully accepted by individual members representing the country within the VC.[9] Another important step of this working process is represented by discussion of the Opinions both within a specific sub-committee, in which the national authorities are invited, and subsequently in the Plenary of the VC in which Ministers and political representatives of the state under scrutiny may intervene publicly, evidencing if and how they disagree with the Opinion. This, although of a peculiar nature and form, is a way of stakeholder involvement (Borrás, Koutalakis and Wendler, 2007) that could account for a positive evaluation and conception of the VC procedure in terms of credibility and fairness.

Moreover, as Bode-Kirchhoff (2014) suggests, the VC in its Opinions refers massively and almost exclusively to existing legal documents, with preference to legal texts produced by CoE bodies, mainly the ECHR. This aspect seems to

9 This was confirmed in three interviews held by the author between March and June 2012 with one individual member of an Observer Country (USA), one former individual member for Spain and one member of the VC Secretariat.

Table 3.3 Working method for Opinions preparation and delivery

Reference to the Commission of a (draft) constitutional or legislative text by a national or international body or Council of Europe Request for opinion may be sent to the President or the Secretary of the Commission by email / fax / post.

↓

Setting up of a working group of *rapporteur* members and experts assisted by the secretariat

↓

Draft opinion on compliance of the text with international standards and proposed improvements

↓

Visit to the country for talks with the authorities, civil society and other interested stakeholders

↓

Final draft opinion

↓

Submission of the final draft opinion to all members of the Commission before the plenary session

↓

Discussion of the draft opinion in a sub-commission and with the national authorities (if necessary)

↓

Discussion and adoption of the opinion at plenary session

↓

Submission of the opinion to the body which requested it

↓

Publishing of the final text of the opinion on the Commission's website.

Source: Table compiled using data from the website of the Venice Commission <http://www.venice.coe.int>

be reinforcing and emphasizing, as its members stress that the Commission is a "technical body, not a political one," with its opinions always rooted in law. Thus, it resembles a court in its method of legal argumentation, but it cannot impose solutions or rely on coercion with regard to the implementation of its opinions, where it is dependent—just like a political body—on the soft power of persuasion, instead. It could be hypothesized that, since it resembles a court by adopting legal argumentation, the VC could benefit from a sort of judicial legitimacy that contributes to reinforcing the institutional legitimacy as a whole (Gibson and Caldeira, 2011).

Concerning topics, the VC has further enlarged its production, elaborating Opinions not only concerning specific country law, but also on European standards of judicial independence, on European Standards of the Prosecution

Service and on judicial appointments.[10] The VC has also produced many Opinions on specific country laws related to the judicial system, judicial appointment and judge's status. Focusing on these documents, it is possible to determine the soft "model of judicial system" they propose. In summary: the VC seems to propose a "Mediterranean model of organization of justice" with a judicial body with members elected by the judges themselves and other members appointed by other powers of the state. This body should be entrusted with the most relevant functions concerning judges' careers and judges should be in the majority. This body should be, consequently, in charge of judges' appointments. Concerning the prosecution service, the VC requires that the independence of the prosecution office and of its holders is guaranteed in relation to the government (Dallara, 2012; Guarnieri, 2011).

As Magrassi (2011) has pointed out, this is clearly a model based on self-government and separation from other legal professions, with very limited links with common law elements and models of judicial governance in place in the Scandinavian countries. This model, proposed by the VC, was, in many cases, at the basis of the judicial reforms adopted in the Central and Eastern European countries during the EU accession stage. This is still the term of reference for the Balkan countries that are currently potential candidates for EU membership.[11] Here the VC suggestions were, and are, spontaneously adopted by countries as a way of international legitimization of national reforms.

The VC impact on judicial governance issues has since increased even more, as already described in the previous chapter. VC Opinions and Recommendations are used as "relevant material" for judgments in ECHR rulings or suggested as "standards to apply" in some European Commission and European Parliament actions. In this respect, the next section will focus on two paradigmatic and vastly debated cases.

The Venice Commission in Two Recent RoL Reversal Attempts

In order to assess the leverage of the extra-conditionality mechanism of external influence on RoL reforms, we decided to focus on two quite well-known and debated cases that challenged the EU and its basis: the constitutional crisis in Hungary (2011–2013) and Romania (2012–2013). In both cases the VC tuned

10 CDL-AD(2010)004, Report on the independence of the judicial System Part I: The independence of Judges adopted by the Venice Commission at its 82nd Plenary Session (Venice, March 12–13, 2010); CDL-AD(2010)040 Report on European Standards as regards the independence of the judicial System: Part II—the Prosecution Service—Adopted by the Venice Commission—at its 85th plenary session (Venice, Dec 17–18, 2010); CDL-AD(2007)028 Judicial Appointments—Report adopted by the Venice Commission at its 70th Plenary Session (Venice, March 16–17, 2007).

11 Dallara (2010); Piana (2010).

out as key-player and is rather the "technical-executive arm" for the international community and for the EU. This is a very important and interesting aspect that we need to examine in depth in order to understand the role of transnational networks in promoting the rule of law.

Moreover, by selecting these two countries we are allowed to test our hypothesis related to external influence in two very interesting cases in terms of RoL performances: Hungary is one of the "new" Member States which entered the EU in 2004 and it performed very well during the pre-accession evaluation process (and in the immediate post-accession) in terms of compliance with RoL standards; Romania, however, which entered in 2007, was defined as one of the "permanent laggards" (Pridham, 2007, Noutcheva and Bechev, 2008, Dallara, 2014) of the east EU enlargement, always scoring negatively in RoL compliance assessments before and, significantly, after accession. In recent times, the two countries experienced similar and convergent political and constitutional crises, affecting in particular aspects of RoL. Why was the internationally driven RoL promotion not effective in inducing the countries to internalize RoL principles?

Why, on the contrary, was VC mediation finally accepted in bringing countries to (at least) declare their willingness to follow its advice? Are the peculiarities of the VC and its working methods causal factors that could explain the success of its mediation?

The Frontrunner of the RoL Reforms: Hungary Before and After the 2004 EU Accession

As Piana (2010) points out, Hungary was one of the first countries to join the CoE after the breakdown of non-democratic rule. Since the very beginning, CoE membership has been a step towards joining the EU. Due to its legacies and the relatively smooth transition, in Hungary the gap in relation to fulfilling EU requests was smaller in almost all policy fields. For this reason, several scholars argue that in Hungary's case the external conditionality has been less persuasive and demanding than in other CEECs (Sasse, 2005; Vachudova, 2007). This also holds for the judiciary (Piana, 2010). The democratic transition, in fact, has been marked by a clear move toward a reform of the judiciary, although without much discontinuity. Many of the staff appointed during the non-democratic rule kept their office, with the exception of high-ranking judges and prosecutors. Therefore, as Piana (2010) explains, the Hungarian newly democratic State benefited fully from the previous experiences of hierarchical (but not democratic) governments, which in Hungary never reached the same peak of totalitarianism as in other countries (such as the Czech Republic, Bulgaria, and Romania).[12] Thus, during all the pre-accession period, the Hungarian government was quite effective in passing the laws requested by the EU.

12 This distinction draws from Linz and Stepan (1996) and has been reaffirmed in Sadurski (2003).

Then, a few years after its accession, Hungary, a frontrunner in establishing a democratic regime, where a Constitutional Court was used to play a significant role in promoting democratic values and citizens' rights, became a serious source of concern at EU level in respect of the independence of its institutions (Coman, 2014).

The 2012 Hungarian Constitutional Revision and Consequent Developments

In 2010, Fidesz, defined by Müller (2013) as a right-wing populist party, obtained a two-thirds majority of seats in the Hungarian parliament, which offered Prime Minister Orban the opportunity to implement a series of reforms aimed at "rebuilding the rule of law" in the country (Coman, 2014).

Among the long list of reforms proposed, including the revision of the Constitution, some were directly linked to independence of the judiciary. Concerning the independence of the judiciary, the new Constitution, drafted in 2011, established only a very general framework for the judiciary, leaving a cardinal law to define the detailed rules for the organization and the administration of courts and the remuneration of judges (Ibid). One of the first moves was directed at reforming the National Judicial Council, re-introduced in 1997. In order to tackle some deficits in the functioning of the NCJ, the Orban government decided to create a new institution—the National Judicial Office (Gyöngyi, 2012). The National Judicial Office is an independent single-person office, run by the president of the office. The president holds all decision-making powers. Instead, the National Judicial Council—the representative body composed of judges—has only consultative powers regarding the activity of the National Judicial Office. In this way, the powers held by the former council of the judiciary were split in two. As Gyöngyi (2012) explains, these changes reveal problems of power imbalance as the tasks entrusted to the new National Judicial Office are the central administration and central management of courts, appointment of judges, training and education of judges. In particular, the new President of the National Judicial Office holds powers to appoint judges, allocate cases to courts, and[13] he/she is responsible for the centralized management and administration of the courts. In exceptional circumstances—demanded by the timeliness of the judicial process—the President of the National Judicial Office may assign a particular case to another court with corresponding jurisdiction.[14] This new institutional solution has been presented by domestic officials as a way to shield the judiciary from government influence. In spite of this, it quite soon emerged that "such important powers [have] been vested in a single person, lacking sufficient democratic accountability".[15] Some concerns

13 Act CLXI of 2011 on the Organization and administration of the courts adopted by the Hungarian Parliament, Section 76, available at: http://www.venice.coe.int/webforms/documents/default.aspx?pdffile=CDL(2012)005-e [accessed 14.7.2012].

14 Ibid. Section 62 para.1.

15 Council of Europe, Opinion no 663/2012, p.7. As cited in Coman (2014).

were voiced by the VC right from the beginning, regarding even the first drafts of the Basic Law. In fact, the first VC Opinion on the new Hungarian Constitution was released in June 2011, proposing several recommendations regarding the text. Many of these recommendations were echoed in the EU Parliament's resolution adopted on July 7, 2011.

In January 2012, when the Basic Law entered into force, the European Commission finally analyzed the Basic Law with regard to its compatibility with EU law. Under EU Treaty obligations, every country is responsible for the implementation of EU law in their own legal system. In case a country does not comply with this obligation—and there is an infringement of EU law—the European Commission has the power to start proceedings in order to end the infringement (Gyöngyi, 2012). Given that the European Commission's responsibility as guardian of the Treaties is to ensure that EU law is upheld, in January 2012 José Manuel Barroso launched legal action against Hungary under Article 258 TFEU.[16] But once initiated, the procedure and the arguments advanced by the institution caused comments related to its legal basis. Even if the European Commission acknowledged that Hungarian democracy was in danger, the infringement procedure did not relate to the separation of power as a fundamental pillar of democracy, but to a breach of the EU legislation on equal treatment and the Hungarian decision to lower the pension age. On 17 January 2012 as a first step of the accelerated infringement procedure, Viviane Reding, Vice-President of the European Commission and EU Justice Commissioner, sent a formal notice on behalf of the European Commission to the Hungarian government.[17] The main concerns were the excessive powers of the newly established President of the National Judicial Office, the transformation of the Hungarian Supreme Court into the so-called "Curia" and in particular the mandatory early retirement of judges and prosecutors at the age of 62 instead of 70, which would allow the government to replace roughly 10 percent of the judges in Hungary. Within the set time limit of one month the Hungarian government replied to the European Commission, but it could not reassure the latter and dispel concerns.

The EU Parliament repeatedly asked the EU Commission to activate EU Treaty Article 7, which is used in the event of a clear threat of a serious breach of EU common values. On March 7, 2012 the EU Commission decided to continue the accelerated infringement procedure.[18] In two areas Hungary had failed to comply with EU Law: the retirement age of judges—which would lead to the

16 EU Commission Press Release, *European Commission launches accelerated infringement proceedings against Hungary over the independence of its central bank and data protection authorities as well as over measures affecting the judiciary* Reference: IP/12/24 Event Date: 17/01/2012.

17 See the document http://ec.europa.eu/commission_2010-2014/reding/pdf/news/20120109_1_en.pdf on the webpage of Mrs Reding, Vice-President of the Commission.

18 Press release. Hungary: Commission continues accelerated infringement procedure on independence of the data protection supervisor and measures affecting the judiciary and asks additional information on central bank's independence http://europa.eu/

anticipated retirement of 236 judges in Hungary—and the independence of the country's data protection authority. The European Commission therefore decided to send two reasoned opinions—the second stage of EU infringement procedure after which the matter may be referred to the Court of Justice of the European Union. In two other areas, the independence of the central bank and further aspects concerning the independence of the judiciary, the Commission sent two administrative letters demanding further clarification. In its administrative letter, the Commission was seeking further clarifications about the independence of the country's judiciary. The Commission asked for explanations relating to the powers attributed to the President of the National Judicial Office, particularly the President's powers to designate a court in a given case and the transfer of judges without consent. The Commission also raised concerns with regard to potentially systemic deficiencies in Hungary's justice system. Hungary was reminded that national courts act as "Union courts" whenever they apply EU law, and therefore need to satisfy minimum standards of independence and effective judicial redress (Dallara, 2012). While the EU Commission's approach in examining the quality of democracy in Hungary was based on a legal and technical analysis, the VC recommendations went far beyond. Without entering here into the detail of a complex case for EU governance, what is relevant is to note that many of the concerns expressed by the EU Commission in its official communications and documents (especially the administrative letter) were cited in the Opinion on the Constitution of Hungary adopted by the Venice Commission on 17–18 June 2011[19] and on the Opinion on the Cardinal Acts on the Judiciary presented in March 2012.[20]

Looking at the EU Parliament and EU Commission press release on the Hungarian case, one can notice the great relevance given to the VC work and to the documents on the Hungarian laws. This was the first case in which the EU Commission explicitly and frequently called for and referred to the VC as a relevant and crucial ally. In his speech before the European Parliament, in January 2012, José Manuel Durão Barroso, the President of the European Commission, stated:

> The issues at stake here may go beyond the European Union law matters that have been raised. These other issues should also be addressed. The Council of Europe is currently considering other points of the Hungarian legislation which

rapid/pressReleasesAction.do?reference=IP/12/222&format=HTML&aged=0&language=EN&guiLanguage=en

19 Opinion on the new Constitution of Hungary adopted by the Venice Commission on June 17–18, 2011, available at: http://www.venice.coe.int/webforms/documents/?pdf=CDL-AD(2011)016-e [accessed 27 July 2015].

20 Opinion on the Cardinal Acts on the Judiciary (CDL-AD(2012)001) on Hungary adopted in Venice, March 16–17, 2012.

are under its remit. The Council of Europe Venice Commission could play an important role in this respect.[21]

In response to international actors' remarks and recommendations, the Hungarian government sent a 100-page response to the EU Commission concerning the infringement proceedings and expressed its willingness to reach a compromise on the retirement age of judges. Although maintaining a close dialogue with the VC, Viktor Orban rejected any form of divided sovereignty and he has been particularly vociferous in protesting against the incursions of the EU on domestic politics. Blokker (2013a), cited in an interview with an international newspaper, underlined that "We do not need the unsolicited assistance of foreigners wanting to guide our hands" (*Guardian* March 15, 2012). In spite of this, the Hungarian government continued the exchange of documents and proposals with the VC, trying to find mediation. Before the summer of 2012, the government submitted to the VC a proposal containing some changes to the issues addressed by the Venice Commission.[22] The Hungarian government proposed a reduction of overarching powers of the President of the National Judicial Office by transferring some of her/his competences to the council for the judiciary.[23] Ultimately, on April 25, 2012 the European Commission announced that it would suspend the infringement procedure regarding the Hungarian National Bank but refer the issue of early retirement of judges to the CJEU.[24]

Concerning judicial governance, 2012 ended with positive developments as the Hungarian government, following intensive exchanges with the VC amended the Cardinal Acts on the Judiciary (October 2012) diminishing, at least on paper, the powers of the National Judicial Office. This was clear evidence of the VC's impact as the entire amendment process was agreed throughout frequent visits and a continuous dialogue between the VC and national authorities.[25]

---

21 José Manuel Durão Barroso, 'A Europe of values and principles', speech delivered in the Plenary debate of the European Parliament on the situation in Hungary, 18 January 2012.

22 European Commission for Democracy through Law (Venice Commission), "Legislative Solutions Proposed by the Government of Hungary In Relation to the Opinion of on Act CLXII of 2011 on the Legal Status and Remuneration of Judges and Act CLXI of 2011 on the Organisation and Administration of Courts of Hungary," available at: http://www.venice.coe.int/webforms/documents/default.aspx?pdffile=CDL(2012)034-e [accessed 27 July 2015].

23 Ibid.

24 On the one hand, the European Commission could initiate action against the Hungarian Government only under Article 258 TFEU. Hence, it was focusing on the mandatory early retirement clauses. The EU rules on equal treatment in employment, in particular Directive 2000/78/EC100, prohibit discrimination in the workplace on grounds of age, which also covers a reduction of the retirement for one profession without an objective justification. This gave the European Commission the link to EU law required by Article 258 TFEU, whereas such links were hard to establish with regard to the other critical aspects of the Hungarian judicial reform.

25 Opinion on the Cardinal Acts on the Judiciary that were amended following the adoption of the Opinion CDL-AD(2012)001 on Hungary, adopted (Venice, March 16–17, 2012).

A second stage of this troubled situation for the EU occurred at the beginning of 2013 when the Hungarian government decided to pass a Fourth Amendment to the Hungary Constitution that signaled a clear step backward, especially with reference to judicial governance. The government in effect again modified the rules on the National Judicial Office along the same lines as improving the powers of the President of the National Judicial Office.

The VC was immediately alerted by the Secretary General of the CoE in March 2013 to assess the compatibility of this Amendment with the CoE Standards and the whole process was re-started. Official communications with national authorities and two VC delegation visits were organized to bring about a new Opinion in June 2013.[26] A direct citation of the Opinion is here necessary to summarize the situation and to offer clear evidence of the VC's role in this game (Fiche 3.3).

Fiche 3.3 Paragraphs 68 and 69 of the VC Opinion CDL-AD(2013)012 on the Fourth Amendment

68. In two earlier Opinions the Venice Commission strongly criticized the extensive powers of the President of the National Judicial Office (PNJO) and the lack of appropriate accountability. The Commission emphasized the need to enhance the role of the National Judicial Council as a control instance.

69. While on the legislative level the situation had been improved in the framework of the dialogue between the Secretary General of the Council of Europe and the Hungarian authorities both by reducing the powers of the PNJO and by increasing those of the National Judicial Council and by making the PNJO more accountable the Fourth Amendment goes in the opposite direction and raises the position of the PNJO to the constitutional level. The PNJO now has the power to exercise the "central responsibilities of the administration of the courts" and "bodies of judicial self-government" merely "participate in the administration of the courts." The supreme body of judicial self-government, the National Judicial Council, is not even mentioned in the Fundamental Law.

Source: Fiche compiled using data from the Opinion CDL-AD(2013)012 on the Fourth Amendment.

The Successful Laggards: Romania Before and After the 2007 EU Accession

For several reasons Romania can be considered as a contrasting case to Hungary, both in terms of legacy and transition patterns and in terms of compliance with the EU during the pre-accession stage. Romanian democracy started its post-1989

26 See page 3 of the Opinion CDL-AD(2013)012 describing the process and listing names and dates of the two delegation visits.

life tackling a more challenging institutional agenda. Romania submitted its application for EU membership in 1995. In 1999 the EU opened pre-accession talks and negotiations started officially in 2000. Political élites were generally in agreement on the EU accession and rarely was the issue disputed. However, in spite of a formal commitment to enter the EU, the pre-accession process was characterized by fake-reforms and partial compliance with EU requirements.

Legacies of the previous state organization were still present and deeply embedded in political élite behavior, even during the decade after the fall of Ceausescu. Judicial reform was one of the fields in which compliance with the EU was difficult and delayed (Dallara, 2014; Piana, 2010; Coman, 2009). The legacies of the Ceausescu regime on the judiciary were deep, as regime control over the judicial power—as in the other sectors of the state—was quite pervasive (Demsorean, Parvulescu and Vetrici-Soimu, 2009). During the 1990s, the legacies of the past were still present within Romanian society and several cases of political interference with the judiciary were reported by Romanian media and by various international or Romanian organizations (Ibid). Also the excessively powerful role of prosecutors inherited from the communist regime had been maintained.

In terms of RoL reforms, Romania was considered a paradigmatic case (Pridham, 2007; Dallara, 2010) in explaining how the influence of EU conditionality is not enough to introduce stable and concrete changes. The case of Romania is well-known as an example of a country that entered the EU without completing judicial and anti-corruption reform and without respecting EU requests. Romania was frequently defined as the successful laggard of the enlargement process obtaining adhesion without judicial reform (Pridham, 2007; Noutcheva and Bechev, 2008). In spite of this, the EU in 2006–2007 accepted a "fake-version" of the judicial reform as the accession day was approaching. Although some Member States claimed the non-compliance of Romania with EU requirements, the EU was not able to find instruments to sanction the country (Dallara, 2013). The judicial and anti-corruption reform stalled at least until 2011, when only some partial measures were implemented. In the last three years, at least in terms of the functioning of the SCM and independence of the judiciary, the situation gradually improved. In Romania there are some powerful judges' associations and many of the Romanian judges are actively involved in the CoE committees of judges and in other international judicial networks.[27] This contributed to strengthening the force of the judiciary as a whole and supported the diffusion of best practices and models for the courts' organization (Piana, 2010).

In spite of these positive signals concerning the functioning of the judiciary, RoL supremacy continued to be undermined, since it was influenced by fragmentation of the political system[28] and by the difficult and challenging inter-institutional relations.

---

27 Ibid.

28 In terms of number of parties (24 parties in 6 elections). Source: Comparative Manifestos Project Data set.

As Stănciulescu (2010) illustrates, the main problems affecting political systems are the frequent contrasts between the head of state, the prime minister and the parliament.[29] For this reason the veto power of non-governmental parties has been exercised by recurring mainly to the Constitutional Court, a fact that has frequently blocked or delayed relevant RoL reforms. In this respect, a huge institutional crisis involving the Constitutional Court and undermining key RoL principles occurred in 2012.

The 2012 Romanian Constitutional Crisis

As had already occurred in 2007, during the summer of 2012 a renewed attempt to impeach president Băsescu was attempted[30] by a newly elected social-democratic government headed by a young leader, Victor Ponta. As Blokker (2013a) explains, Ponta's government not only called for the impeachment procedure against the supposed unconstitutionality of Băsescu's actions but it went further, in a clearly unconstitutional direction,[31] using Emergency Ordinances, dismissing the speakers of both chambers of parliament (who were replaced by allies), as well as the Ombudsman, by restricting the powers of the Constitutional Court and threatening its judges with impeachment, and by issuing a decree (as well as a draft law) on the Law on Referendum in order to drastically increase the probability of a successful impeachment referendum. Blokker (2013a) reminds us that the actions of the Ponta government were strongly criticized internationally, not least in a progress report on Romania by the European Commission. The EU Commission exhorted the Romanian government to return to serious reform in the name of the rule of law, as recent events "raised serious doubts about the commitment to the respect of the rule of law or the understanding of the meaning of the rule of law in a pluralist democratic system."[32]

---

29 The executive-legislative relations fall under the premier-presidential category (Shugart and Carey, 1992) with a directly elected president who may dissolve the parliament, a cabinet responsible only to the parliament and a president who may be impeached by the parliament.

30 In 2007, the Parliament suspended Basescu as president and called a referendum on the grounds he had exceeded his authority and pushed the country into a political deadlock. On this occasion, 74 percent of Romanians voted against impeaching Basescu on charges that he overstepped his authority. See http://www.reuters.com/article/2007/05/20/us-romania-referendum-idUSL2026723720070520.

31 The Romanian constitutional scholar Ioan Stanomir has argued that the "Romanian constitution has become an insignificant and irrelevant element" in Romanian politics, commenting on the Ponta government's actions, see http://www.evz.ro/detalii/stiri/ioan-stanomir-constitutia-romaniei-a-devenit-un-element-insignifiant-991426.html

32 It is worth mentioning that the Commission's report triggered a response by a large number of Romanian intellectuals and representatives of civil society that replied with a Letter to the EU, in which they argue that the Commission ignores the fundamental legal principle of "audiatur et altera pars" and thereby underestimates the unconstitutional and

Among the various issues that hugely affected the inter-institutional accountability,[33] some were directly linked to dismantling the RoL core: the idea of restricting the competences and jurisdiction of the Constitutional Court using an Emergency Ordinance, action taken by the government creating a Commission within the Senate to investigate abuses of the Public Prosecutors[34] and, more generally, the idea (denounced by the VC in its Opinion in paragraph VII—Pressure against the Judiciary) of publicly disrespecting judges of the Constitutional Court, asking explicitly for their dismissal.

The remarkable nature of the Ponta government's assault on the Constitutional Court was confirmed by two very unusual letters of complaint (in July and August 2012) sent by The Court to the Council of Europe's Venice Commission, as well as to European officials to ask for help against "virulent attacks" on its independence by the government (Blokker, 2013a).[35]

Before these letters, the Secretary General had already asked for a VC Opinion on the compatibility with the constitutional principle of the RoL of the actions taken by the Romanian government.[36] It is worth noting that Mr. Ponta, just after these facts, himself sent a request to the VC for an Opinion regarding the two Emergency Ordinances he issued. Given that the two requests overlap, the VC decided to prepare a single document. Then the usual process for an Opinion preparation was undertaken and in December 2012 it was issued.

---

undue political behavior of Băsescu. The response was restated in the European Parliament on September 12 by the MEP Renate Weber. See http://actmedia.eu/daily/heated-debates-among-mep-groups-over-the-political-situation-in-romania/42025.

33 Many issues were at stake including the excessive use of Emergency Ordinances, the idea that the Parliament does not accept any type of control, the idea of dismantling the Ombusdman, of modifying the rules for the Impeachment Referendum and so on. For the detailed analysis of all these aspects see Opinion CDL-AD(2012)026 on the compatibility with constitutional principles and the rule of law of actions taken by the Government and the Parliament of Romania in respect of other state institutions and on the government emergency ordinance on amendment to the law no. 47/1992 regarding the organization and functioning of the constitutional court and on the government emergency ordinance on amending and completing the law no. 3/2000 regarding the organization of a referendum of Romania adopted in Venice, Dec 14–15, 2012.

34 Decision n°38/2012 of October 2012. Romanian Parliament. Senate chamber.

35 The Constitutional Court has clearly also showed some strength in resisting the attacks, by, first of all, issuing a negative decision on the amendment of the law on public referenda (against the government's intent to implement a simple majority), and second, in its decision on the invalidity of the referendum held on the impeachment of Băsescu. This referendum, held on 29 July, failed to reach the quorum of 50 percent of the electorate, as upheld by the Constitutional Court in its earlier ruling. Therefore, the Constitutional Court ruled that the referendum was void, which meant that Băsescu was re-installed. Ponta ultimately accepted the Court's decision.

36 See page 3, Opinion CDL-AD(2012)026.

This was discussed and presented in the Plenary Session of December 15. As expected, the VC evidenced huge problems in respect to many issues, in particular regarding the use of Emergency Ordinance to reduce the jurisdiction of the Constitutional Court and the blaming of judges by political authorities. Moreover, interesting and useful information could be drawn from the discussion of the Opinion that took place during the Plenary Session. A huge delegation of the Romania government was present that day together with national individual members of the VC: the Ministry of Justice, the Ministry of Foreign Affairs and some other government officials. After the preliminary discussion of the Opinion in a private sub-committee (as the working method allows for), President Buquicchio gave the floor to the two rapporteurs[37] who summarized the VC Opinion on the Romania situation evidencing that

> There is a lack of respect among Romanian institutions. There is something missing in the implementation of the RoL, that is not only a provision of the law, but moreover the implementation of the RoL is embedded in the relations, mutual respect and legal cooperation among institutions in Constitutional practice. The problem in Romania is the practice of Constitutional culture. I'm not saying it is missing but, it needs to be improved in practice … The problem of Constitutional practice is typical of the new democracies. This could be seen as an example of how new political majority tries to diminish the power of the Const Court when it enters in power.[38]

After these comments, the Romanian ministers took the floor and replied that they were profoundly committed to respecting RoL and the Constitutional Court but that some specific issues needed to remain in the hands of the national government and needed to be evaluated considering in detail the national context. They also added abundant technical information about the administrative and legal procedure in Romania. After that, the EU Commission Delegate asked to intervene and his words are summarized in Fiche 3.4.

What it is particularly interesting is the reaction of the Romanian Minister of Foreign Affairs to the EC Delegate speech. He asked Mr. Buquicchio to underline that the Opinion is a document of the VC, which is a technical body, and cannot be used by another political body such as the EU Commission. The President, on the contrary, explained how the EU Commission is absolutely entitled to use the VC Opinion as it is an official member.

After this episode, the Romanian government did not officially reply to the VC Opinion but, starting from 2013, initiated a broad project of Constitutional

37 Mr Bartole and Mr Tuori were the two speaking in the name of the delegation. Please note that these two rapporteurs are among the most experienced and active members of the VC.

38 This is a transcript of the debate made by the author who attended the Plenary Session as auditor.

Fiche 3.4 Transcription of the speech of the EU Commission Delegate in the VC Plenary Session held on December 15, 2012

Firstly, thank you very much for this intervention.

You (VC) have a tortuous task. Thank you also to the Romanian authorities.

The EU welcomes the fact that VC has analyzed the Romanian situation as the events of last summer in Romania also attacked the functioning of the EU itself. The EU is in fact worried about the fact that in an EU member state judicial independence was not respected, nor the RoL. The EU will insist on the need for this respect for judicial cooperation in the EU. The Constitutional Court is the core of the RoL, thus the EU Commission asks to respect it! The EU Commission asks the Romanian government to respect the July 2012 advice on cooperation and verification mechanisms. All the Constitutional amendments in each member state of the EU must respect the values of the EU; the role of RoL and separation of power. Each member state needs to respect RoL and separation of power as these are at the base of the Treaty of adhesion that Romania has signed.

The EC will intervene with a report on Romania on precisely this point. In this document the VC opinion will be explicitly taken in consideration.

Source: Transcript made by the author attending the Plenary Session.

revision announcing on several occasions that the recommendations of the VC would have been taken into account during the whole process. In mid-March, an informal Constitutional Forum was also established. The Forum tries to brand itself as a "partnership between civil society and the parliament," but scholars evidence that "there has been very little consultation of the general public. This is hardly indicative of good things to come" (Kanterian, 2013). The Constitutional Forum recommends the modification of many points; for example, the impeachment of the president, the Constitutional Court, the limitation of political migration of parliamentarians and the structure of the Parliament. Without entering into detail of the work and the composition of the Constitutional Forum, for our purpose it is sufficient to evidence that Prime Minister Ponta officially asked (in a visit in Strasbourg) the VC to assist the Romanian government with the whole process of Constitutional revision, declaring his willingness to accept and respect all VC suggestions.[39] An important visit by the VC to Romania was organized in July to assess and discuss the results of the Constitutional Forum.

39 Government of Romania. Press Release, May 8, 2013.

Conclusion: Which Impacts and Which Mechanisms?

In terms of concrete impact on judicial governance issues, the two cases analyzed offer clear results. The Hungarian government tried again to intervene in the powers of the highly criticized National Judicial Office but, soon after, the VC replied with several and explicit criticisms. The result was that just after the Opinion was made public, with another consequent mobilization of international organizations and NGOs, the Hungarian Justice Ministry filed a bill that would revoke the law which allowed the head of the National Judicial Office to reallocate trials to other courts. The Foreign Minister recently announced that the change will be made in response to the European Commission, which has launched infringement proceedings against Hungary (*The Budapest Times*, 2013).

Similarly, in Romania, the prime minister declared his willingness to follow the VC's advice. These are, at least, the results in terms of official declaration. However, the description of the two troubled cases shows that the VC continued to monitor the two situations, guaranteeing its ability to quickly intervene when requested.

Which factors could explain this ability to act as the "technical-executive arm" of the EU international community? In spite of the considerations already advanced—concerning the perceived legitimacy of the VC and its working method that surely account for its positive impact—other causal factors may be found.

First of all, the VC is related to the ECHR both formally and informally. Regarding the formal connections, we have already described how VC documents are used in ECHR judgments. As for informal connections it is worth noticing that the personnel of the ECHR and the Venice Commission are closely connected. As Bode-Kirchhoff (2014) points out, whereas some of the judges of the ECHR have also become members of the Venice Commission at a later stage, the opposite is also true. The author lists that, in the first years, it was the VC which would benefit from the expertise and experience of former or even still active judges of the ECHR—namely Franz Matscher (Austria, ECHR Justice 1977–1998), Peter Jambrek (Slovenia, ECHR Justice 1993–1998), Pieter van Dijk (the Netherlands, ECHR Justice 1996–1998) and Marc Fischbach (Luxembourg, ECHR Justice 1998–2004). Then, in the reverse direction, starting with Giorgio Malinverni (Switzerland, ECHR Justice 2007–2011), who was a member of the Venice Commission before being elected as judge at the ECHR. Finally, on February 1, 2008 three former Commission members were appointed as ECHR judges: Ledi Bianku (Albania), Mirjana Lazarova-Trajkovska (Former Yugoslav Republic of Macedonia) and Luis López Guerra (Spain), then in 2011, Angelika Nussberger (Germany).

Secondly, apart from the formal participation of the EU in the VC as member, in the last 10 years increasingly formal ties with the EU can be identified. In the context of the enlargement policy, the EU has several times invited the Venice Commission to take part in activities such as the negotiations on the State Union of Serbia and Montenegro and its dissolution, judicial reforms in Serbia and Turkey or constitutional issues in Bosnia and Herzegovina, Moldova and Ukraine. Accession states are required to achieve *inter alia* stability of institutions guaranteeing democracy, the rule of law, human rights and respect for minorities together with their protection. Hence, it was no wonder that the EU made use of the Council of Europe and its Venice Commission in order to help accession states in fulfilling these goals. In effect, membership of the Council of Europe became one of the first steps on the long road to membership of the EU. In the ongoing process of the accession of Serbia, for example, the Venice Commission was involved in the drafting of every major piece of legislation in Serbia, starting with the Constitution but also including election legislation and, above all, legislation on the judiciary. The majority of requests for opinions of the Venice Commission were initiated by the Government of Serbia, arguably upon invitation of the EU.

The example of Hungary, and in some way also Romania, is other evidence of formal ties and official cooperation between the VC and the EU.

The idea that could be advanced is that the VC functions as a sort of external change agent that can penetrate the national domain by virtue of the participation of each country as a member. Frequently, it is the country members themselves that ask the VC to intervene with Opinions on specific national laws, as the VC is used as an anchor to internationally legitimize new national laws (Magen and Morlino, 2009): this fact makes the national domain more accessible and permeable, also regarding Opinions that are requested by other international bodies, even if in cases of negative assessments. The cited interview with Hungary's Prime Minister Orban in this respect is quite telling, as he speaks about the other international organizations as "unsolicited assistance," while in the case of the VC it was the Hungarian government itself that asked for dialogue and advice throughout the process. The same goes for Romania, in which it was the government that, in spite of the negative assessment, continued to ask for assistance from the VC. This type of reflection will be recalled and deepened in the book's conclusion, in which the empirical case of the VC will be used to verify the hypothesis we listed in the Introduction. Indubitably, it is worth noting that by analyzing the activity of the VC one should confirm the existence of the highly debated EU "policy of double standards" (Grabbe, 2006) towards the newly democratic or transitional countries. In fact, the list of Opinions produced by the VC in the last 10 years includes very few old EU Member States.

Chapter 4
The Cross-Fertilization of Judicial Training Models[1]

Between High and Low Politics

The nexus between rule of law promotion and judicial training stems from an abstract principle, which deems judicial professionalism to be an effective barrier against any kind of (unlawful) influence endangering the impartiality of the adjudication. As a matter of fact, this reasoning does not exclusively refer to the context of the rule of law promotion. In any political system, whether more or less advanced, the judicial function works in two ways: on the one hand, it represents a way of dealing with conflicts (Shapiro, 1981), while, on the other hand, the law must be correctly applied and judges are entrusted with the task of doing so. A sound and legitimate system of judicial education is required in order for both functions to be carried out adequately (Guarnieri, 2004 and 2007). The impartiality of adjudication therefore depends on the effectiveness of the judicial education system, and it is this second aspect that is the crux of constitutional democracies. Indeed, only impartial judges can legitimately adjudicate. Hence the reform of programs of judicial education is a turning point in the transformation of a non-democratic regime into a democratic one.

In transnational systems, such as the European system of governance, judicial education seems to play an even more complex role. Judges should be able to handle conflicts not only by applying the law, but also by interpreting legal principles, constitutional norms and international laws (Slaughter, 2001; Baudenbacher, 2003; Jacob, 2000) and by referring to norms and procedures that have validity across national borders. They play a fundamental role in adapting domestic legal norms to supranational principles and jurisprudence (Garapon, 1997; Groppi, 2012); accordingly, in such an institutional setting, legal expertise is also used to create, select and interpret legal norms.

What should be highlighted is also the fact that judicial professionalism is not built only by means of judicial training. Learning how to behave as a judge is a much more comprehensive and somehow partially tacit process than the one that is triggered simply by being exposed to judicial training programs.

Surely by training judicial staff any institution is aiming to build capacities and skills. This does not only target the individuals—judges and prosecutors—but also the offices where these individuals work. Therefore, the comprehensive analysis

1 This chapter is authored by Daniela Piana.

of the mechanisms of capacity building that takes place within the judiciary to make the judicial staff capable of performing its role properly should cover in principle the analysis of the judicial training as well as the analysis of the mechanisms of intra-organizational control that hold within the judicial offices where the appointed judges are trained. This notwithstanding, one cannot deny the crucial role played by the latter in ensuring a well-functioning judiciary. Furthermore, and even more importantly for the EU, judicial actors and in a broader sense legal scholars and experts are expected to share a common language which creates a professional group or, in some cases, especially where judges and prosecutors are appointed according to a bureaucratic scheme. In any case, legal knowledge is a platform and a symbolic divide, which creates a boundary between those who do not master it and those who handle it with skill.

Within the promotion of the rule of law the emphasis put on judicial training has seemed always to follow the endorsement of these general considerations. In particular in those countries where the legacy of the past does not bring any experience of a government limited by the law, the existence of a well-functioning, modern, and independent judiciary goes hand in hand with the existence of powerful mechanisms which ensure the professional autonomy and the competence of those actors who are vested with the responsibility of imposing the law even upon the other branches of the State: namely judicial actors.

These abstract concepts are conveyed in a vast array of strategies, policies, and programs of rule of law promotion and, within this broad policy stream, of judicial training. It is far beyond the scope of our work to map extensively all these actions and policies. The main lesson one can draw from them is the dominance of one principle, working underneath as an inspiring guideline for all these activities: if judges and prosecutors are trained, this will help the absorption and the implementation of the rule of law principle and of the EU laws.

In the European Union the first embryonic attempt to have a say about judicial training is made by the European Parliament with a series of Resolutions starting from 1991. However, the launch of a European discourse regarding judicial training took place in 1997 when the European Commission embarked on the pre-accession strategy whose main goal was regulating and ensuring the process of institutional and legal adaptation of the candidate countries located in Central and Eastern Europe (Piana, 2010; Dallara, 2012; Benvenuti, 2013). Among the actions undertaken in this context, judicial training can be considered as one of the key tools used by the European Commission to promote the rule of law. Due to the specific context represented by CEECs, the European Commission often and with preference worded the support of new programs and delivering mechanisms of judicial training as a way to convey to the candidate countries a "European rule of law." By this means, presumably the European Commission aimed to promote a European conception of law and more pragmatically a skillful, competent judiciary. In fact, the concern of the European Commission (acting as agent of the Member States) was twofold. On the one hand judicial actors appointed during the non-democratic era were to be re-socialized in order to re-orient their legal culture toward a standard closer to the European concept of rule of law. On the other hand these countries, which were at that time experiencing a comprehensive process of legal change entailing the transformation of domestic laws, were asked to accomplish a supplementary effort, namely to adopt the *acquis communautaire*. Judges and legal practitioners, trained in national legal disciplines, were now under a double pressure: to renew their knowledge of the domestic legal system (since this was changing rapidly) and incorporate the competence of EU law into their knowledge. Despite judicial training being treated as a minor policy issue, far away from the contested issues of hard politics such as reform of the institutional setting governing the magistracy, in fact it represents a terrain where many resources and capacities have been spent in order to speed up the process of 1) modernization of the judiciary; 2) European rule adoption; 3) European integration.

This has not been without conflict and resistance. For the purpose of the research we are presenting here, it is necessary to introduce a double distinction. The promotion of judicial training institutions has been framed—and this happened in an unprecedented way—within the pre-accession strategy adopted by the European Union in the context of the Eastward enlargement. However, this ran in parallel—and in some cases with interconnections—with the promotion of a closer coordination among the judicial schools already set up in order to pave the way for better and closer cooperation among judges and prosecutors located in the different areas of the EU. Therefore we need to keep separate the two policies: one for the candidate countries and the other for the Member States. A second level of distinction, which partially intertwines with the first level, concerns the target of European standards in this field. Two key aspects should be mentioned. European standards are founded on the idea that a European judicial culture should be either disclosed—being that it already exists but is somehow forgotten—or strengthened and enhanced. The target of European influence is accordingly the content of the judicial training programs. They are expected to include EU law courses and courses of comparative law to provide a general knowledge of the European legal systems and of the European legal system as a whole (Figure 4.1).

The second aspect is the need to ensure that judicial training is not captured or kept hostage by the budgetary policies of the executive. In other words, the idea here is that the judicial school should be autonomous not only with regard to the design of the programs but also with regard to the budget. Much less pressure has been applied to this second aspect for obvious reasons. European standards are less controversial if they promote the introduction of EU courses. More controversially, they raise conflicts within domestic politics if they ask the political elite to create a new judicial school with an autonomous budget where this does not already exist.

Twenty years have passed since European activities in the field of judicial training began. This chapter aims to answer the following questions:

1. Did these activities create favorable conditions for a convergent pattern of change?

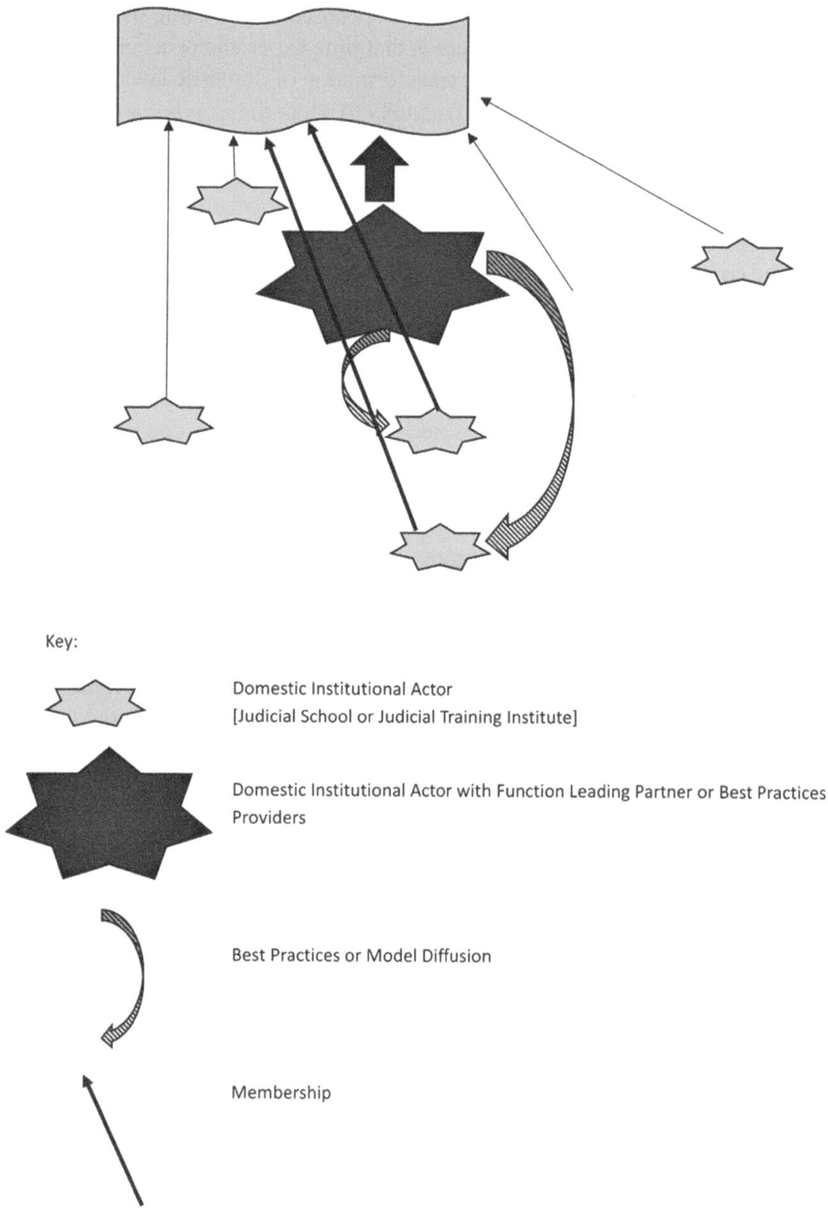

Figure 4.1 The European model of judicial training: actors and levels

2. To what extent do the domestic systems of judicial training resemble each other?
3. Finally, have the networking activities, which have been prominent in this field, created a sort of epistemic community all around Europe? Do judges and prosecutors actively participate in the creation of a European judicial culture? And if so, how do they do this?

Networking with a Leading Actor

When communism fell and pro-democratic elites took power in the CEECs, several different logics of action drove Western policies toward post-communist countries. Opportunities for economic exchanges were the first concern of Western political actors, who pushed national governments toward the definition of strict conditions in order to allow private enterprises and public institutions to open up economic and political dialogues with those countries.

The legal environment has turned out to be a turning point in the process of reform initiated in a post-communist setting and leading to a truly constitutional democratic one (Krygier, 1999; Morlino and Magen, 2008; Sadurski, 2004). This was in any case true even before the European process of pre-accession started, since the Council of Europe itself was pushing the legal reforms through the norms included in the European Convention of Human Rights and the principles of constitutionalism endorsed by each of its members (Piana, 2006).

Judicial education has shown itself to have dramatic leverage in transforming the legal environment of CEECs. Indeed, if only judges and prosecutors can be entrusted to be fair and predictable actors in implementing the law, economic transactions can be realized efficiently, without the supplementary costs that may arise as a result of arbitrariness and patronage in legal enforcement. Judicial education has been considered one of the key conditions allowing judicial actors to be independent from possible influence by political and corporate power, a requirement laid down by the Council of Europe on behalf of the international community. In particular, in the early 1990s, the Council of Europe started step-by-step monitoring of the implementation of constitutional principles within the new constitutional charters (see Chapter 3 of this volume). In that field, the Council of Europe has progressively developed a set of recommendations dealing with the independence of judges, which also touch upon judicial education (Oberto, 2003).

Furthermore, in the late 1990s, European institutions went ahead with the process of judicial cooperation and tried to set up platforms and arenas where old and new Member States could coordinate their domestic judicial policies. This process has become even more challenging for new members, since they have already had to come to terms with the communist system of recruiting judges. The Council of Europe and the European Commission have asked the Central and Eastern European Countries (CEECs hereinafter) to fundamentally reform their systems of judicial education because judges who had previously been recruited on the basis of their political loyalty have been expected to become 'apolitical,' competent and legally accountable (Dietrich, 2000). Furthermore, enlargement has also increased the participation of CEEC judges in the process of European judicial cooperation (Moore and Chiavario, 2004; Council of Europe, 2005). All this accounts for the huge amount that European institutions have invested in judicial education for new members. While the EU has no power to force Member States toward a common model of judicial education, the European Commission has provided public institutions with a number of opportunities to improve, reform and adapt judicial training programs.

Finally, several NGOs and professional associations have provided the standards for re-assessing judicial systems with regard to their independence and institutional capacity. Both were held to be deeply influenced by the legal expertise and skills of judges, clerks and prosecutors. In particular, the Soros Foundation—through the EuMap and Justice Initiatives organized by the Open Society Institute—and the American Bar Association—through its CEELI program—have funded seminars, consulting sessions and peer reviews of reform projects by local Ministry of Justice think tanks. In all these activities judicial education has been included in the agenda and has featured as the main lever in reshaping judicial behavior. In each country, international watchdogs have interacted with certain local actors including Judges' Unions, where they have merged as representative and effective actors (in Poland, Hungary and the Czech Republic), and think tanks particularly devoted to the monitoring of judicial reforms (in Romania and Bulgaria). These actors have been also involved in the organization of seminars and training sessions for judges and prosecutors (Ottaway and Carothers, 2000). The IOs and the international NGOs have therefore paved the way for the reform of the systems of judicial education that were requested by the European Union when the pre-accession negotiations began in 1997. The pressure of such rules upon national governments is therefore cognitive and also normative (Schimmelfennig and Sedelmeier, 2004: 12). The attention paid by the Council of Europe and the European Commission to judicial education is largely justified by the legacy of post-communist countries. Indeed, in these countries the previous political elite had transformed judicial systems into institutional instruments aiming at fundamentally controlling the economic and social behavior of their citizens. Under communist rule, policy making was realized through the action of judges and prosecutors, who were expected to behave according to political commands issued by exclusive and partisan policy makers. Judges and prosecutors were not trained to behave according to legal norms but were socialized to obey and to be accountable to political powers (Ajani, 1996). When the regime broke down, this legacy needed to be dismantled. Both international watchdogs and domestic democratic elites have applied pressure aimed at eliminating political attitudes, arbitrary decisions and unfair and unreliable rules of behavior from judicial practice. The creation of a well-equipped and skilled judicial staff has been on the agenda of all democratic reforms. When the pre-accession process started, the European Commission nudged this process along and asked that judicial staff learn the *corpus juris* of the *acquis communautaire* and be adequately trained in order to work cooperatively within the European legal space.

The recommendations drafted by the Council of Europe set guidelines for the pressure exercised by the European Union in the area of reform of CEEC judicial educational systems. However, strategies and initiatives of judicial training also stem from bilateral projects of judicial cooperation. With the pre-accession strategy, the European Commission decided to allocate 30 percent of the Phare funds to institution building and to the diffusion of administrative capacity within the public administrations of candidate countries (European Commission, 1998). At the beginning, the targeted countries were the CEECs. To promote the exchange of information and international communication, the European Union introduced twinning, a political instrument adopted in 1997 within the strategy of streamlining pre-accession, as outlined in Agenda 2000 (European Commission, 1998). Twinning—which is a praxis commonly used in the German administrative tradition—relies on the appointment of experts within public administrations who introduce experiences and patterns of problem-solving which have been successfully adopted in other agencies of public administration. Thereafter, twinning was extended, and was widely adopted in the neighborhood policy and in the stabilization process enacted. In fact, since 1998 the training of judges and prosecutors has been strongly supported by the European Union throughout the "twinning exercise" (Papadimitriou and Phinnemore, 2004). This is organized in two steps: first, candidate countries issue a call for tender addressed to any potential administrative partner in the old Member States; then, the administrations of old Member States submit a proposal to the European Commission, which ensures that the selection of a partner and the implementation of the project is procedurally correct and substantially coherent with the National Plan for the pre-accession strategy that each candidate had previously agreed with the European Commission. Twinning projects are intentionally aimed at supporting a transfer of best practice from the old member to the prospective new member. Indeed, the experts appointed in the project can come from the administrative institutions of the old Member States or from independent think tanks or NGOs working in the field targeted by the call for tender (Stone Sweet, 2000). Therefore, twinning projects have represented a model for exporting patterns of behavior, procedures and rules. The calls for experts issued by the Commission are formulated such that the national public administrations of candidate countries search for partners within the set of public administrations of old member countries. The selection of partners is done on the basis of their capacity to deal with the specific problems that the candidate country has. Once the winner has been notified, the public administration of the old member appoints one or more experts, who spend a short period within the public administration of the candidate country in order to transfer policy instruments, solutions to problems and procedures and patterns for the management of human resources. The basic idea of twinning is therefore to focus on the agency in the process of change: actors bridge the knowledge gap in candidates, profiting from knowledge obtained in old members' administrations.

The channel opened by the European Commission is therefore a specific incentive for candidate governments to enact policy transfer and to intentionally adopt exogenous policy inputs to achieve better policy making at home.

In the period 1998–2004 the European Commission, through the Phare program, funded 64 projects directly related to judicial reform: 59 addressed judicial education, either because they aimed at reforming judicial education programs or because they included training sessions in projects primarily addressing other aspects of the judiciary such as governance, administration or procedural rules. Of those 59, in 19 projects judicial education was the main objective of the cooperation.

Experts who take part in the projects and are involved in the exchange of models, templates, policy solutions and know-how, are mostly representatives of judicial organizations or think tanks specializing in judicial matters. Among them, the German Foundation for International Legal Cooperation (IRZ) and the Ecole Nationale de la Magistrature (ENM) are clearly the leading partners for CEECs. ENM has not only provided expertise, but also a model for organizing training programs (Dallara, 2012). Twinning projects currently represent the bulk of large-scale activity in international cooperation based on bilateral exchanges between old and candidate members. In the process of enlargement, several experts moved from western countries to CEECs to disseminate know-how and to bridge gaps between their own country and the host administration located in candidate countries. Even though judicial education was not included on the agenda of any project, training sessions, and exchanges of views, legal expertise (for instance, doctrine or interpretative patterns of legal norms) and ideas were somehow encouraged in each judicial cooperation project. Twinning and bilateral or multilateral cooperation projects have entailed large-scale training activity. Training thus covered not just specific objectives of cooperative projects, but also spillover effects of other projects, most of which were based on peer review, cross-border discussion or teaching. In actual fact, the attention paid to the judicial education systems of new members is not distinct from the Western legacy. The model promoted by the Council of Europe and the European Commission is based on a view of the judiciary that is clearly imbued with a civil legal tradition. It relies on a model of bureaucratic judiciary, in which the judges are appointed, promoted and directed in the same way as the staff of a centralized bureaucratic structure (Guarnieri and Pederzoli, 2002). Therefore, the judicial school is a crucial institution in achieving a truly independent judiciary. It is for this reason that the reforming elites of CEECs searched for a successful model of a judicial school and it is not therefore by mere chance that the ENM has been the leading actor in 71.4 percent of projects, including 63 projects directly aimed at reforming judicial education.

Here the combination of forward-looking policies adopted at domestic level and a policy window opened up by the European pre-accession strategy by means of twinning programs can explain the relatively high success of the influence played by the model instantiated by the French ENM as the EU model of judicial training. In fact, in the late 1990s the French government decided to invest in the field of judicial cooperation. In 1998 the Ministry of Justice (Garde des Sceaux), with the approval of the Bar Association, the Clerks' Association and the Union of Judges (though these latter bodies were not among the donors), created a specialized administrative unit that became a leading actor in the field of judicial cooperation: ACOJURIS. The mission of ACOJURIS is to act within the field of judicial cooperation, not only within the European legal area, but also with external countries.

French legal experts have represented the main channel through which to disseminate a model of governance via the law. Certain specific areas were placed on ACOJURIS' agenda, including judicial ethics and the law relating to the Internet. More generally, ACOJURIS has taken advantage of the opportunities created by the Council of Europe and the European Commission. The cooperation projects consist of mobility projects from France toward the beneficiary or, vice versa from the beneficiary toward France. The main outcome of this process is the establishment of consolidated relationships between French judges and the judges of the other countries. It may therefore be said that ACOJURIS is an agency that has provided beneficiary countries with legal experts socialized in French legal culture who belong to a judicial network. In the judicial field, French administration has international legitimacy: its model is disseminated by experts who provide not only a model per se, but also a link to an influential international network (Checkel, 2005). ACOJURIS has now been replaced by the GIP JCI (Groupement d'Intérêt Publique Justice Coopération Internationale, Benvenuti, 2013: 3, n. 6)

This premise makes sense of the force of attraction the French model has for European incomers. When the pre-accession period began, the international network of centers for judicial education represented one of the most promising tools for linking national systems to international scenes. The multilateral meeting "The training of judges and public prosecutors in Europe" held in Lisbon in April 1995 aimed at promoting European cooperation in the field of training for judges and prosecutors. The participants supported the implementation of a European information exchange network between persons and bodies in charge of the training of judges and public prosecutors. The Lisbon Network took advantage of the support given by the ENM, and today it is part of the network coordinated by the Council of Europe Directorate of Legal Affairs. French foreign policy is very sensitive to the opportunities for multilateral coordination created by European judicial cooperation. In October 2000, the French Presidency of the European Union proposed an initiative to formally create a European judicial training network that would improve mutual understanding of Member States' legal systems among judges and prosecutors, and increase the practical implementation of judicial cooperation within the European Union. This network, the European Network for Judicial Training, has obtained the support of the European Commission, which in 2005 made a financial contribution for the administrative facilities of the building and the secretarial offices located in Brussels. The Network includes representatives of institutions in charge of the training of judges and prosecutors in Member States.

It acquired legal status in June 2003; it receives subsidies within the framework of the civil program and the AGIS program. The network focuses its activities on criminal and civil matters. The aims of the network are: to further mutual knowledge of legal and judicial systems; to improve the knowledge of European and international instruments; to exchange experiences and identify training needs; to encourage the coordination of judicial training programs planned by Member States; to develop training curricula for members of the judiciary. The European Judicial Training Network was welcomed by the European Union because it fits perfectly with the European Council's call for increased judicial cooperation in the European legal arena. Once again, the role played by the ENM is a leading one. The ENM was one of the founding members of the European Judicial Training Network and is still one of the main promoters of judicial cooperation activities through the mutual exchange of knowledge and best practices.

Of 64 twinning projects carried out in the field of judicial policy from 1998 to 2004, 19 explicitly concern the training of judges and prosecutors while 10 of them directly include the creation ex novo or the reform of centers for judicial training (Piana, 2005). The new institutions share two key characteristics. The first is the connection with the ENM. Here a mechanism of institutional isomorphism is at play. The second is membership of judicial networks. If we consider the European Network for Judicial Training (see the next paragraph for a detailed description) all new schools created in the CEECs have become members.

Membership of European networks is therefore not only a means of socializing legal experts but also a channel to interact with frontrunners in international judicial cooperation. Twinning projects with the ENM enforce the legitimacy of national legal experts (Franck, 1990), for whom the ENM is:

- a successful and internationally acknowledged institution;
- a public institution created in accordance with a bureaucratic view of the judiciary; and
- an institution experienced in dealing with international judicial cooperation.

From this point of view, bilateral cooperation established with the French legal elite has a dual value for the national legal elite engaged in the sub-system policy of the candidate States by:

- opening the door to an international epistemic community; and
- providing the judiciary with a model that is legitimate in the eyes of the international community.

Thus, cooperation with the ENM seems to be an opportunity to enter the 'club' of legal experts who participate in the definition of standards defining a fully legitimate system of judicial education. While these premises seem to allow us to argue in favor of the full diffusion of the French model of judicial education among the CEECs, this was not actually the case. If we take as an empirical study the series of ENM-led twinning projects carried out in the judicial field from 1998 to 2004, we notice that all included the transfer of courses and handbooks drafted with the support of the ENM, all provided for the training of judges and prosecutors. All training was in house or in Paris in the ENM building. A totally different matter is whether these training systems are convergent and whether, in terms of content, they still feature the requested characteristics of an integrated judicial system that the European Union is supposed to be or is aiming to become.

However the new judicial schools have all been involved in networking activities, carried on with the praise of the EU under the umbrella of the EJTN.

A Condition Necessary for Mutual Confidence: The Stockholm Program and the EJTN

In 2000 at the crossroad of a three-fold agenda, encompassing judicial training, mutual trust, judicial cooperation, the European Network for Judicial Training has been set up. Located in Brussels and having among its members the judicial schools and the institutions delivering judicial training within the member States, the ENJT's mandate is to foster the exchange of practices, know how, skills, and approaches in top quality judicial professionalism in the EU. Therefore it would be interesting to see if the new judicial schools, those set up after 2000, have become members of the ENJT.

In Table 4.1 we answer the question of whether networking has ended up by engaging all judicial schools. According to the EJTN, its 30 members include all the judicial schools and especially those created over the last 20 years as an effect of the pre-accession strategy. Table 4.1 shows that membership is an integral part of the institutionalization of the new judicial training authorities set up in the Central and Eastern European countries. None of them, once created, remained outside thc EJTN.

Why then is EJTN so important in the European context? And why is networking so centrally positioned at the present time in the 28-EU? In 1999 heads of States met in Helsinki and decided to delegate to the European Commission the task of drafting a breakthrough program to enhance the cooperation in the field of the (at that time so-called) "Third Pillar." This is the starting point of the Hague Program. Among the measures recommended by the European Commission to reach the ambitious goal of tightening up links among Member States in such a delicate and sensitive field, the promotion of a "European policy of judicial training" was already emerging as one of the most important points. The rationale behind this can be expressed as follows. In a highly differentiated system, where legal and judicial settings diverge, the possibility of enhancing cooperation depends on the capacity of individual actors—the judicial staff—to rely on the cooperation of colleagues that are located in other countries. This requires trust. Mutual trust is, accordingly, inserted in the European approach to judicial cooperation as a key mechanism. In a way, if one wants to make explicit the reasoning behind all this, one may safely say

Table 4.1 Members of the EJTN

Judicial authority	Pre-accession creation with transnational leverage
Austrian Federal Ministry of Justice	No
Belgian Institut de Formation Judiciaire	No
Bulgarian National Institute of Justice	Yes
Croatian Judicial Academy	Yes
Cypriot Supreme Court	No
Czech Judicial Academy	Yes
Danish Court Administration	No
Estonian Supreme Court	No (but partner in Phare)
Finnish Ministry of Justice—Training Unit	No
French Ecole Nationale de la Magistrature	No
German Federal Ministry of Justice	No
Greek National School of Judges	No
Hungarian Judicial Academy	Yes
Irish Committee for Studies Institute	No
Italian Scuola superior della magistratura	No
Latvian Judicial Training Center	Yes
Lithuanian National Courts Administration	No
Luxemburg Ministry of Justice	No
Malta Judicial Training Committee	No
Dutch Training and Study Centre for the Judiciary	No
Polish National School of Judiciary and Public Prosecution	Yes
Portugal Centre For Judicial Studies	No
Romania National Institute for the Magistracy	Yes
Judicial Academy of Slovakia	Yes
Slovenian Ministry of Justice—Training center	Yes
Escuela Judicial Consejo General del Poder Judicial	No
Courts of Sweden Judicial Training Academy	No
UK England and Wales Judicial College	No
The Judicial Studies Board for Northern Ireland	No
The Judicial Institute for Scotland	No

Source: EJTN, http://www.ejtn.net/About/EJTN-Affiliates/Members/

that trust is considered as a favorable condition which should be first put in place and then left to act as a catalyst for enhanced patterns of cooperation. Since trust presupposes knowledge and mutual knowledge, judicial training—and especially the share of judicial training programs and opportunities— becomes, along this line of reasoning, a key lever in creating trust. This argument is even more evident in the document adopted by the European council which met in Stockholm in 2009: "The Stockholm program: An open and secure Europe serving and protecting citizens." Mutual confidence and trust depends notably on the certainty that all judges, prosecutors and judicial staff (such as assistants, law-clerks and registrars) in the European Union receive suitable training. The training provided to judges, prosecutors and judicial staff is thus a vital tool for fostering mutual recognition (preamble art. 7).[2] Adequate judicial training requires that all judges, prosecutors and judicial staff be provided with sufficient knowledge of European cooperation instruments and that they make full use of the European Union's primary and secondary law. Such training should cover all the aspects that are of relevance to the development of the internal market and of the area of freedom, security and justice. It should contribute to adequate knowledge of the law and legal systems of the other Member States of the European Union and promote relevant courses of comparative law (preamble art. 8).

Training in official languages of the European Union, other than the mother tongue of the person concerned, started to be considered very important in enabling and facilitating direct contacts between judicial authorities of different Member States, and in order to create an interest in and openness toward the legal culture

Box 4.1 The European policy of judicial training: the principles and the instruments

Mutual trust between authorities and services in the different Member States and decision-makers is the basis for efficient cooperation in this area. Ensuring trust and finding new ways to increase reliance on, and mutual understanding between, the different legal systems in the Member States will thus be one of the main challenges for the future.

In order to foster a genuine European judicial and law enforcement culture, it is essential to step up training on Union-related issues and make it systematically accessible for all professions involved in the implementation of the area of freedom, security and justice. This will include judges, prosecutors, judicial staff, police and customs officers and border guards. The objective of systematic European Training Schemes offered to all persons involved should be pursued. The ambition for the Union and its Member States should be that a substantive number of professionals by 2015 will have participated in a European

2 Resolution of the Council and of the Representatives of the Governments of the Member States meeting within the Council on the training of judges, prosecutors and judicial staff in the European Union (2008/C 299/01).

Training Scheme or in an exchange program with another Member State, which might be part of training schemes that are already in place. For this purpose existing training institutions should in particular be used.

Member States have the primary responsibility in this respect, but the Union must give their efforts support and financial backing and also be able to have its own mechanisms to supplement national efforts. The European Council considers that EU and international cooperation aspects should be part of national curricula. For training of judges, prosecutors and judicial staff it is important to safeguard judicial independence while at the same time the emphasis should be placed on the European dimension for professionals that use European instruments frequently. CEPOL and Frontex should play a key role in training of law enforcement personnel and border guards with a view to ensuring a European dimension in training. Training of border guards and customs officers is of special importance with a view to fostering a common approach to an integrated border management.

and traditions of other Member States. Language training can also contribute to allowing judges, prosecutors and judicial staff to participate in exchange programs, as well as in training activities which are held in other Member States (preamble art. 17; and Box 4.1 above).

The wording adopted by the Stockholm Program reveals the attempt to keep the balance between the constraints represented by national traditions embedded in the legal and judicial cultures of the Member States, and the opportunity to open up a new policy window, i.e. the European policy of judicial training.

This policy has been boosted by adoption of the Treaty of Lisbon:

> In recent years, the approach and the influence of the EU seems to change. Partly, because of the changes the Treaty of Lisbon brought. Last September the Commission published an ambitious plan in the field of European judicial training towards 2020. European judicial training is seen as a cornerstone for the development of a "European judicial culture," or in the words of the Commission a "true European judicial culture." It forms an important part of the implementation of the Stockholm Program on the development of a European area of freedom, security and justice. Article 67 of the Treaty on the Functioning of the European Union (TFEU) is the founding provision for the establishment of the area of freedom, security and justice. It stipulates in paragraph 1 that "the Union shall constitute an area of freedom, security and justice with respect for fundamental rights and the different legal systems and traditions of the Member States." For the purpose of the development of the area of freedom, security and justice the EU has gained specific competence in Articles 81 (2)(h) and 82 (1)(c) TFEU for support of training of the judiciary and judicial staff in civil and criminal matters. The Commission's Communication of 13 September 2011 provides concrete goals and objectives within the framework of its "newly" gained competence in this field. (Van Harten, 2012: 7)

The policy stands at a juncture of two different streams. The first is the incremental development of the European policy of pre-accession. Within this field the instruments of twinning and generally of bilateral cooperation are considered welcome and fruitful. The second is the multilateral cooperation that had already been unfolded in the framework of the Council of Europe by the leading activity of the French ENM. Already in 2000 the "adoption of the Bordeaux Charter during a meeting hosted by the ENM resulted in the creation of an informal network of national judicial training institutions" (Benvenuti, 2013: 3). The network in Bordeaux, active since 2001, ended by promoting the creation of a European network of judicial training.

It is not pure coincidence that the EJTN was founded in 2000 precisely under the impulse of the Bordeaux network. This initiative was welcomed by the European Parliament as well as by the European Commission.

The European Commission has granted to the EJTN the "monopoly in the implementation of the Exchange Programme," (founded in 2003) which provides EU legal practitioners, judges and prosecutors, as well as judicial trainers with a short- and long-term exchange platform where Member States open their initiatives of judicial training to the judicial staff and legal experts of other Member States. As the EJTN presents it:

> The Exchange Programme was launched in 2003 at the European Parliament's initiative. The first edition of the Programme has been implemented jointly by two members of the Network (ENM-France and CSM-Italy). In 2006, EJTN became the sole promoter of the Programme and it's been awarded a de facto monopoly by the European Commission in the implementation of judicial exchanges. Since 2005 the annual number of beneficiaries of the Programme has increased sevenfold. Over the period 2005–2012, nearly 4300 judges, prosecutors (including future judges and prosecutors), judicial trainers and members of the superior councils of justice took part in the Exchange Programme.[3]

The Exchange Program fits perfectly with the overall aim stated in the Stockholm Program, since it tries to develop mutual knowledge among the judicial staff of the Member States. The expected target of impact is twofold. On the one hand, the professionalism of judges and prosecutors is expected to be created in a truly transnational arena, across domestic borders. In fact, the program promotes the participation of judges and prosecutors to training initiatives set up in different Member States than the one where they work. On the other hand, the fact that trainers and trainees get in touch also creates a transnational communication mechanism, which enhances possible imitative behaviors among the judicial training institutes. One of the key points on the EU agenda is in fact the integration of EU law courses in the initial and in-service training. This also happens by means of mutual knowledge. The possibility of observing EU law programs offered in

3 http://www.ejtn.net/Exchange-Programme/.

different countries might help in adopting similar ones or ones focusing on the sub-topics that are most requested.

We already have empirical evidence to see to what extent the networking process set up by the European Union in the field of judicial training has originated the desired effects.

In terms of participants the exchange program can now count 4,323 judges and prosecutors taking part in exchanges: 38 percent are judges, 17 percent are prosecutors, 28 percent are future judges/prosecutors, 7 percent are trainers and 10 percent administrative judges (EJTN, 2007: 7). The largest part of the initiatives consist in short term-exchanges: "those can follow a one-to-one scheme, in which the visiting judge/prosecutor shadows a counterpart (tutor) in their daily practice in a court/prosecutor's office of the hosting country or they can be organized as a group exchange, in which several judges/prosecutors from different countries go on the same exchange, thus increasing the 'cross-fertilization' aspect of the experience" (EJTN, 2007: 5). In terms of coverage and impact the number of judges and prosecutors involved in the exchange program still remains low. If we consider that there are about 700,000 magistrates in the EU (CEPEJ, 2012), it is evident that only a small proportion of judges and prosecutors are targeted by this activity. Yet, the judges and the prosecutors that profit from the opportunity offered by the EJTN are those that most probably in the Member States are more active in promoting modernizing reforms or in any case in creating new frames and references for public discourse on the judicial function. In this respect we need also to consider that there is an element of spontaneous selection which is determined by the self-motivation of each attendee.

A recent study financed by the European Parliament and carried out by the European Legal Academy of Trier (ERA) has mapped the diffusion of EU law courses within the EU. This study shows that despite the fact that "88% of judges and prosecutors who responded to the survey knew another EU language in addition to their principal working language, of whom 81% cited English, 40% French, 17% German and 10% Spanish," only a small number can use the language to attend a course or a seminar (Coughlan et al., 2011: 4). Consequently, the exchange program can target only those judicial staff that can understand the language of a different Member State. Secondly, "Almost all new entrants to the judicial professions today have studied EU law as part of their university degree. This is not true for older generations, of whom only a minority covered EU law, the European Convention on Human Rights or another Member State's law as part of their university studies," whereas only 53 percent has received continuous training in the EU law.

To sum up the main results of this study, the diffusion of EU law is constrained, or at least not facilitated, by a lack of linguistic mastery; by EU law not being considered as a fundamental topic but a complementary topic, especially by senior judges and prosecutors; and by the fact that domestic legal systems are still dominant in determining legal reasoning.

Patterns of Convergence?

Judicial training is, among the many different fields and sub-fields where the networking processes are prominent, one area where the European Union has recognized a political priority. Only a well-functioning space for Justice, Security, and Freedom can allow European citizens to feel part of a whole, as beneficiaries of rights enforced in a homogeneous manner across Europe. Moreover, most of the crimes that have an intrinsic transnational dimension can be tackled by means of enhanced patterns of judicial cooperation. Therefore, it is unquestionably important that trust and knowledge are created and maintained across domestic borders among the judicial authorities. If these are the goals, the actual results seem to witness a weak Europeanization and patchy patterns of influence. A recent research project carried out by a network financed by the European Commission, DG Education and Culture, showed that European Member States are not in agreement toward a European model of judicial training, neither in terms of training delivery mechanisms, nor in terms of training programs, nor finally in terms of teaching methods. The results achieved through comparative analyses of the training systems still in place in the European Member States show the co-existence of two ideal types, one centered on the judicial school – or judicial training institute or similarly named organization – and the second centered on the role played by the ministry of justice in delivering training programs for judicial staff. In a smaller number of cases we have also the Supreme Court as the key actor delivering training. For instance, in Belgium, France, Italy, the Czech Republic, Hungary, Romania, Poland, the Slovak Republic, Bulgaria, Spain, Portugal, Netherlands, Latvia, and Croatia the judicial school is the authority with competence to deliver judicial training. In Austria, Denmark, Finland, Lithuania, Estonia, Luxemburg, Germany, Slovenia, and Sweden the judicial training is handled by an in-service authority, which does not have autonomous status. This also has some specificities. For instance, in Germany the European Legal Academy is considered an autonomous institute but it does have competence in the field of judicial training for all Germany. In general, we can distinguish between a neo-Latin model (almost all European Member States where the High Judicial Council is vested with the responsibility of appointing judges and prosecutors) where the judicial school is autonomous and a Nordic model where the judicial training is an endogenous function of the judiciary. In the Nordic model the judicial staff is trained through a process of learning by doing, which takes place within the premises.

Finally, the target of influence of the networking process also includes the programs, i.e. the training content. The transnational inputs are twofold in this context. The request of the European Commission, which promotes the diffusion of EU law courses, is combined with the inputs from the networks that operate within the Council of Europe, especially the CEPEJ (see next chapter). The CEPEJ promotes the introduction of IT tools, which entails that judges, prosecutors, and clerks are trained adequately to use them. Similarly, the CEPEJ promotes high

Table 4.2 Diffusion of EU law and non-legal disciplines in judicial training programs

Country	AT	BE	CZ	DK	UK	FI	FR	DE	IE	IT	LV	LT	LU	MT	NL	NO	PL	PT	RO	SI	ES	SW
Political Sciences																						
Sociology				X			x											X			X	X
Anthropology																					X	X-P
Psychology	X	X					x				X	X-J						X	X		X	X
Philosophy and Ethics		X		X			x				X	X-J	x					X	X		X	X-J
Economics	X						x			X								X	X			X-J
History	X						x															
Foreign Languages	X						x				X-J		x					X	X		X	
Communication	X	X			X		x		X		X-J	X-J	x		X				X		X	X
Information technology	X				X		x		X	X	X-J		x					X	X		X	X-J
Management	X	X					x		X		X		x					X	X		X	X-J

Source: Based on Menu for Justice, data set, available at https://www.academic-projects.eu/menuforjustice/default.aspx.
Note: X-J indicates for judges, X-P for prosecutors.

quality communication between users and courts as well as high awareness of judges and prosecutors in terms of interaction with the media and the society in general. How are skills and competences provided? By means of reliable training programs. Table 4.2 gives an overview of the diffusion of non-legal disciplines in judicial training programs.

The empirical evidence we have at our disposal allows us to test Hypothesis n. 2 developed in the Introduction: that domestic cultural legacy plays a favorable role in the compliance of a judicial training policy with European standards. According to current socio-legal scholarship we can distinguish between two models of legal culture. They can be located along a continuum which goes from the model displayed by the Nordic and Central European countries (Bell, 2006; Bobek, 2013) to the model displayed by the Southern European countries (ibid). In the first model, legal knowledge is handled by senior judges and high ranked courts. Accordingly the judicial school, as autonomous legal entity, does not exist in these countries. The second model considers that judges and prosecutors are equal and that they can differ only in terms of functions, but not of status. The judicial hierarchy is much weaker in this model than in the one featured in the Nordic countries. Here the judicial school can be seen as a mechanism to legitimize the judiciary, to provide a clear, visible, and reliable guarantee of competences. In both models the legal knowledge, and especially the doctrine, is transmitted by professors of law. These latter are often trainers within judicial schools whereas they are influential in the Nordic model by means of their publications. The European standards require a judicial school which is an autonomous entity. Moreover, the possibility of becoming a member of the EJTN represents an incentive for a judicial school to strengthen its position within its country. To what extent can we say that the standards have been applied within EU Member States? We consider six countries, grouped in three sub-groups, each sharing the same degree of involvement in the European integration process: Italy and France (old members); Poland and Czech Republic (new members); Macedonia and Turkey (candidates for membership).

In Table 4.3 we offer an overview of the timeframe and the final outcome of the reforms adopted in the field of judicial training. As we can see, in Italy and in France the external influence results are very weak. Even in the case of Italy, where the Scuola superiore della magistratura has been introduced by a law decree passed in 2007 and implemented only in 2011, the endogenous mechanisms of negotiation among the political forces are much more prominent than the external influence of the EJTN. As a matter of fact, the High Judicial Council, which has been always very active at the transnational level, had developed, till 2011, good relationships with the EJTN since it was vested with the responsibility for initial and continuous training. In the case of France we have shown that the Ecole Nationale de la Magistrature has played a leading role in uploading the transnational agenda and in transferring models of training abroad.

Table 4.3 Compliance of six countries with EU standards of judicial training

Country	Time frame of judicial reforms	Influence of European standards on the judicial training authority
France	Before EU policy has been launched	None
Italy	After EU policy has been launched	Weak in the creation; however the institution status fits with the EU standards
Poland	After EU policy has been launched	Financial; institutional; partial compliance
Czech Republic	After EU policy has been launched	Financial; institutional; partial compliance (the Judicial Academy is not fully autonomous)
Macedonia	After EU policy has been launched	Financial; institutional; full compliance
Turkey	After EU policy has been launched	Financial; institutional; partial compliance (the Judicial Academy is not fully autonomous)

Sources: Data set of Menu for Justice; Lisbon Network, country reports 2006.

We have mentioned here the cases of Poland and Czech Republic. In both countries the twinning instrument has acted as an external lever to promote the creation of a judicial school. This latter has been created because it was strongly requested by the European Commission. However, we can't say that at the present time the judicial schools of these countries are fulfilling the standards of the European Union in terms of institutional and financial autonomy from the executive. In the case of the Czech Republic, the Judicial Academy has been created with strong commitment from the Ministry of Justice, who entered into a twinning partnership with the Open Society Institute and the European Commission in 2002 (Piana, 2010).

The third pair of countries, Macedonia and Turkey, also differ in terms of adaptation to the EU standards. In Macedonia the Judicial Academy has been created as a prominent signal for transnational institutions and international watchdogs, also because of the pro-active role played by its director (Dallara, 2012). In this respect, full compliance is attributable to the need to follow the institutional isomorphic logic of change. In Turkey the Judicial Academy has been created with the co-participation of exogenous financial resources. However, Turkey's negotiating power is still higher than that of Macedonia. Moreover, inertia and domestic legacy still play an important role in pre-setting the agenda and in leading the policy-making process. In the end, the Judicial Academy is not fully autonomous.

It would be difficult to explain these differences on the basis of legal culture, since the countries belonging to the same area and to a similar legal culture differ enormously in terms of paths and results in the judicial reforms that related specifically to the judicial training authority. Much more likely, we would argue, is that what makes the difference is the existence of a change agent within the country which is confronted with a set of incentives that clearly makes relatively more profitable the adoption of a judicial school, either because of the endogenous political situation (Italy) or because of a commitment to the pre-accession strategy (Poland and Czech Republic), or because of a commitment to be recognized as a democracy at an international level (Macedonia).

A further pattern of change can be detected in the judicial training programs. As we have understood from Table 4.2, the training programs have integrated only partially the types of discipline that seem to be praised by the judicial networks, especially IT, communication, and management. This has been facilitated by the domestic tradition: a user-oriented public sector helps in general to introduce programs of judicial training covering court management.

It does not seem that membership of the EJTN is conducive to a convergent pattern in methods and topics adopted to train the judiciary.

Macedonia, which does not belong to the EJTN, seems to be more compliant than other countries, such as Czech Republic. Hence, it would be incorrect to argue that networking activities have entailed a convergent pattern of change.

The importance of multiple networks has already been pointed out (Wedel, 2009) and stresses the different impact that networks have on the identity of the actors who are in a position to adopt input from abroad and implement them at home. Such actors are vested with a *de facto* power as gatekeepers and are influenced by the pressure exercised by supranational institutions through non-coercive instruments (Scott and Trubek, 2002). As far as the Europeanization of candidate countries is concerned, scholars have identified several mechanisms of influence that go far beyond the coercion of political conditionality (Schimmelfennig and Sedelmeier, 2004; Dimitrova, 2002). Empirical research has shown that social learning and lesson drawing have been channels of democratization 'from abroad' for EU candidates.

In particular, studies acknowledge that the European normative inputs aimed at promoting democracy (Kubicek, 2003) and the rule of law differ considerably in terms of their compulsory force (Grabbe, 2002; Kochenov, 2004; Schwellnus, 2005).

Where, as is the case in the Member States, the absence of legal constraint opens the door to social learning (Checkel, 2001) and lesson drawing (Rose, 1993), actors involved in judicial networks are best placed to shape the process of creation, selection and diffusion of norms. Pro-active judicial schools or entrepreneurial judges and prosecutors who invest time and professional reputation in fostering cooperation and communication along with the development of judicial networks are facilitating conditions to create exchanges of ideas. Indeed, actors moving across national and supranational policy sub-systems are vested with the power to take norms and adapt them to national institutional settings. Moreover, experts are also in the best position to fully exploit their competence to interpret inputs before they enter the domestic system (Stone Sweet, 2000). In the field of judicial education, the EU is not vested with any coercive power. Norms that apply to that field are not legally binding. Thus, the diffusion of models and policy solutions tried out in other countries represents a key mechanism of Europeanization. The participation in epistemic communities involved in the process is a key variable in the process of Europeanization (as intended above) and accounts for the differences among countries equally subject to external opportunities for imitation and transfer. Accordingly, the low degree of legalization (Abbott and Snidal, 2000) of the "pro-rule of law" norms—the ones that become the normative guidelines for judicial education programs—does not simply represent a pitfall in the European policy of judicial training, but can be also seen as an opportunity to test the other mechanisms that work above and beyond legal coercion. Indeed, the absence of legal constraint opens the door to an entrepreneurship by domestic policy makers, a phenomenon that helps the interpretation of European standards and their integration into the domestic institutional context.

The crucial platform that gives incentives to the process of transfer is the network, that is, a network of actors that exchange information and ideas within a particular policy sector. Experts belonging to epistemic communities (Haas, 1992), that is to say policy networks that cross national borders, are only part of a variety of networks which may be set up in a multi-level system of governance. To the extent that policy makers move across national borders and between domestic and European arenas, they progressively enforce the domestic ties that the policy sub-systems have with the transnational policy network.

The phenomena depicted in this chapter also have an impact on the reference group of the judges and the prosecutors. This is a point already raised in the literature (Vauchez, 2013; Piana, 2010 and 2012). In sociology the concept of a "reference group" was introduced by Robert Merton to refer to the group of people to which an actor longs to be accepted (Merton, 1949). Compliant behaviors and adherence to specific clusters of values that are thought of as being constitutive or preferred by this group represent the clearest indicator of likelihood of being accepted by a reference group. The reference group also comprises individuals from whom one learns behavioral norms and values. Generally speaking, these individuals are higher ranked when the reference group is functionally associated with the work environment. Training is tightly related to the identification of a reference group. People trained in a particular organizational environment by a specific type of teacher will be affected by the values transmitted by her/him. This is due to the peculiar relationship that exists between actors who are willing to enter into an organization and actors who are recognized as the embodiment of values and norms that are constitutive of that organization. Usually these actors are senior or higher ranked staff who have been working in that organization for a long time.

In the judicial field, seniority and prestige by and large determine the type of actors who are entitled to teach and transmit values to incoming judges and prosecutors. In some countries, which adhere more strictly to a *Rechtstaat* model of judicial governance, legal values have been developed by legal scholars, i.e. professors of law (van Caenegem, 1991). Patently, in this sector, cultural and institutional traditions exercise a fairly large influence on the type of reference group (Guarnieri, 2003; Guarnieri and Pederzoli, 2002). Even staying at the very surface, while in bureaucratic judicial systems lawyers and judicial actors are trained and socialized on two different and rigorously separate paths, which may cross each other only in an advanced stage of their career (Bell, 2006), in professional judicial systems judges and lawyers follow the same career path and consequently they end up belonging to the same reference group. A reference group is strictly associated with some sort of professional accountability. *Professional accountability* refers to the control exercised by peers on the basis of their knowledge and expertise. They also transmit and enforce legal ideologies. Professional accountability is strongly linked with the allocation of moral and cognitive costs. If a judge wishes to be held in high esteem by her colleagues, she will be encouraged to argue and to decide according to the mainstream doctrine. This has also an impact on the career path followed by individual judges.

Training activities are of the utmost importance in socializing judicial elites and in allowing them to enter into a permanent relationship with a reference group. The choice of trainers, of topics on which judges and prosecutors are taught, and ultimately the choice of the type of mechanisms by means of which training programs are delivered, all these factors deeply affect the type of reference group judicial elites recognize and by which judicial elites are recognized.

In this scenario, the role of the EU is unclear and, at least to some extent, contradictory. On the one hand, European institutions, by means of standardization, push toward uniformity and generalization. Legal cultures are bound to disappear from the screen of the "quality of justice" promoters. On the other hand, exactly because of its influence, the EU is challenging the bureaucratic order held so far by judicial institutions by virtue of the sovereign power of national states to which they belong. Indeed, the coherence and consistency of those values and norms that are enforced within judicial institutions by means of judicial training are ensured by the closeness of domestic borders. Once they have been opened up, consistency and coherence are by consequence questioned and likely to come out weakened.

What then happens to the values transmitted to incoming judges? And what should be the approach in judicial training if it has to provide judges with adequate instruments to deal with this new scenario? In bureaucratic judicial systems, such as those which dominate in Europe, judicial and administrative functions overlap and interact. They are not deeply and systematically integrated and coordinated to the point that they become easily critical for the functioning of the whole system. This overlapping affects the identity of the judge. Judges' professional identity should encompass both managerial dimensions and judicial dimensions, which makes their decisions and their actions intrinsically more complex than other types of public actions accomplished by state-based agencies. Moreover, the legal order is becoming trans-nationalized and fragmented (Santos et al., 1996). For good or bad, judges need to cope with this new scenario. Principles and standards that identify a professional judicial profile should be responsive to the needs societies address and witness before the courts: transparency, public accountability, but also the importance of public communication. This means in practice that training programs need to touch upon not only the law, but also extra-legal knowledge. Recent developments in the judicial field have created a space for legal pluralism. Fragmentation and pluralism are destined to be joined with a process of new assemblage of pieces of norms, whose sources are located in different political and cultural settings. Courts still remain at the crossroads of this process of assemblage. Each case represents a potential arena in which norms produced by different sources can be combined in many different ways. Margins for judicial creativity and judicial innovation are increased accordingly. If this argument holds, judicial decisions would be more discretionary than they were in the traditional setting. For that reason, if not for others, judges are in strong need of adequate ethical codes. Which ethics, however? It seems that legal pluralism also entails some sort of professional pluralism (Salas and Epineuse, 2004). Different values are retained to be constitutive of judicial professions in different cultural settings. It is already occurring in relation to the bulk of law cases and jurisprudence produced by constitutional courts in different European countries. This allows us to heavily question the commonality of principles and values and the existence of a common grammar that might be advocated in a code of judicial ethics for all European judges. However, judges will be forced to perform a complex set of different roles, some of them contradictory, and also to learn the grammar of different legal cultures (Allard and Garapon, 2005). Mobility, international communication and social learning that take place across domestic borders challenge the self-awareness of a judge that is becoming multi-national (Kuhn, 2004; Priban, 2007). The point raised here does not speak in favor of a unified, top-down imposed ethical code. Judges are not in a need of a repertory of commands. More likely and more adequately, one may argue in favor of a kind of judicial training that is, beyond anything else, training in self-awareness. Tools to assess the need for training (Thomas, 2006), tools to make explicit normative premises from which judicial decisions take legitimacy, tools to enter into a comprehensive and durable collective discourse about who we are, what our institution is for, which law for which society. The task in front of us is not the easiest. However, institutions should take responsibility for providing judicial actors with adequate instruments to contribute to the construction of a new narrative, which "takes part in the story's movement, in the dialectic between order and disorder" (Ricoeur, 1995).

Chapter 5
Transnational Standards of Quality of Justice, Domestic Judicial Reforms[1]

Standards of Quality of Justice

Standards, benchmarks, policy guidelines, and indicators are tools of European governance, which complement the wide range of tools made available by European institutions to enforce a traditional and top-down functioning mechanism of government (Héritier and Rhodes, 2011; Jacob, 2011; Piattoni, 2012).[2] This is the general premise we endorse in this chapter following on from what we argued in the previous chapters. The activity of actors through the arenas created by the judicial networks consisting into the promotion of the rule of law and the quality of justice is a kind of governing strategy, i.e. leading and influencing social processes and institutions. In this sense, someone claims that standards have the promising characteristic of overcoming cultural and institutional resistance shown by national States toward any possible influence from an external actor and targeting their systems of justice administration. One may safely claim also that standards create policy windows, displaying low-conflict ideas and principles, where actors can invest their resources or obtain new resources.

Standards can also be conceived as normative ideas, which do not determine any specific behavior. Therefore, the context where standards are implemented provides elements and factors determining what specifically standards signify *within this context at that time in history*.

In the judicial sector the double nature of standards—objectivity and non-legally binding nature—create unquestionably a puzzle for the homogeneous implementation of the rule of law. The questions the following pages try to address are therefore twofold:

1 This chapter is authored by Daniela Piana. The argument unfolded herein refers strictly to the timeframe considered in the cases studies described. It should be noticed in fact that since 2014 the ministry of justice in Italy launched a new round of reforms which is not considered in this chapter. On the new round of judicial reforms see Piana 2015.

2 The definition of a new mode of governance refers to a combination of the hierarchical structures still in place, with new practices to organize and coordinate collective actions, such as networking, policy transfer, quality management, and social budgeting. On this topic, a vast literature has been developed. The purpose of this chapter is not to provide a critical review. See however Piattoni, 2010 and Radaelli and Schmidt, 2012.

1. Do these instruments matter as driving mechanisms triggering more or less effective processes of judicial reforms?
2. To what extent do standards create favorable conditions for actors with leadership and skills who are willing to promote change processes?

Our response is based on:

- the analysis of one prototypical case of standard setting via the activity of a judicial network, CEPEJ.
- the analysis of the process by means of which the reference to transnational standards has penetrated into a domestic system. This will be done by focusing on Italy.
- the analysis of two countries, Italy and France, with regard to the governing capacity of national institutions to lead judicial reforms.

The reasons prompting a focus on such a narrowed down empirical field are manifold. Firstly, the CEPEJ is the judicial network displaying the strongest commitment in the field of court management (Fabri, 2005; Langbroek, 2010). Its agenda covers a large number of policy issues, ranging from the collection of data about national judicial systems, to the adoption of policy guidelines, to the formulation of roadmaps to successfully implement judicial reforms, to the provision of a permanent platform where representatives of national judicial offices meet and exchange experiences and information. In this respect, for the quantity and the quality of the resources devoted to these purposes, the CEPEJ is the most prominent network in Europe with a specific focus on the managerial and organizational quality of judicial systems.

Secondly, the legitimacy of the standards of quality of justice that are set up by the CEPEJ creates a potential anchor for domestic reformers and policy makers in promoting judicial reforms and policies. Yet, as we all know, standards are not legally binding instruments (Kerwer, 2008). Their application can be easily undermined by a lack of political will or a lack of institutional capacity (Héritier, 2005).

CEPEJ played a critical role in defining transnational standards of quality of justice. These standards are considered legitimate because of the method adopted by CEPEJ in setting them. Once this prototypical process of standard setting is analyzed, the focus of this chapter zooms in to unveil how standards intervene in domestic systems where the demand for better quality of justice is prominent. In fact, standards do not enter domestic systems only by means of the legislative process. In some cases, the Ministry of Justice or any other actor promotes a law decree, influences thereby the parliamentary agenda, and finally ends up with a new legislative act, which impinges upon the institutional setting of the judiciary (Dallara, 2014; Piana, 2011; Dehousse, 1998; Honnige, 2012). It is not only via the central representative institutions—the government or the parliament—that the standards become relevant to the domestic debate on the quality of justice.

Here we need to distinguish between the mechanism of influence exercised by the standard of quality of justice, and those set by the CEPEJ and the mechanism of influence exercised, for instance, by other networks, such as the Commission of Venice (see Chapter 3 herein).

In the case of the standards of quality of justice, actors still matter enormously. This statement holds both at the transnational and at the sub-national level. Consider for instance the case of the CEPEJ, once again. Representatives of the judicial offices which participate in the meetings that are hosted in Strasbourg or the experts that are closely connected to the judges and prosecutors in a country and, at the same time, attend the CEPEJ's meetings can operate as bridging actors between the transnational arenas (where the CEPEJ is) and the local context, i.e. a specific judicial office where some (not necessarily all) standards might be implemented. As described in detail in the next paragraph, the CEPEJ exists in a large and inclusive arena where experts and judicial actors can participate. They gain prestige, recognition, and knowledge. These resources can then be spent in the country where they operate, on the basis of and in relation to the specific, contextual conditions they find.

For these reasons we decided to focus on a comparative analysis of judicial offices, located in the same country, to show that local conditions can make a huge difference to the actual influence exercised by European standards when they promote quality of justice within a specific country. It should be noted however that the rise of a standards-driven discourse on judicial policies is not exclusively due to the actions undertaken by CEPEJ. Furthermore, CEPEJ's standards join in a way and stretch their hands to a wide and variegated range of standards that have been developed during the last decades to measure the rule of law (Kenneth et al., 2010). So, the reader should not interpret the analysis offered here as a way of saying that the CEPEJ has determined the policies adopted in the member states of the Council of Europe. The causal chain looks much more complex and definitely not linear. We selected Italy for the domestic context, because this is one of the countries most targeted by the recommendations and warnings from transnational and international organizations in terms of length of proceedings, trial timeframe, backlogs, transparency and public accountability of the administration of justice, and access to justice (especially physical access to the courthouses). Italy is therefore a very relevant subject for this analysis. A comparative analysis of three cases which share the same domestic institutional setting is not yet enough to cast a bright light onto the mechanisms of influence triggered by the dialogue, the communication, and the standard setting which take place within judicial networks. In order to assess the relative weight of the variable "strength of the centre" which is meant to cover the meaning assigned by the international organizations to the governmental capacity of the cenytral domestic judicial institutions, we also consider a different country, France, which shares Italy's system of judicial governance but differs in the degree of centralization of the decision making-processes. The selection of the cases relies on the following reasoning. We need two countries that differ in terms of their position within the EU—an old Member and a new Member State. Secondly, we need two countries that have promoted reforms over the last 10 years. Thirdly, we need to avoid the bias that might be created by selecting a country—such as the Netherlands, Sweden, Denmark, Austria—which notably is leading in the development of instruments and experiences of effective court management (Smolej, 2012).[3] These countries, in fact, might be conceived as agenda loaders rather than agenda recipients. In fact, and just as an example, they have brought their expertise and their experiences within the CEPEJ discourse. Therefore it would be not possible to compare them on an equal basis with a new Member State or to generalize from the inductive reasoning that can originate from their comparative analysis.

The European Commission for the Efficiency of Justice: An Ideal Type of Standard Setter

The European Commission for the Efficiency of Justice was created with a *Resolution* of the Committee of Ministers of the Council of Europe in 2002[4] "recognizing that the rule of law on which European democracies rest cannot be ensured without fair, efficient and accessible judicial systems." The *Resolution* refers to the macro themes that have occupied the core of the CEPEJ's agenda ever since: 1) access to justice and proper and efficient functioning of courts; 2) the status and role of legal professionals; 3) administration of justice and management of courts; 4) use of information and communication technologies. These four items are permanently on the agenda of the CEPEJ's meetings and works (Oberto, 2012).

The *Resolution* also refers to a "normative anchor" (Kelley, 2004; Morlino, 2001) which consists in the European Convention of Human Rights art. 5 and 6 and creates a semantic bridge between the abstract and universal principle of "fair trial" and the concrete and practical conditions where courts operate. In other terms, the premise which stands at the basis of the CEPEJ's creation claims that the right to a fair trial, stated in the ECHR, will be undermined or not fully enforced if judicial offices are not capable of ensuring equal access to administration of justice for all citizens, if they do not ensure a reasonable timeframe, if they do not administrate efficiently and effectively the human resources at their disposal, and finally if they do not rely on solid and reliable implementation of IT tools. These last tools do not have a normative value in themselves. They are instrumentally valuable, since they might be very effective in reducing backlogs, in speeding up the length of proceedings, in making the services of the courts etc. more easily accessible for users and citizens.

Box 5.1 offers a synthetic view of the tasks assigned to the CEPEJ and highlights its working method. In short the CEPEJ has been vested with the responsibility of intervening within the judicial systems of States, though without being vested with the authority of sanctioning the States that do not follow its recommendations. Nor

3 http://www.coe.int/t/dghl/cooperation/cepej/Delais/GestionTemps_en.pdf

4 Resolution RES (2002) 12.

is the CEPEJ conceived as a supervisory body. Therefore, the relationship that is set up between the CEPEJ and Member States is not one that can be described in terms of hierarchy. The mechanism of influence, consequently, does not work with a top-down scheme of governance. States are not under the direction of the CEPEJ. We observe instead the creation of an arena where participants are expected to contribute to an institutional game where the normative inputs come from multilateral dialogue with all of them and the intervention of a representative of CEPEJ takes place only if a State requests it.

Which resources are put in the hands of the players of this game? The Council of Europe provides for a budget covering the costs of a regular calendar of meetings whereby the goal is building four types of cognitive instruments:

1. Indicators to collect data;
2. Country reports and comparative analysis;
3. Pilot studies; and
4. Blueprints and guidelines.

Box 5.1 Statute and working methods of the CEPEJ

Statute of the European Commission for the Efficiency of Justice (CEPEJ)

Article 1—Aims

The aim of the European Commission for the Efficiency of Justice (hereinafter referred to as "the CEPEJ") is (a) to improve the efficiency and the functioning of the justice system of member states, with a view to ensuring that everyone within their jurisdiction can enforce their legal rights effectively, thereby generating increased confidence of the citizens in the justice system and (b) to enable a better implementation of the international legal instruments of the Council of Europe concerning efficiency and fairness of justice.

Article 2—Functions

1. Without prejudice to the competence of other bodies of the Council of Europe and taking into account the work they have already carried out on the subject, the CEPEJ shall encourage and enable member States to co-operate with each other and with participating international institutions concerning specific themes. It shall have the task:

a. to examine the results achieved by the different judicial systems in the light of the principles referred to in the preamble to this resolution by using, amongst other things, common statistical criteria and means of evaluation;
b. to define problems and areas for possible improvements and to exchange views on the functioning of the judicial systems;
c. to identify concrete ways to improve the measuring and functioning of the judicial systems of the member States, having regard to their specific needs;

d. to provide assistance to one or more member States, at their request, including assistance in complying with the standards of the Council of Europe;
e. to suggest, if appropriate, areas in which the relevant steering committees of the Council of Europe, in particular the European Committee on Legal Co-operation (CDCJ), may, if they consider it necessary, draft new international legal instruments or amendments to existing ones, for adoption by the Committee of Ministers.

2. The CEPEJ shall not be a supervisory or monitoring body.

Article 3—Working methods

The CEPEJ shall fulfill its tasks by:

a. identifying and developing indicators, collecting and analysing quantitative and qualitative data, and defining measures and means of evaluation;
b. drawing up reports, statistics, best practice surveys, guidelines, action plans, opinions and general comments;
c. establishing links with research institutes and documentation and study centres;
d. inviting to participate in its work, on a case-by-case basis, any qualified person, specialist or non-governmental organization active in its field of competence and capable of helping it in the fulfillment of its objectives, and holding hearings;
e. creating networks of professionals involved in the justice area.

Source: Committee of Ministers, Resolution 2002, 12.

The bodies of CEPEJ "are a plenary session with representatives from all member states that meets twice a year; a bureau with four members elected from the representatives that function as the board of CEPEJ; one to three (or more) working parties or working groups with a maximum of six expert members; a secretariat provided by the Secretary General of CoE" (Johnsen, 2012).

This resulted in an impressive task of singling out indicators and measurement methodology. The first two Reports, published in 2008 and 2010, are in this respect to be welcomed as an innovative way to go about the justice administration assessment (CEPEJ, 2008; CEPEJ, 2010). The idea underpinning this work can be summarized as follows: justice administration is a public sub-sector and should be held accountable from the point of view of its capacity to deliver a good service to users—citizens—and of its capacity to allocate money with a strict instrumental rationality. Remedies suggested come from best practices utilized in more advanced countries—countries that rank high in court efficiency[5]—and

5 The overall effect of this comprehensive change consists of a broad and extensive growth of innovation within the realm of justice administration. Innovation has been praised alongside the development of several exercises of monitoring and policy transfer (Rose, 1993; Dolowitz and Marsh, 2000), all of them supported by transnational judicial networks

from the development of common standards which serve as common transnational reference points to assess the quality of national and sub-national judicial offices. Judicial offices respectful of the rule of law should be efficient in delivering judicial decisions in due time and be transparent in the way they manage their resources. They should also introduce a comprehensive installation of IT instruments to facilitate information processing and public communication. To put it briefly, innovation has become common sense when policy makers are asked to cure the illnesses affecting the judicial sector, such as unreasonable time frame, difficult or unfair access to the courts, the general public's lack of confidence toward the bench, etc. (Frydman, 2011). This has entailed a growing commitment to inject new organizational practices and policies, originated in other systems or offices, into the traditional systems of judicial governance, new organizational practices and policies originated in other systems or offices.

A functional incremental development of CEPEJ's agenda should also be examined. We will now observe the flourishing of specialized groups working within CEPEJ, whose mandate spans from singling out a checklist for quality management to monitoring the implementation of user-oriented tools to supporting the transfer of policies and organizational practices through a network of pilot courts—where "pilot" indicates a keenness to innovate their organizational structure.

As Michael Power rightly notices, increasing audit commitment and expanding accounting practices go together with the decrease of systemic trust. To be sure, within the European area trust among judicial institutions would never have been possible if a persistent effort to bridge national boundaries had not been made by transnational and international institutions such as the Council of Europe. It is not out of pure coincidence that the Stockholm Program, launched after the European Council held in Stockholm in December 2009, prioritized the enhancement of mutual trust in the judicial field, a necessary condition for implementing EU policies of judicial cooperation (European Council, 2009: 11 ff.).

A more realistic view would argue however that the transnational arenas created to single out standards of quality of justice are not egalitarian worlds. Countries with better experiences of court management seem to gain visibility and prestige, whereas countries with systems of judicial governance that look more prone to protecting the judicial independence both of the individual judge and of the court system seem to press ahead in promoting their model of judicial governance renamed under the promising flag of the EU model of judicial independence and rule of law.

All these sides are, however, not the focus of this chapter and they should be left for further and deeper investigations. What the reader should bear in mind is the existence of this unexpected and still astonishing process of standardization and quality of justice audit and monitoring which is now taking place in the European continent, presumably one of the regions in the world where national traditions

and welcomed by users and the legal professions as recourse for the problems encountered by increasingly overloaded judicial organizations.

of law and judicial politics has resisted more jealously the attacks of history. If a curious reader accesses the CEPEJ web page for the first time, she may be surprised by the gap between the amount of resources devoted to establishing standards concerning court management and the amount of resources devoted to establishing standards concerning public prosecutor's offices. This is not a coincidence. Being relatively more involved in fighting crime, public prosecutor's offices are more sensitive than courts to the local context in which they are located. Most of the time, proactive attitudes are not only expected but also required of public prosecutors in order to enact successful investigations. The validity of this statement depends of course on the institutional framework adopted by the public prosecutor. The more the public prosecutor employs an active role in launching investigations and driving prosecuting strategies, the more a strategic rationality applies in her daily work. From this point of view, European countries exhibit a large variety of cases (Bell, 2006; Di Federico, 2012). In some of them political accountability plays an important role. Accordingly, the avenue through which prosecuting can legitimately run is determined by central government. In this respect political accountability and managerial accountability must be considered as components of the same system of governance.

Variations also exist among courts. Adjudication takes place in several different ways in European countries depending on the civil and criminal procedures in place within the country in question, the organization of the jurisdiction, etc. However, the logic behind legal reasoning and judicial decision making is more clearly visible through standardized lenses which observe equally defined components of court management: court accessibility, communication with users, timeframe, etc. Whereas courts are supposed to deliver a service, public prosecutor's offices may be conceived as organizations whose output will be inevitably processed by courts.

Despite these differences, once standard practices of quality management have been established, they need to be implemented in everyday life. This touches directly upon a critical point raised by scholars. Accounting is, among other things, a collective activity of sense-making (Preston, 1986; Czarniawska, 2000). Moreover, accounting through common standards is subject to "local variations in activities constituting best practices" (Baxter and Chua, 2009: 68). Therefore, the standards of quality management, of which audit and accounting seem to be prominent practices ensuring institutional performance, need to face the terrain where they will be implemented. This requires a bridge that is to be built in context, not *in vacuum*.

External Anchors for Policy Entrepreneurs. The Odd Path of the "Quality of Justice" in the Italian System

In a nutshell, standards of quality of justice cover a wide range of aspects, which all pivot on a key fundamental idea. Justice is legitimated if its administration is transparent, efficient, effective, and if the delivery mechanism is based on a friendly, user oriented and accountable pattern of interaction with citizens and stakeholders. Alongside this general idea, not only has CEPEJ developed its recommendations and benchmarks, but also other judicial networks have started a process of standard setting which refer to 1) judicial independence; 2) society and courts relationship; 3) courts and media relationship; 4) judicial training, to mention but the most salient topics.

The diffusion and the enforcement of these standards—as normative anchors playing a role in shaping and leading the policies adopted in domestic judicial systems—cannot rely but on a non-legally binding mechanism. Standards are not mandatory. Countries which join the Council of Europe and whose representatives join the judicial networks are not obliged to apply the standards they contribute to setting. However, standards do have the comparative advantage of soft norms, embedding a kind of soft power into guidelines, recommendations, and best practices. This soft power goes hand in hand with the capacity of these standards to sum up the experiences developed in EU countries. The most successful experiences are key to inspiring new policies and launching learning processes across domestic borders. Judicial networks, in this context, act as facilitating conditions for sharing knowledge and information.

The point this paragraph aims to address is therefore the following. Do standards matter? To what extent are they keen to be completely transformed and localized by means of the process that some scholars qualify as "hybridization" (Eymeri-Douzans, 2005)?

To investigate this field, we have decided to focus on the reforms adopted in Italy. Italy represents a paradoxical case in terms of judicial governance (Piana, 2011: 117) The Consultative Committee of European Judges, which operates in the frame of the Council of Europe, proposed to the Committee of Ministers an Opinion to recommend the institutional features of a High Judicial Council. If one reads this text, which has finally been adopted by the Committee of Ministers, one discovers that the European model of the High Judicial Council resembles in almost all the characteristics recommended the Italian Consiglio superiore della magistratura. In other and more explicit terms, from the point of view of the institutional guarantees of judicial independence, which are the ultimate goal pursued by the High Judicial Council, Italy scores high enough to be considered a benchmark. This institutional setting is however combined with a low rank in the efficiency of court administration. In comparative terms, Italy is well below the average of the high income countries for the efficiency of its legal system and trust in the judiciary (Tables 5.1 and 5.2).

These indexes, despite having been criticized for relying on experts' surveys, seem to agree with objective data, such as the number of violations of the European Convention on Human Rights due to court delays and the unreasonable timeframes of trials. Table 5.3 shows that Italy scores far above the average for CoE Member

Table 5.1 The efficiency of the legal system in Italy and in high income countries, 2002–2010

Efficiency of the legal framework									
Name	**2002**	**2003**	**2004**	**2005**	**2006**	**2007**	**2008**	**2009**	**2010**
Other (High Income)	5.31	5.26	5.23	5.06	4.51	5.24	5.09	4.81	4.75
Italy	3.8	4.2	3.2	3.1	5.3	3	2.8	2.5	2.6

Source: http://www.iadb.org/datagob/

Table 5.2 The rule of law in Italy and in high income countries, 1996–2009

Rule of law														
Name	**1996**	**1997**	**1998**	**1999**	**2000**	**2001**	**2002**	**2003**	**2004**	**2005**	**2006**	**2007**	**2008**	**2009**
Other (High Income)	1.3	N/A	1.35	N/A	1.35	N/A	1.36	1.29	1.29	1.28	1.29	1.29	1.3	1.3
Italy	1.05	N/A	0.83	N/A	0.87	N/A	0.8	0.77	0.66	0.49	0.31	0.4	0.38	0.39

Source: http://www.iadb.org/datagob/

Table 5.3 ECHR violations by country, population and period (1998–2011)

	Violations	**Violations**	**Violations**	**Pending cases**	**Pending cases > 5 years**
	1998–2003	**2004–08**	**2009–11**		
Av/TotAll	2372	5800	3759	1435	399
Italy	1065	329	156	2569	33

Source: Cavallini, Dallara, Guarnieri and Piana (2013) on the dataset of the ECHR.

States, for the number of violations and for the number of pending cases[6] because the sentence of the ECtHR has not been implemented or properly implemented. From this point of view Italy ranks above only Russia and Turkey.

Therefore the Italian judicial system displays a paradox: high compliance with the EU standard of judicial independence and low compliance with all EU norms—both legally binding and soft law—of trial timeframe and court management. This results in a low synthetic index of rule of law (Table 5.2). This state of affairs has been a dominant issue in institutional agendas only very recently.

6 The cases are pending before the Committee of Ministers of the Council of Europe.

During the nineties the key topic of public discourse regarding the judiciary referred intensively to the role played by some public prosecutor's offices in dismantling political corruption, especially with the so-called Clean Hands operation (launched against Tangentopoli, or the system of bribery practices in political institutions and among the economic and the political elite). Only after 2001 did court delays become a policy issue. In 2001 in fact the Italian parliament passed a law called *Legge Pinto* (l. 24 March 2001 n. 89) which states that each Italian citizen, in cases where s/he has suffered from an undue delay in a proceeding, can lodge an appeal with the Court of Appeal of a different district to the one where the initial proceeding is pending, to ask for "reparative justice," a reimbursement proportional to the costs originating from the delay. The unacceptable delay is calculated on the basis of ECtHR case law.

The *Legge Pinto* is the first act in the direction of taking on board in the institutional agenda the issue of the right to a fair trial conceived as comprehensive of the right to a reasonable trial timeframe.

The significance granted by the European institutions to the trial timeframe and the bad image reflected by the ECtHR's sanction represented a facilitating context for one of the first Italian magistrates that devoted his entrepreneurship to improving the performance of a judicial office: the president of the Turin court of first instance.

The idea of reducing the trial timeframe originates from the early experience of Mario Barbuto between 1993 and 2000 when he was president of the first civil division of the court. This was when the case law of the Court of Strasbourg was for the first time condemning Italy for the slow progress of its trials. This external input worked as a "cognitive anchor." In 2001, when Barbuto became president of the Court, he decided to try the "Strasbourg programme," with the help of those colleagues in the civil division who had followed his experimental experience. Files have been classified, considering the risk factor, known as the "Strasbourg risk," which is the risk that a file may give rise to proceedings before the European Court of Human Rights (ECHR) for violation of art. 6 of the European Convention on Human Rights. The Strasbourg program started in 2001. The first step was to classify the files by date. This inventory of pending cases led to a more rational handling of the backlog. A key mechanism that allowed for organizational learning was progress checking throughout the process. Judges were aware of the stage of each case. The transparency and efficiency of the Strasbourg program and the fact that its effects were shared knowledge resulted in a slash in the costs of settlements in the judicial council. Between 2001 and 2009 the number of pending cases of over three years went down to zero. The Council of Europe recognized the importance of the program and awarded the Turin court of first instance with the Crystal Scale, an award granted to those judicial offices that create new practices worth diffusing and consolidating (Barbuto, 2009).

Whereas the Turin court of first instance was experiencing the effects of the Strasbourg program, a further judicial office was moving toward the innovation of management and the relationship to the territory: the public prosecutor's office in Bolzen.

The practices of quality of justice introduced in the PPO in Bolzen represented a case of genuine bottom-up agenda loading. From 2004 to 2008, under the lead of chief prosecutor Cuno Tarfusser the PPO introduced:

- public sector charter of services;
- social responsibility budget;
- a map of all production cycles, i.e. the breakdown of processes necessary to process cases; and
- permanent control of expenses.

How was this possible?

In 2004 the need to improve the quality of justice administration was already explicit and well known in the Italian public discourse. The experience of the PPO in Bolzen goes in the direction of providing an answer to the demand for more quality, in terms of more accountability and transparency. This direction has been taken on the basis of what can be rightly qualified as a change of paradigm: the PPO has been reframed as the center of a wide network of actors, stakes, and capacities, all of them spread all over the territory. Consequently, to improve the quality of PPO management, all actors interacting with the PPO have been taken into consideration and embarked on a participative process of mapping, innovating, monitoring, rewarding, and learning (Tarfusser, 2008).

The project "progetto pilota di riorganizzazione e di ottimizzazione della Procura della Repubblica di Bolzano," financed under the ESF of the Province of Bolzen, produced several practices and products fitting with the "quality of justice approach." First, a customer satisfaction survey, whose main function is to provide suggestions and ideas to the PPO. Second, a program to trace in a timely and transparent manner the costs of each action undertaken in processing files and cases. Third, a flowchart to break down case management into sequential steps, allowing the PPO to inspect each step, detect weaknesses and strengths, and finally improve punctuality.

The Bolzen experience received national and international attention. The PPO has been certified ISO 9000 (a method of external legitimization completely new for the judicial sector). The reduction of costs, and of backlog, and the positive impact on the organizational culture of the PPO were echoed in those scholarly arenas where innovative experiences of quality management in the judicial sector were presented to the broad public (such as EIPA, among others).

Therefore, despite being local rather than national in their extension, from 2001 to 2007 two internationally recognized practices of quality of justice were experienced by the Italian system. Furthermore, several offices started to offer micro programs aimed at improving performance following cuts in resources by the Ministry of Justice (Castelli, 2014). However, due to the highly conflicted character of judicial reform, Italy has for several years been almost unable to formulate a comprehensive reform incorporating those measures that were needed to tackle the length of proceedings, especially in civil matters. What the public debate reveals is confirmed by empirical research. The issue of managerial accountability of judicial offices has been framed for several years as a potential challenge to the independence of the judiciary and by this means to the impartiality of the courts. Worded in this manner, the achievement of a better level of performance, which would have entailed the introduction of mechanisms of organizational control, has often been belittled as a minor policy goal.

The MPG Program—A Policy Window Between Strong Agency and Weak Structure

In 2006 and 2007 policy discourse started to incorporate the issue of judicial accountability, worded in terms of efficiency of court management. We can track this process of change by using qualitative analysis of the official speeches given by the presidents of the biggest Courts of Appeal in the country: Turin, Milan, Rome, Naples, and Palermo.[7] The topic of the efficiency of the judicial district is present in all the official speeches by presidents of the Courts of Appeal at the beginning of the year, during the celebrative ritual that takes place each year in January in each Appeal Court of the country.[8]

The reference to the recommendations put forth by the Council of Europe—and to the sanctions issued by the ECtHR—became a successful anchor in legitimizing a domestic discourse that would otherwise presumably have been perceived as an implicit attack on judicial independence. The impact of the policy discourse permeated by the values of efficiency and transparency can be detected at the national level in the 2006–2007 reform called Castelli-Mastella, which tries to tackle the lack of intra-organizational accountability in judicial offices (control of the chief justice and the chief prosecutor on the court and the management of cases). Unquestionably the policy discourse has been influenced by the CEPEJ by means of individual or bilateral connections between policy makers operating in the Italian system and members of the CEPEJ, such as Fausto de Santis.[9] However, one cannot argue that this influence is strong enough to lead reform processes once the legislative measures—adopted in 2006–2007, as said above—are to be implemented. This is also due to the structure of the Italian system. The judicial

7 The size of the court of appeal is here calculated on the basis of the extension of the judicial district where the court of appeal has jurisdiction. The source is the High Judicial Council, www.csm.it.

8 Annual Reports of the President of the Appeal Court (Turin, 2009–2013; Milan, 2010–2013; Rome, 2009–2013; Naples, 2012–2013; Palermo, 2009–2013). The solemnity of the events that occur in parallel—during the same week usually—allows us to consider these speeches as significant sources to measure the salience of the policy issue "efficiency" and to see if the reference to the CEPEJ's standards is explicit. The reference to CEPEJ has occurred in official speeches in Turin since 2009 and in Milan in 2013.

9 Speech delivered in Strasbourg, 2008, available at www.coe.int/CEPEJ.

offices still retain a certain flexibility in the way they organize human resource management and management of the office in general. This flexibility creates a space for individual entrepreneurship (Carnevali, 2010; Zan, 2011). If the chief justice—namely the President of the court—or the chief prosecutor—and more often in large-sized offices the vice-chief prosecutor delegated to look after the organization and the management—demonstrate managerial capacities, have managerial knowledge, act as policy entrepreneurs, the system does not prevent the emergence of a divergent pattern of court management. As a matter of fact, in a system like Italy's, we expect to find divergent patterns of influence of the CEPEJ standards.

Generally speaking these standards are inspired by a user oriented approach to court management, highlight the importance of the performance driven legitimacy of the judiciary, and stress the pivotal role played by all tools of transparency, open communication, and efficiency in the judicial sector.

In Italy, the link to an objective, external, non-conflictual, and non-partisan frame turned out to be successful in 2006–2007. The turning point however is represented by the opportunity offered by the European Commission with the 2007–2013 round of structural funds. In 2006 the Ministry of Justice Clemente Mastella and the then general director of the Italian directorate on judicial organization (Dipartimento per l'organizzazione giudiziaria) recognized in the actions undertaken in Bolzen a potential lever for change. The Italian government was at that time drafting the six-year plan (PON), which was expected to be submitted to the European Commission under the European Structural Fund regulation. By this means, six actions regarding quality of justice, inspired by the Bolzen experience and reworded according to ESF regulations, have been incorporated into the Italian ESF plan:[10]

1. analysis of judicial offices aiming at reducing costs and improving performance;
2. assessment of IT diffusion and assessment of the functional needs displayed by judicial offices in terms of IT tools;
3. introduction of a public service charter;
4. budget of social responsibility;
5. ISO 9000 certificate; and
6. effective use of web-based communication with users, parties in trials, and stakeholders.

Despite the lack of a reliable and coherent implementation process which puts the reforms adopted into motion, Italian judicial offices have shown during the last ten years a high number of instances where the standards of quality of justice, the guidelines adopted by the CEPEJ and more generally the policy discourse

10 http://qualitapa.gov.it/fileadmin/mirror/i-perfgiustizia/materiali/1._Abstract_Progetto_Esecutivo_MPG.pdf

developed within the CEPEJ seem to have permeated local policies. Hence, the map of the different factors which interact during the processes of policy formulation and implementation offers a considerable benefit in terms of understanding of the engines of the rule of law networking.

Here we consider two cases of organizational reforms. To follow a comparative design, we will focus on the professional profile and attachment to the judicial networks of change agents, the organizational context, favorable/resistant conditions, and finally, where possible, explicit reference to the CEPEJ policy discourse. These cases consider the court of first instance in Milan and the public prosecutor's office in Naples.

Budgeting and Accounting in the District of Milan: The Entrepreneurial Strategy of President Pomodoro

The judicial district of Milan is one of the most relevant in Italy for visibility of cases and the density of economic and financial transactions that take place in the region of Lombardy. It is a fairly extensive region, with more than 4 million inhabitants. From the point of view of the resources available in the external environment this region can be considered as one of the richest in Europe and surely the richest in Italy. The relationship with local authorities and with economic and civil society has traditionally been a co-operative one. In the district there are more than 10 universities, some of them leaders in the country. Livia Pomodoro, currently President of the court of first instance in Milan, demonstrates all the characteristics that we have mentioned before. She has solid connections with central government, having served as deputy chief on the ministry advisory board with the Rognoni Ministry and then as chief on the ministry advisory board with the Castelli Ministry (which initiated the efficiency-oriented reform passed under the name of Castelli-Mastella). Awarded for her civic engagement, President Pomodoro's personality has permeated the managerial, goal oriented, and system vision of the court. She "likes responsible chiefs and goal oriented management."[11] Since her presidency began the court has been largely transformed. First, given the size of the office, where more than a hundred magistrates work, she introduced the presidential board, which has the same functions that can be performed in a private enterprise by the advisory board of executive directors. She enjoys a highly positive reputation among magistrates as well as experts who, during the years, have been appointed to introduce specific measures in the court, such as the digitalization of dockets, the setting up of an innovation office, etc.

In 2010, within the framework of the national program "Diffusion of best practices in judicial offices," financed by the European Structural Fund (Xilo, 2010; Vecchi, 2013) the court of first instance in Milan launched the implementation process concerning a number of measures all addressing the efficiency and the transparency of the judicial organization. According to the report by experts

11 Speech delivered in Bologna, May 25, 2013.

who have been working on this comprehensive modernization project, several instruments have been adopted, including:

- re-organization of the front-office;
- introduction of bar codes to identify trial folders;
- a program to constantly monitor office costs;
- witness projects (services to the witnesses);
- rationalization of external consultants costs;
- self-evaluation assessments;
- introduction of an Evaluation Committee to assess the Court's performance;
- service chart for users; and
- social budget report.[12]

As reported by one of the experts working on this project: "Distinctly different from the Italian judicial tradition, the Law Court of Milan is testing a close interaction with local public administrations and other external stakeholders, among which the Lawyers' Association is the most relevant. This collaboration has been formalized through the creation of the Milan Justice Table, where they take part both as financial partners and/or direct participants to the implementation of on-going projects. Since 2010, the Law Court of Milan has adopted a Strategic Plan and built up a specific innovation office led by a magistrate in order to better manage the projects developed together with other partners".[13] Does the CEPEJ matter in this context? It does. In the Social Budget Report it states:

> The CEPEJ (Commission Européenne pour l'Efficacité de la Justice / European Commission for the Efficiency of Justice) analysis is one of the main information sources for the comparisons of the organizational performance of the Italian justice system with those of the other European countries.[14]

and it adds a few pages further:

> In the last years, the law Court of Milan has been trying to deal with the inefficiency of the Italian justice system issue through the continuous modernization of the working processes and their digitalization, through strengthening the staff's competencies and through a continuous attention to demands of citizens, professional users and enterprises. The Strategic Plan that we are drafting includes actions regarding the improvement in the quality of the services offered by the Court of Law with particular reference to the reduction in the duration of trails, to solving the backlog inherited in the civil justice field,

12 Source Vecchi (2013).

13 Interview with expert working in Milan, May 25, 2013.

14 Tribulane di Milano (2013), p. 20.

to the simplification of the magistrates' work, reducing also the costs of the trials management and citizen's easy access to justice services.

What are the local conditions that create a favorable context for project implementation? First of all, the co-participation of the university. The polytechnic of Milan is intensively engaged in providing expertise and an external monitoring capacity during the entire process of policy making. Second, a wealthy region, which has supported this comprehensive policy in various ways. Third, the connection between the President of the court and the central governing institutions, something that has speeded up those processes of deliberation which are necessary for all interventions in the field of IT, court management, and human resources management.[15]

Agreement with the University: From the Change Agent Melillo to the Innovation Office

The judicial office in Naples is unquestionably one of the most relevant in Italy because of its size, the complexity and the number of cases it handles, and its visibility in the media. This institutional prominence is combined with a very critical location, since Naples is one of the districts in Italy with the highest density of criminal organizations. Generally speaking, the system of local institutions wherein the Southern judicial districts are situated features a low rate of diffuse trust, which comes from a negative attitude toward the political and administrative elite (Costabile, 2009). These features altogether create very unfavorable conditions for building a reliable system of inter-institutional collaboration, especially for judicial institutions. Interaction with the external world is unavoidable nonetheless. The PPO of Naples regularly needs to enter into pattern of communication, exchange, collaboration with other local institutions, in terms of institutional dialogue as well as in terms of knowledge and information exchange. This latter can also take the format of expertise supply, as happens when a prosecutor appoints an expert in order for her or him to draft a survey or a report on a technical aspect involved in the investigation or generally speaking in management of the case. The University of Naples is one of the biggest further education institutions in Italy and one of the more prestigious ones for studies in law and medicine. During the last ten years favorable conditions emerged for the university to be able to set up a new organizational unit with the task of raising money and managing research projects. This unit is still working and has expanded its competences and its staff under the label of COINOR, Center of Specialized Projects Coordination (COINOR). The mission of this unit mostly consists in raising funds and managing projects, going through the entire project cycle (from the design to the final evaluation and accounting). Meantime, starting from 2010, within the public prosecutor's office in Naples the vice-chief prosecutor promoted the introduction of organizational

15 Interview with expert working in Milan, May 25, 2013.

innovation within a comprehensive strategy aiming to foster managerial accountability of the office. Among the proposed instruments is the development of a regular and formalized cooperation with the university. In November 2011 the University Federico II and the PPO signed a framework agreement. This joint partnership created a new policy window for bespoke services provided by the university or some of its sub-units. Up to now this has been put into motion by means of a number of micro-instruments, such as an agreement for the provision of expertise and knowledge in the fields of toxicology, or information technology (to mention just a couple) and prospectively in statistics. Table 5.4 shows a synoptic view of these micro-instruments.

The reader can easily see the added value not only in terms of content—knowledge and expertise—but in terms of method—the process whereby inter-institutional trust has been built and strengthened. To make this happen, actors involved have been forced to overcome internal barriers in both organizations. Therefore, the individual commitment to the first steps proved to be a dramatically important favorable condition to set up this partnership. For the purposes of criminal justice administration, expert surveys are regulated by Italian procedural law and within each prosecutor office by a regulation issued by the chief prosecutor and implemented under her/his own control or, in the case of large offices, under the control of a vice-chief prosecutor. In the last three years the use of expert surveys within the PPO of Naples has occurred along the criteria and the limits fixed in a specific regulation "Guidelines and organizational criteria to appoint experts and interpreters and to pay off the corresponding fees."[16] Overall, the goal of this document is to ensure a high level of managerial accountability, without jeopardizing the quality of the prosecutorial activity. The points addressed in it are twofold. First and foremost, the guarantee of a plural, open, but still checked list of experts out of which each ordinary prosecutor can opt for the one she or he wants to give responsibility to for the expert survey in a specific case. The second point consists in the limitation of costs, given the high number of incoming cases. We should also note that since the regulation was issued, the entire list of experts has been cross-checked and updated. This represented a first achievement in coming to terms with the legacy of the past and establishing a system capable of ensuring a high degree of transparency and answerability. As a matter of fact, due to the highly sophisticated tasks and the highly specialized matters surveyed the updated list included—and still includes[17]—a certain number of scholars and researchers who serve as professors or assistants at the university but are nominated as experts by an ordinary prosecutor, not in their capacity as public employees but in their capacity as legal professionals.[18] This system has been in place for quite a long time with positive results on the overall and some potential criticalities. In fact,

16 Regulation issued in Naples, February 23, 2010.

17 This regulated system is based on a directive issued by the chief prosecutor.

18 The Italian law allows people to serve within a higher education institution—such as a university—and to practice as a legal professional—such as lawyer, engineer, architect, etc.

Table 5.4 Instruments and goals of the cooperation with the university (updated 2013)

Instruments	Goals of the cooperation with the University
Framework agreement	Development of research activities and applied research aiming at fostering processes of technological innovation, rationalization of the production cycle and of the services offered by the PPO
Joint agreement between COINOR and the PPO [JA 1]	Methodological and professional back-up support: administrative activities; management; human resources empowerment
Addendum to the joint agreement N. 1	COINOR is vested with full competence as the administrative and technical unit managing the IT platform used to trace the entire management of seized cars (two institutions involved: PPO and Prefecture)
Joint agreement between the Department of Chemistry, the PPO and the District Carabineers Headquarter	Highly specialized toxicological analysis of narcotics
Joint agreement between the Department of Advanced Biomedica Sciences	Highly specialized toxicological analysis of narcotics
Joint agreement with the Department Experimental Medical Sciences	Highly specialized toxicological analysis of narcotics
Joint agreement between the Department of Electric Engineering and Information Technology	Support for the development of IT tools
Joint agreement with the Department of Political Sciences	Training of judicial police staff; support for collection and analysis of statistical data with specific significance for the PPO management.
Work Experiences – joint agreement between UNINA, the Naples first instance court and the PPO	Start-up September 2012; WEs last six months; extended under a national governmental financial agreement.

Source: Piana (2013).

practicing as private professionals, experts were free to charge an almost non-negotiable cost. In truth, regular interaction and good collaboration with the PPO led in several cases to a reasonable level of costs, but this was in practice left to the individual and not ensured in the normative framework adopted by the office as a whole. Furthermore, the ability of individual experts to deal with particularly highly sophisticated cases might be limited as a consequence of the unaffordable sunk costs that specific technical endowments, which are necessary in these cases, entail. Finally, for all cases regarding drug dealers and drug consumption the surveys were assigned to public institutions, such as customs and the police. The number of toxicological analyses started to load these offices to the point of jeopardizing their capacity to respond to the demands of the PPO. This has been the "functional reason" pushing toward the creation of new mechanisms to deal with this large demand for expertise within a sustainable, reliable, and transparent framework. The functional reason matched the existing opportunity and entailed thereby a number of spillover effects.

In 2011 the PPO of Naples and the University Federico II signed a framework agreement establishing the general conditions for what can be properly called an exchange of knowledge. The driving mechanism is the supply of opportunities for students, interns, and researchers to learn and be trained through participation in the activities of the PPO and the supply of knowledge, expertise, and technical support by the above mentioned departments of the university. A further type of efficiency-oriented cooperation is work experience. The "Work Experience Program" (WEP) was the initiative of one of the vice-chief prosecutors of Naples, Giovanni Melillo, who heads up managerial competences developed throughout the experience made as delegated vice-chief prosecutor for the PPO management. The program has been designed to tackle three major problems faced by the public prosecutor's office and, most likely, by most Italian judicial institutions of significant size: a lack of change in personnel within the administrative staff which reduces the motivation of clerks and administrative operators to engage in innovative experiences; a lack of specialized non-legal training for administrative staff; low levels of intra-organizational knowledge transfer and knowledge management (this latter problem affects the judicial and administrative staff as well). The design of the work experience is inspired by the possibility of a mutually profitable exchange between judicial offices and the university. This is to be measured in terms of knowledge management, whose main components are knowledge production and knowledge transfer. With the financial resources provided by the ESF and in practice put at the disposal of the work experience project by the region, the university launched a call for graduates or undergraduates—but in their last year of enrollment. The winners will benefit from an integrated training program which will be deployed within judicial offices in Naples, i.e. the court of first instance and the public prosecutor's office. The call covers 165 places: each of them corresponds to a monthly salary of €500. Appointed interns are assigned to specific administrative units according to what they opted for in their application. For administrative units such as financial units, preferably interns with a degree (or about to graduate) in Economics would be appointed. Interns assigned to prosecutors' assistant offices have a degree in or are about to graduate in law. The coordination of the entire WEP is ensured from two sides. On the one hand, all persons assigned to a sub-project, which shares the same type of tasks and the same type of organizational problems they have been asked to deal with are under the coordination of a tutor. On the other hand all staff units that interact with students assigned to a specific administrative or judicial organizational unit (such as the human resources department, IT department, etc.) are coordinated by the Steering Committee and the Staff of the Innovation Office.

The entire machinery works only because of the full engagement and the personal commitment of the head of the innovations office. This is in fact ensured on the basis of three mechanisms. The first is the human satisfaction of interacting with the interns. Senior clerks feel valuable in transferring their tacit knowledge to these young employees. Second, communication among all the people involved has been fostered and guaranteed by the innovations office coordinator. He has performed the function of a "complexity reduction" mechanism and, at the same time, has acted as the creator of a collective memory. The time spent in the different rooms where the administrative staff were working next to the interns has been an investment of temporal and cognitive resources. This has paid off, especially concerning the fact that after three months all people involved were aware of what was going on in parallel in the other units. A collective knowledge has been created and this has also facilitated the creation of a reflexive knowledge. The last mechanism consists in scheduling regular informal and formal meetings, and engaging the judicial staff. The governance of the entire project performed well in terms of effectiveness. All persons surveyed declared that they felt supported all along the process. Horizontal mechanisms of exchange and mutual supports among WEP beneficiaries have also been set up. This has been facilitated by the informal training sessions organized within the specific services where they have been assigned.

Beyond Local Change Agents—In Search of a Regulative Center

The two cases presented provide strong empirical evidence to support the following claims:

- in loosely coupled systems, where the intra-organizational ties are weak and flexible, the relative weight of individual (micro) variables in promoting the implementation of efficiency-oriented judicial policy making is increased;
- the existence of external financial leverage proves very effective in speeding up such a type of policy making since it forces the involved actors to do this in a goal-oriented manner;
- the professional profile of the change agents which promote the change from the inside is crucial;
- the more the national government displays weak governmental effectiveness the more the local offices become leading actors in networking activities; and
- the networking takes place across different levels of governance, from the local to the supranational.

This last claim is portrayed in Figure 5.1, where the connections among the levels of governance are shown for the two cases.

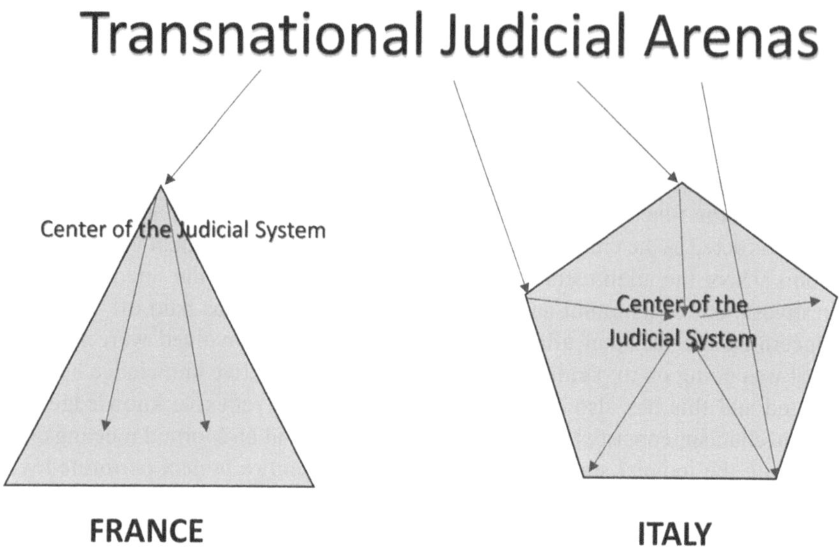

Figure 5.1 Transnational judicial arenas

Note: The arrows linking the transnational judicial arenas and the domestic systems are punctuated because the influence does not work linearly nor directly. The influence is made in terms of reframe, reword, and lastly reprioritize the policy goals.

However, can we test the relevance of the macro variable? By macro variable we mean those variables that depend on the national structure of the judicial system and on the domestic pattern of judicial policy making. The French experience is analyzed to test this point.

The judicial system in France features a highly centralized governance, centered on the Garde des Sceaux and the Conseil supérieur de la magistrature. The majority of organizational reforms are initiated by the minister whereas the CSM is engaged in human resources policies (such as judicial appointments and promotions). The issue of the quality of justice had entered the system as far back as 2001, as the outcome of the combination of several factors: prestigious and reputed judicial and governmental actors launching the debate by means of the institutional arenas that have national visibility; a multiplying effect resulting from the proximity between France and the CEPEJ; the framing of judicial reforms in the broader context of a) the constitutional reform (*loi organique*) and b) budgeting policy (LOLF, *lois des finances*).

In 1999 in the context of an academic colloquium hosted at the Ecole Nationale de la Magistrature the President of the Court of Cassation, Guy Canivet, launches the topic of the quality of justice and the efficiency of the judicial system as a service to the citizens. Guy Canivet is a highly reputed judge, known internationally and on the verge of becoming the President of the Network of Supreme Court

Presidents. The prestige helps him in influencing the national debate, even though other favorable conditions are at work. Among them are the actions of the Mission de Recherche de Droit et Justice (MRDJ), a small unit created within the Ministry of Justice to promote scientific research exploring the main evolutions of the judicial system. It is not in itself the MRDJ which is to play a key role, but rather its director. Jean-Paul Jean, director of the MRDJ and justice at the Court de Grande Instance in Paris, becomes a very visible and reputed interlocutor of CEPEJ. He drafts several reports for the CEPEJ group on the quality of decision making and bridges between Strasbourg and Paris, praising the integration in the judicial policy-making discourse on the topic "quality of justice."[19] In a text published in 2002 he highlights the positive effects resulting from the introduction of the New Public Management in the Netherlands and he refers to the implementation of the *loi organique des finances*, passed in August 2001, as a unique chance to change the approach to justice administration (Jean, 2005). In fact this law forces all ministries to plan their activities and to adopt a goal-oriented approach: "In France, the assessment of justice is a recent phenomenon which can be explained by two movements. First, increased justice budgetary needs have made politicians more responsive to justice performance. Second, scarcity of public funds has deepened the phenomenon of 'control' and courts only obtain what they ask for if they can show their needs to be justified. From these recent events many concerns and tensions in the dialogue between politicians and judges have emerged. The infringement of the independence of the judiciary by the concern of a more efficient administration of justice is regularly highlighted" (Jean et al., 2012: 39). The need to prioritize the needs and the actions to be taken would be—this is the argument endorsed by Jean-Paul Jean—a positive leverage for the judicial system as well. Some years later the issue of quality of justice in relation to user satisfaction is stressed as a key challenge for the French judicial system (Cadiet, 1997).

Therefore, the key actors involved in the French discourse on the quality of justice are national: the judicial school, the research unit of the Ministry of Justice, the court of cassation. The possibility for change is related to the legislative decisions taken at the national level again. The *loi organique* passed in 2001 and more recently the aggregation of the administrative services offered to the appeal courts at the level of the Departments (*loi organique* March 2009) represent the unique tools to promote the efficiency-oriented approach in judicial policy making. No local actor is allowed to take free and flexible initiatives. The connection between the national and the transnational level is ensured by individual bridges, authorized by the governmental authorities.[20]

---

19 https://wcd.coe.int/ViewDoc.jsp?id=1725861&Site=DGHL-CEPEJ

20 http://www.coe.int/t/dghl/cooperation/cepej/thematiques/Measuring_perf/Study_session_14th_plenary_contrib_jean_eng.aspThis text, authored by Jean-Paul Jean, interestingly recognizes the cultural differences existing in Europe in the judicial sector and in the public sector in general.

In this different scenario is the CEPEJ more effective than in the Italian one? Can standards be more effective in triggering changes if the change agents are located at the national level? The evaluation of French scholars and experts remains open on this point: "In France … it seems difficult to analyze a policy of quality of justice because of its heterogeneity and its dispersion, and even its weakness. As part of the promotion of quality of reception in public services, the courts' welcoming and information policy led to the certification of a few of them, when reforming the judicial map removed, without joint action, 178 district courts [*tribunaux d'instance*] and local courts [*juridictions de proximité*]. User satisfaction surveys consisted of a single national survey led by the Justice Public Interest Group in May 2001 and since 2007, in surveys of victims of infringements. At the local level, only one local survey was led in 2010 under the auspices of the European Commission for the Efficiency of Justice. Beyond a few limited initiatives, the discussion on the quality of justice has not managed to diffuse the French (ordinary) judicial justice which is caught up in its functioning problems as well as in implementing a system by the central administration that does not allow the accountability of local actors" (Jean et al., 2012: p. 40). It seems that different barriers are operating in the two systems. In Italy, one major problem resulted from the several attempts to implement a quality oriented and efficiency-oriented reform in the judicial sector without following up with proper policy implementation (Cavallini et al., 2013). The capacity of the center to steer processes of policy making is reduced also by weak intra-organizational connections. The mechanisms of control are loosely coupled and the functions can be performed under a general framework which ensures judicial independence but does not introduce national mechanisms of managerial accountability. On the other side, however, individual judges and prosecutors, with managerial competence and the political resources (political is meant here in terms of prestige and reputation) can afford the moral costs of a locally driven reform on the basis of the resources available in the context of the judicial district. In France these patterns of change are not emerging. The central government and the national institutions play a major and monopolistic role in bridging between the CEPEJ, the transnational discourse on the quality of justice and the domestic policy-making processes. This difference does not in itself skip the major barrier that both countries share, which consists in the original frame through which the quality assessment is perceived, notably as a danger for judicial independence.

Therefore, one might draws the conclusions that cultural barriers do filter the external inputs, but domestic change agents are the real engine of the CEPEJ's standards adoption or diffusion in the domestic system.

Conclusion

Networked Rule of Law: Explaining and Assessing the Rule of Law in Action[1]

In authoring this book and conducting the research which forms its basis we wanted to focus on rule of law as has emerged from a complex, multi-layered and multi-faceted process of networking across different levels of authority—both of law making and law enforcement—and between and across different national borders. Our study has developed from a simple yet compelling fact: the rule of law, intended as the primacy of impersonal rules over the dominance of the rules of men, may be comprised only in a transnational setting, whereby the laws are shaped and released and their primacy is ensured by means of a compound system of enforced laws. We also wanted to give serious thought to the challenge launched by the promotion of the rule of law and the quality of justice. Our perspective has been the vast repertoire of rules, ranging from the most coercive to the most flexible and negotiable ones, that have been used in different countries, in different times and moments of their history, under different cultural premises, to bridge between the principle of the rule of law and the rule of law in action.

One of the strongest beliefs underpinning our work can be phrased as follows: it is necessary that the law on the books must aim to entrench the set of formal rules of the constitutional principles, included the division of power, the checks and balances, the right to a fair trial, the presumption of innocence, all of them being the heritage of the constitutional experience. Yet, it is not sufficient to say that a citizen, in a given country, enjoys in fact and fully his rights. Much more than this is requested. This "more" is what we call the shift from the principle of the rule of law to the rule of law in action.

The bridge between law on the books and law in action has gained, to the present time, an unquestionable and indisputable importance. This bridge is made of bricks and concrete whose nature is not legal nor formal. Rather, it relies on actors who *each day* take decisions endorsing the law as a regulative behavioral principle together with other normative principles, such as transparency, efficiency, effectiveness, accountability. In that sense, our scientific concern, which leads us to investigate the actors' strategies and the resources at their disposal is framed in a non-positivistic view of the EU rule of law (Vauchez and de Witte, 2013; Priban, 2012).

If strategies and resources matter in building a bridge between law on the books and law in action, the arenas and the contexts where these strategies and

1 This chapter is authored by Cristina Dallara and Daniela Piana.

these resources are built and shaped gain *ipso facto* a scientific relevance in our analytical approach. For this reason, this book explores the emerging phenomenon of transnational judicial networks in order to ascertain if, and how, these networks can be conceived as actors and/or arenas for a supranational governance of justice.

Having this purpose in mind, we have introduced the concept of *networked rule of law*. This is to say that the rule of law in action, as it emerges from the many different, compounded and multilayered strategies, actions and initiatives undertaken in all the countries targeted by the European institutions committed to the promotion of the rule of law (including then the Council of Europe in "European institutions"), is also affected by the broad and widely spread process of networking. What is networked? Standards, models, organizational practices, templates, hard and soft laws. Who is networking? Actors involved in the promotion and the adoption of the rule of law. Who are these actors? In some cases they are individual actors, in other cases they have the configuration of a collective actor, whose cohesiveness and degree of institutionalization are so high that it can be observed as speaking with one voice and acting with one authority. When these actors are promoters of judicial reforms or changes in judicial policy making, we refer to them through the concept of *change agents*.

As already mentioned, rule of law networking could be conceived as a process through which these actors, located at different levels of governance, create, diffuse, enforce, and dismantle procedures, routines, policies and standards of RoL and quality of justice. Different instruments, which range over a wide spectrum, from advising to standard setting to training, are used and put in place by each of the actors to promote and, in some way, to protect the RoL.

In this context, judicial networks and communities could be conceived as groups, conferences, commissions or organizations of legal experts, judges and academics (coming from different countries) established at a transnational level. Overall, the activities of these networks can be summarized as an exchange of ideas and practices, in the production of recommendations, opinions and best practices, concerning different fields of law and the functioning of the judicial system, and in the organization of seminars, conferences and training of judges and legal experts (Amato and Dallara, 2012). Throughout these actions, judicial networks put in place mechanisms of influence and interaction on different judicial governance dimensions, as described in Chapter 1, i.e., the system of rules by means of which individual actions performed in a judicial organization are regulated, shaped and constituted in a way that makes them 1) compliant with the law; 2) reliable and predictable for the public's sake; 3) replicable for judges and generally speaking for judicial personnel; and 4) responsive to citizens.

We identified five main mechanisms: legal harmonization, judicial cooperation, judicial dialogue, standard setting, and monitoring. Each mechanism could be activated using one or more instruments. According to our analysis and to the existing studies, five main instruments are applied in RoL networking. Mechanisms and instruments are detailed in Table C.1.

Table C.1 Mechanisms and instruments of EU influence

	Law making	Standards	Training	Communication	Twinning and legal advice
Legal harmonization	X		X		X
Judicial cooperation	X		X	X	X
Judicial dialogue		X			X
Standard setting		X		X	
Monitoring		X			X

Why should this overarching process of deep transformation in the matter of the rule of law, as well as in the matter of the relationship between States and rights holders, be taken as a truly scientific challenge in social sciences? We will provide some major reasons as a response to this question. The first reason why the process of networking the rule of law should be investigated further in social sciences is that the overall effect is revealed in the balance between external and domestic actors. In performing as if in arenas, where the rule of law is defined as a principle, judicial networks create new incentives and channels by means of which domestic actors enter into multilateral patterns of interaction. Domestic actors thereby gain resources, such as legitimacy, learn to do things, or in some cases simply learn how to refer to things with different words, framed/enclosed in a transnationally accepted policy frame. Generally, judicial networks impact upon the balance between domestic and external actors, between truly international organizations—such as the Council of Europe—or supranational organizations such as the European institutions—and the judicial national authorities. The second reason this phenomenon deserves more attention and why it stands at the core of the research agenda in social studies, refers to the new ways through which actors interact with the system where they are located. By actors we mean judges, public prosecutors, attorneys, lawyers, legal experts and policy makers involved directly in the processes of judicial policy making. All these actors, with their own professional, cognitive, political, and symbolic resources become more prominent as determinants of the processes of change as the rules become looser and the possibility to play as entrepreneurs is more likely. What are the concomitant factors that could facilitate this? We will consider in our analysis all the instruments which do not stem from a legally binding mechanism of influence—such as legal harmonization—but, rather promote actions and provide incentives and arenas where these actions can be undertaken. Courts' dialogue across domestic borders, transnational standards of quality of justice, cross-national training sessions, all these actions are made possible, even more profitable, where transaction and communication costs are reduced by the existence of judicial networks. Nonetheless, these actions are not compulsory. Therefore, actors who are willing to play/perform can do so, accepting the risk of failure or the possible loss of legitimacy. Finally, this phenomenon is interesting for social scholars because it stands as a good example of coordination without convergence.

Judicial Networks in the EU Space of Justice

We firstly conceive of networks as *arenas*. Thus, change agents are members of the networks that activate processes of change at the domestic level. In this respect what is important in our analysis is the level of governance and the institutions through which change agents act. Our analysis shows that there are some cases where judicial networks are recognized by external institutions such as the European Commission, and in these circumstances they act as *unitary actors*. The nature of a unitary actor is, consequently, not intrinsically that of the network. It can emerge under certain conditions. Specifically, it occurs when the working method adopted by those networks is insomuch accepted and shared that other international or supranational institutions, such as the EU or the CoE, recognize them and their activities as norms and standards producers. In these cases networks themselves could be conceived of as change agents. An instance of this type of situation is the role played by the Commission of Venice (see Chapter 3).

In the European context, the activity of RoL promotion was mainly exercised throughout two different, but increasingly convergent, policy streams. The first is the European policy of pre-accession under which RoL and judicial reforms promotion were among the main goals to achieve for countries who were involved in the enlargement process. Although the criteria did not originally specify reform of judicial systems as one of the conditions to fulfill for EU accession, the interpretation given by the EC to the 'rule of law' concept has been largely built on the notions of judicial independence, judicial capacity, fair trial, and efficient functioning of the court system (Dallara, 2014). Starting from the 1970s, the European Commission recommended that judiciaries become self-governing entities, and called for non-interference by other branches of power in the judiciary, the independent training of judges, an independent system of appointment, and, more technically, systems and programs to modernize judicial administration through the use of ICT and management tools (Piana, 2010; Kochenov, 2004).

It is worth mentioning that the EU strategy of rule-of-law promotion was largely constructed together with other international organizations working on rule-of-law assistance. Among them is the Council of Europe, which may be the EU's "partner for prestige" (Piana, 2010) in identifying standards and criteria for judicial reforms in Eastern European countries.[2] The first problem faced by the European Commission was the lack of common and uniform structures for the organization of the judiciary in Europe. Each Member State had different institutional frameworks related to balance of power, judicial review and, more generally, the organization of judicial systems (Guarnieri and Pederzoli, 2001). Nevertheless, it should be emphasized that, although the EU had the formal asymmetric power to force candidate and potential candidate countries to adopt its recommendations, the content of these recommendations and the details of the reforms suggested (the so-called "Priorities to be fulfilled"[3]) were defined together with other international actors, especially as regards judicial reforms.

With reference again to the candidate countries for EU membership, some scholars argued that transnational legal and judicial communities exerted a sort of "extra-conditionality" on candidates in the field of judicial governance (Parau, 2013). Judicial networks become particularly relevant when the accession conditionality goes over and when the asymmetric power between the EU and the countries decreases. With reference to some specific cases, such as the constitutional crisis in Hungary and Romania, it is possible to hypothesize a sort of delegation from the EU to the CoE, and in particular its judicial networks and commissions, for monitoring and influencing national developments. In this respect, we aimed at analyzing in which way, and under which conditions, some of these transnational legal and judicial communities could act as "external agent of change" promoting and protecting the RoL principles.

The other policy stream is more recent and is related to the process of building a common and reliable Area of Justice based on cooperation and trust among Member States and national judicial institutions. In doing this, the EU (namely the EC) together with the Council of Europe, is actively engaged in a process of externally promoting harmonization and cooperation among national judiciaries (Piana, 2012). Thus, the existence and the enforcement of common Rule of Law (RoL) standards and principles is a pre-condition to fostering these goals.

With the beginning of the new millennium the EU started to devote more attention to justice issues, even outside the pre-accession enlargement policy and began to effectively realize its policy in the field of judicial cooperation.

In more recent times, the Stockholm Program has placed direct contacts between judges and officials in areas covered by Justice and Home Affairs among the key mechanisms in fostering mutual trust and an effective cooperation inside judicial systems. Along the same lines, the Lisbon Treaty has also promoted the

2 Piana (2010) has extensively developed this argument by showing how the various organizations contributed to defining priorities and details in relation to reform of the judiciaries.

3 In its official documents monitoring the progress of countries towards accession, the EU defined a set of "Priorities" that each country must fulfill each year in order to continue with the accession process.

use of even more intense collaborative forms among national judicial systems with a view to favoring EU integration.

The EU's new future goal is the creation of a European Area of Justice as a "common judicial space," based on the principle of mutual recognition of judgments and judicial decisions. As a consequence, the functioning of this area is strongly dependent on a higher degree of mutual confidence among the members involved. Operational cooperation among courts and judicial authorities would be easier if a minimum standard of harmonization in the EU judicial systems could be reached. The bulk of the research on judicial systems in Europe underlines how harmonization could be more efficiently fostered by relying not only on the application of EU legislation, but also by diffusing practices and routines already internalized and developed by national courts and actors in a bottom-up perspective (Piana, 2010, 2012; Lazara and Contini, 2009; Guarnieri and Piana, 2011). The Hague Program also emphasized that the effectiveness of existing instruments on mutual recognition should be increased, by standardizing procedures and documents and by developing minimum standards of information-delivering, procedural law, judicial and extra-judicial documents to start proceedings, enforcement of judgments and transparency of costs. Here, relevance and the area for judicial networks are immense, so that they are explicitly mentioned in a variety of official documents as target actors in the future EU area of justice.

On September 13, 2011, the European Commission adopted the Communication "Building trust in EU-wide justice: a new dimension to European judicial training," whose aims are explained thus: "The Commission is encouraging national and European level networks, professional organizations and training structures to work together, exchange best practices on training methods, build consortia, and set up trans-sectorial training activities." Then, in the Proposal for a Regulation of the European Parliament and of the Council on the Justice Programme COM(2011) 759, this specific action is described as a "support for main actors, … support for key European level networks whose activities are linked to the implementation of the objectives of the Programme; networking among specialized bodies and organizations, … funding of experts' networks." Finally, the EC Justice Program 2014–2020, with a budget of 416 million euros, aims at the creation of a European area of justice by promoting judicial cooperation in civil and criminal matters. Specific actions to be supported in the program will be: "Strengthening EU cooperation on justice and rights issues through networks of legal practitioners, non-governmental organizations and policy-makers."

It seems also that the European Commission is starting to involve judicial networks in a more official way in some specific areas such as judicial training. In fact, recently, the DG Justice launched a Tender for a study on judicial training in Europe, stating that one of the specific aims of the project that will be financed has to be the "Promotion of cooperation between judicial stakeholders concerned by European judicial training" and in particular "the cooperation between the European Judicial Training Network and its members with judicial training providers and with the European level judicial organisations such as the European

Network of the Councils for the Judiciary, the Network of the Presidents of the Supreme Judicial Courts, the Association of the Councils of State and Supreme Administrative Jurisdictions and the Network of the General Prosecutors of the Supreme Judicial Courts of the EU" (European Commission, 2012).

Endogenous and Exogenous Factors

As pointed out in the introduction, the first focus of our book is related to assessing how domestic and international factors intervene and trigger processes of change in the judicial governance at a national level. In this respect, we aim to address the following research questions: which causal role do external factors play? Are they concomitant factors? Or is it rather the domestic dimension that dominates, whereas the international influence comes in only to the extent to which it makes sense for national players?

The role played by "international" (Diamond, 1995) and "transnational" factors (Carothers, 2003; Mattina, 2004) in the transition and democratic consolidation became one of the most important questions for the scientific political literature since 1990s and is still at the centre of a broad scientific debate. While some scholars remark on the anchoring effects enhanced in the new democracies by international watchers (Morlino, 2005), others stress that international factors give domestic actors the opportunities to enhance their leadership and to reach the legitimacy needed to open the transition toward democratic regimes (Pridham, 2005). More in general, scholars are convergent in arguing that international pressure, created also by means of comprehensive processes of institutional imitation and isomorphism, drove national institutional changes and somehow created opportunities for these latter to converge.

Some others have been rather inclined to support a different view where national policy makers and elites managed to exploit and take benefit from international resources, such as financial programs, legitimate norms and values, and ended up with being influenced by international conditionality only to the extent to which this latter impacted upon the expected pay-off of the different options and strategies they had found useful in undertaking national reforms.

This debate, which is now enriched by the scholarship, has developed around the European Union and the EU enlargement conditionality. To be sure, European studies have included the concepts used to identify the processes through which international actors are to create the conditions for democratization and institutional changes. The concepts of "imitation," "consent," "coercion" and "conditionality" (Whitehead, 2001) are explored in studies addressing the policy of European enlargement (Pridham, 2005). These studies show that new European Member States have been influenced through the socialization of political élites (Checkel, 2005; Schimmelfenning, 2000); the provision of resources if institutional and structural reforms are enacted (Zielonka and Pravda, 2004); the horizontal extension of a system of rules integrating neighboring countries in a political community (Grabbe and Hughes, 1998); and the offer—even if non-intentional—of models of governance, which could be used by political élites to shape new domestic regimes. Institutional adaptation is meant to be the effect of the transfer and of the implementation of European rules and standards within national political systems.

The main theoretical assumption of these studies was thought of as follows: the EU influences the development of governance in Central and Eastern Europe through its accession process in ways that go well beyond its official competences in the current Member States (Grabbe, 2002). The causal chain is one of the Europeanization concepts, therefore it starts with adaptation pressure created by the incompatibility between the EU's policies and policies at the domestic level. Europeanization rapidly became one of the main conceptual tools used to explain the processes of change in CEE candidate countries in reaction to EU conditionality pressure (Noutcheva, 2012). Although the first studies on EU conditionality in the enlargement process considered the importance of facilitating factors at a national level,[4] they mainly perceived the relation between the EU and the country as a top-down process in which the requirements suggested by the EU are (quasi) automatically implemented in the name of conditionality (Schimmelfenning and Sedelmeier, 2004). Thus, these contributions on Europeanization and conditionality hypothesized that there are clear causal relationships in the use of conditionality to ensure policy or institutional outcomes (Hughes, Sasse and Gordon, 2004).

These theoretical considerations are at the core of the first research on Europeanization aimed at assessing the impact of European integration on the politics, policies, and polities of Member States in general, and on the judicial institutional designs and the politics of judicial governance in particular.

Although the first generation of studies was still mainly focused on EU action, as Coman et al. (2014) suggest, it was throughout the results of this research that the top-down Europeanization approach was partially denied. In fact, accounts of the poor records of reforms, especially in Romania and Bulgaria, showed that the EU's capacity to influence institutional reforms was strongly mediated by various national domestic factors in each country. Whilst EU conditionality was quite effective in promoting the adoption of EU-driven rules, especially in the years just before accession, the implementation of those rules was instead a longer and more difficult process strictly linked to national actors' willingness and capacity (Dallara, 2014).

The shortcoming of several studies is partially due to the conception of "institutional fitness" (Börzel, 2002; Featherstone and Radaelli, 2003). Indeed, it is held to be (apart from an exception in Giuliani, 2004) the adoption of rules and the formal adherence to EU standards (Falkner, 2003). This conception limits the

4 Some authors (Hughes, Sasse and Gordon, 2004) emphasized that Europeanization also requires the existence at the national level of "some facilitating factors—be it actors, be it institutions—responding positively to the EU external pressures."

understanding of stabilization and consolidation of political institutions that take place after compliance, behind the formal reception of rules (Morlino, 2000).

Magen and Morlino (2009), when analyzing the results of the EU's rule-of-law promotion toward candidate and potential candidate countries, from 2005 to 2008, focused more on the domestic factors which they considered necessary when assessing the influence of the EU. According to the authors, these factors are broadly related to decision making by the domestic élite, distribution of power among domestic actors and their interests (in particular the presence of change agents and/or veto players), political momentum and possible political fluidity, the presence of alternatives to the political regime promoted by the EU and/or the presence of alternative directions in foreign policy, and last but not least, the existence of an organizational, institutional and administrative setting suitable for adoption of the changes suggested by the EU. Among the specific factors that Magen and Morlino (2009)[5] found crucial in determining the rule-of-law reform outputs there is the presence of change agents or 'norm entrepreneurs' (Finnemore and Sikkink, 1998) within the judicial policy field. Thanks to the studies on the Eastern EU enlargement, the theoretical approaches used to analyze judicial reforms in democratizing countries shifted from a framework strictly focused on domestic factors toward a more comprehensive theory of judicial reforms. They also considered the role of international actors and, in particular, the interaction between the two levels of action (Coman et al., 2014).

In line with the theoretical developments presented above, we can identify two main hypotheses to test with reference to judicial networks. The first is a broad hypothesis related to the leverage of external factors.

HP1: Domestic changes are determined by external factors; if external factors change, domestic policy frames, norms, policies, and routines change accordingly. Alongside this view, we should expect a fairly homogeneous change in the judicial governance at the national level once transnational frames, norms, policies, and routines of RoL are changed as well.

We could affirm that, from a general point of view, our case studies falsify this hypothesis as the analyzed changes in our sectors of judicial governance cannot be attributed only to the influence of exogenous factors.

More specifically, Chapter 3, on the Venice Commission, confirms that both Romania and Hungary introduced important changes before the accession to comply with EU conditionality; thus it confirms that the EU conditionality was a powerful mechanism to induce changes at least in terms of rule adoption. As explained in Chapter 2, EU conditionality was largely based on standards and criteria elaborated by judicial networks themselves and thus this substantiates the leverage of the standards mechanism and monitoring (as listed in Table C.1) as a means to influence judicial governance. Even Chapter 4 on judicial training and Chapter 5 on organizational innovations confirms the importance of standard

5 The study by Magen and Morlino (2009) focuses on four case studies: Romania, Serbia, Turkey and Ukraine.

and monitoring mechanisms, although both chapters underline the presence of change agents at national level as the key factor in explaining changes in judicial governance.

Moreover, Chapter 3 shows, as in the case of new Member States, that EU external leverage drastically decreases once membership is acquired. The political élites attempt, in both countries, to reverse the judicial governance structure that they have adopted as an EU requirement before the accession, a clear evidence of how national actors' behavior and attitudes are crucial in determining concrete and tough changes. These results partially confirm our second hypothesis:

HP2: Domestic changes are determined endogenously; if external factors change, domestic policy frames, norms, policies, and routines change only if change agents are in the position of taking benefit from a compliant strategy of reform.

Both chapters on judicial training and organizational innovations demonstrate that, even if standards and monitoring are important in creating a potential anchor for domestic reformers, their application can be easily undermined by a lack of political will or a lack of institutional capacity (Héritier, 2005).

As a matter of fact, standards enter into domestic systems only by means of the legislative process, namely because the Ministry of Justice or any other actor promotes a law decree, influencing thereby the parliamentary agenda, and finally ending up with a new legislative act which impinges upon the institutional setting of the judicial system. It is not only via the central representative institutions—the government or parliament—that standards become salient for the domestic debate about the quality of justice. In the case of CEPEJ as described in Chapter 5, actors still matter enormously.

In the case of judicial education, the EU is not vested with any coercive power. Norms that apply to that field are not legally binding. Thus, the diffusion of models and policy solutions tried out in other countries represents a key mechanism of Europeanization. The participation in epistemic communities involved in the process is a key variable in the process of Europeanization (as intended above) and accounts for the differences among countries equally subject to external opportunities for imitation and transfer. Accordingly, the low degree of legalization (Abbott and Snidal, 2000) of the 'pro-RoL' norms does not simply represent a pitfall in the European policy of judicial training, but can also be seen as an opportunity to test the other mechanisms that work above and beyond legal coercion. Indeed, the absence of legal constraint opens the door to an entrepreneurship by domestic policy makers, a phenomenon that helps the interpretation of European standards and their integration into the domestic institutional context.

The crucial platform that gives incentives to the process of transfer is the transfer network, that is, a network of actors that exchange information and ideas within a particular policy sector. Experts belonging to epistemic communities (Haas, 1992), that is to say, policy networks that cross national borders, are only a part of the variety of transfer networks which may be set up in a multi-level system of governance. To the extent that policy makers move across national borders and between domestic and European arenas, they progressively enforce the domestic ties that the policy sub-systems have with the transnational policy network. Thus, in cases where the mechanisms at work are more related to judicial cooperation and dialogue, they are exercised through the instruments of training, communication and, in some way, twinning.

The case of the Venice Commission seems also to confirm the hypothesis of the "extra-conditionality" exercised by judicial networks, meaning that when the accession conditionality ends (due to the timing of the accession process), other actors could come on the scene trying to exercise external influence in line with the EU conditionality principles. On judicial governance topics, the "extra-conditionality" is mainly applied by the Venice Commission that, by virtue of its working method and legitimacy, acts as an "external change agent" pushing countries to maintain and respect the RoL priorities.

The role of the Venice Commission as "external change agent" in the new Member States could suggest also that in the countries involved in the enlargement process, the RoL maintenance needs a shift from a dominance of the Monitoring and Standards mechanisms toward a more relevant use of other mechanisms such as judicial dialogue and cooperation exercised mainly by communication, training and legal advice.

Are Judicial Networks Generators of Epistemic Communities?

A promising way to view the spectacular growth of judicial networks and networking activities spanning the domestic borders of the judicial systems in the EU is supplied by the broad scholarship developed to investigate the processes of policy diffusion and policy transfer. Especially in the last two decades, these phenomena have gained a central position in the international scientific agenda (True and Mintrom, 2001; Simmons and Elkins, 2004; Gilardi and Füglister, 2008). Several reasons might be recalled in explaining this state of affairs. First of all, in many policy sectors, we observe a pattern of policy coordination: in the welfare sector, in political economic policies, in regulative policies, in environmental policies, not to mention the education and schooling sector. The interdependence of domestic policy systems has grown continuously during these years and thereby has offered to comparative scholars convincing reasons to state the existence of a pattern of convergence among different States. This holds especially in the EU, where transnational and supranational mechanisms of policy coordination have been set up in order to circumvent and somehow to overrule the jealously guarded sovereignty of Member States. In those sectors where European institutions do not enjoy exclusive competence—such as labor, pension, fiscal, and education policies—coordination among Member States has been seen as the possible outcome of a structured horizontal dialogue based on monitoring, peer reviewing, etc. This has been called an open method of coordination. However, beyond the labels used by the EU, what matters seems to be the possibility for domestic policy makers and experts to meet and to learn from one another (Gilardi, Füglister and Luyet, 2009). Following the same path, several scholars have tried to test the hypothesis which identifies a positive correlation between membership in an international organization and the inclination to be inspired—as policy makers and decision makers—by those experiences that have been successfully tried abroad. Accordingly, the international arenas would act as facilitating mechanisms in lowering communication and information costs and thereby they would allow policy makers located in different—and sometimes far away countries—to find out about the positive results achieved by innovative solutions to specific policy problems (Risse, 2000; Greenhill, 2010). However, one should not forget the stream of research which tries to show to what extent the influence exercised by international or supranational arenas has to be detected not so much at the level of the cost of information as much as at the level of the values and the ideas that are endorsed by members of IOs or transnational networks in making or re-making their professional identity (Checkel, 2005). In this view, the convergence originated by the transnational networking would be due not to the exercise of a strategic rationality oriented toward adopting the most promising and less risky solution to a policy problem—less risky, better known. Rather, the convergence would be due to the exercise of a normative rationality, shaped on the basis of common transnational values and ideas. This seems to be fairly appealing in explaining the rise of the human rights discourse, to mention only the most prominent and significant example.

This volume offers three different sub-sectors to test both hypotheses. Do judicial networks create conditions for a convergent professional identity? Are norms and values promoted through the judicial networks absorbed into the domestic systems to the point of originating from the inside the changes that are praised by members of the networks? Are the information and ideas that circulate through the judicial networks useful tools to make more effective and efficient choices of judicial policies when they are in the hands of domestic judicial actors?

The empirical evidence offered in the Chapters 3, 4, and 5 shows different trends and encourages disentangling among different levels of analysis. On the one hand, we can say that some general, and not contended key ideas, which are promoted through the judicial networks, reach the domestic judicial communities. In the field of constitutional policies, the need for an independent judiciary and the importance of a constitutional court which champions the defense of fundamental rights, even against—when this is necessary—the intrusive power of the legislative branch, has gained a level of the domestic policy system which might be described as "policy principles." In most of the EU democracies that have afforded the reform of States—as has been the case in all new Member States—these ideas, these principles acted as a beacon lighting the way for future reforms. However, if one distinguishes between the level of policy principles and ideas and the level of policy implementation, which is made of practices and diffuse enforcement, then the hypothesis according to which judicial networks are effective mechanisms in making judicial policies convergent is far from being verified. This emerges for instance in the chapter which focuses on the policies of judicial training. There is no doubt that the institutional mechanisms which deliver judicial training have been progressively designed according to the general guidelines adopted at the transnational level and promoted through the judicial networks. However, the differences among the domestic legacies and legal cultures arise as intervenient variables differing considerably in the policy implementation that takes place within EU Member States. Despite being inspired by the idea of an independent institution delivering the training—and this is mirrored in the number of schools that have been created all over the European Union—the contents and the relative weight of the disciplines taught to judges and prosecutors still retain the traces of the legacies of the past and of the cultural heritage. This said, nonetheless, one cannot say that legal culture determines judicial policies in the reality of judicial training. In fact, countries with similar cultures seem to differ and diverge in the way they design programs. Therefore, it seems to be that in terms of policy implementation, the context and the existence of capable and legitimate institutions promoting ideas that are in tune with transnational guidelines is a key variable.

The importance of the context and of capable and legitimate actors also emerges from the comparative analysis of the practices of judicial modernization that are described in Chapter 5. Here, the general idea of quality of justice as a user-oriented service seems to have penetrated the domestic systems, both in Italy and in France. However, the effective implementation of this general idea is up to the capacity, the opportunity, and the competence of the "engine" of the change. In Italy this is locally distributed and takes the shape of a bottom-up process of change. Actors driving the change are located in some key, visible, judicial offices. They translate the general ideas promoted through the judicial networks and pick up those parts of ideas that might be used as leverage to encourage the domestic élite in designing innovative policies. In France this is handled by the central government, but again according to the context in which the process of justice modernization is framed. In the case of France we observe a comprehensive process of modernization that takes place in the public sector, and whose pivot is its transparency to the public and the satisfaction of the users. Much less attention is devoted in France than in Italy to organization of labor—such as the problem of the assignment of proceedings which has been of particular focus in the Turin office.

The empirical field we have taken into consideration allows us to respond to further key questions. If we fully endorse the idea that policy convergence should be assessed by disentangling policy formulation, policy implementation, and the internalization of norms and ideas—which agrees with the distinction put forth by Morlino and Magen (2008) for rule adoption, rule implementation, and rule internationalization—the third chapter provides evidence to say that in fact judicial networks are very weak mechanisms in ensuring the internalization of norms. Which is a way to say that the identity building effect created by the judicial networks is fairly limited and reversible.

Is then the approach suggested by Haas (1992) here suitable to explain the patterns of policy transfer? Is there a regular pattern? Does it lead to any convergence? To reply to these questions it is crucial to recall the Haas's words: "Recognizing that human agency lies at the interstices between systemic conditions, knowledge, and national actions, we offer an approach that examines the role that networks of knowledge-based experts-epistemic communities play in articulating the cause-and-effect relationships of complex problems, helping States identify their interests, framing the issues for collective debate, proposing specific policies, and identifying salient points for negotiation" (Ibid.: 2). Judicial actors have nowadays the opportunity to enter into experts-epistemic communities, whose influence targets in a homogeneous manner all judicial actors serving in a country. Only those who represent judicial institutions by the transnational networks are directly affected by the ideas and the principles that circulate in an informal way in meeting, reporting, exchanging, and communicating activities. Surely, in cases where the technical dimension of knowledge is exchanged, it is crucial that this knowledge is legitimized by the fact of its having its origin from or through a judicial network—as in the case of the Commission of Venice or in the case of the CEPEJ—giving to the knowledge a sort of qualification. This means the CEPEJ becomes—or may become—a leverage of change if used at home—in the national systems—by those actors who are willing to invest political and cognitive resources to promote a change that is in tune with transnational ideas. A completely different story comes out of the telling of the policy implementation. Moreover, the epistemic communities that may facilitate the promotion of certain frames and policy tools to check the entrenchment of the principle of the rule of law into the domestic system and the quality of justice seem to be much less effective in creating conditions to diffuse socialization. The chain of ideas does not flow without any obstacle, so to say. For sure, however, the members of judicial networks are involved in a process of transnational socialization. A strong argument for this comes from the reconstruction of the professional profiles of the domestic representatives which are members of the judicial networks. They gain legitimacy by belonging to these networks. The other side of the coin is that the networks gain legitimacy by making up a common identity, a common grammar and a common way of referring to this. This certainly happens in the two networks that come out as being more institutionalized, the Commission of Venice and the CEPEJ.

Whither (is the) Rule of Law?

The "*guerre des dieux*" fought for centuries in modern societies consisted of a headstrong attempt to bind the overwhelming power of the king and, afterward, of the executive branch to the point of affirming, above any other possible source of authority, the primacy of the law (the rule of law). Today, in societies that several scholars call "post modern," the battle to be fought is rather different and somehow less heroic and emptied of its ancient epic tension but not less important and challenging. Where the formal rules of the right of fair trial have been written into the legal codes, the critical aspect of the judicial system is not the status quo as it is reflected in the law in the books. What matters are the strategies, resources, ideas, and possibilities, which actors invested with institutional roles have to use to bridge between law in the books and law in action, or eventually use actions to change law in the books. In other terms, the rule of law as an ideal principle has been transformed into the rule of law as a set of conditions, fixed by formal rules, whereby judicial actors move and exercise their functions. However, this function does not consist any longer of the strict application of the law. Rather it consists of shaping justice administration as a service offered to citizens whose horizon—both culturally and socially speaking—is now going beyond national borders.

This book tries to cast light on this huge and deep transformation, whose consequences seem to go far beyond what one may even imagine from the perspective offered by the present time. We have engaged in the difficult exercise of combining an analysis of constitutional and ordinary justice, in order to show a common thread shared by judicial institutions in terms of transformation and future scenarios. As already mentioned in the introduction, this book points the finger at a phenomenon which triggers profound changes in the life of European citizens showing that justice administration is the backbone of any democratic civil society.

What citizens ask for, in a pressing manner, is quality of justice. This also happens in those countries where the constitutional rules, which had been written in the constitutional charters, have been subverted. As we seem to have a babel of doctrinal interpretations of the rule of law as an ideal, the same seems to happen in the realm of quality of justice. Langbroek explains that "often three concepts are applied: 1) quality assessment; 2) quality assurance; 3) quality management" (Albers, 2007: 58). Generally speaking, "in the judicial branch the terminology of quality is often applied, especially as regards legal reasoning or the identification of errors made by judges and as regards the existence of a system of appeal" (Ibid.).

Together with the description provided in the fifth chapter, the broad topic of the quality of justice has been deconstructed into several sub-dimensions, touching upon the access to justice and thereby the possibility for any individual to effectively enjoy the right of an impartial bench and of a fair trial; the efficient administration of courts and thereby the disposal of proceedings in due time; the transparent and reliable interaction with the external environment and thereby openness of the budget.

The effort to keep the unitariness and the consistency of national legal systems in check is reflected by the punctual distribution of a way out and a way in for transnational hard and soft laws which are today allowed to penetrate national systems. This happens via the preliminary rulings activated by ordinary judges, as well as through horizontal dialogues activated by constitutional and generally high courts or, in a less dramatic but not less compelling manner, through the individual strategies adhered to by judges and public prosecutors who play the role of bridging transnational ideas and standards and transferring them to the local judicial offices where they are serving. This transfer of rules—both of hard law and soft law—also entails a sort of translation and adaptation. In fact, in order to make the standards suitable for regulating the institutional behaviors of judicial actors—such as their legal reasoning, their sentencing or their managerial decisions—the standards and the rules need to be rewritten in order to make them a consistent part of a national, if not local normative order. (An example could be the organizational matrix which regulates the behaviors of judges, prosecutors and clerks serving in a judicial office or such as the institutional[6] setting which regulates the behavior of constitutional judges).

The weakening of the internal consistency of the national legal and judicial systems goes hand in hand with the expansion of power that individual judicial actors enjoy. These latter are situated in a totally new context, whose constraints have a completely different shape, and they have the opportunity to confront them. This point is extremely important and it highlights a number of consequences for the type of justice citizens may expect to enjoy.

In the modern setting reflected by a traditional demo-constitutional order, the power of the judiciary was limited to an extreme point, in such a manner that any judicial actor was obliged to take decisions always and only on the basis of the national law. Legal accountability was tightly linked to the organization of judicial offices. The more legal accountability was considered as the pivotal principle of judicial legitimacy, the more the organization of the judicial office was marked by a legal, procedural, formalistic assignment of the proceedings. This requirement is released in those countries where criminal justice was subjected to a criterion of political—see democratic—accountability. Generally however, the idea that any decision taken by a judicial actor is led by a rule-oriented rationality has been the cornerstone of European—continental in particular—constitutionalism. History, and especially recent history, has put this idea under great pressure. The reality we observe nowadays deviates from this ideal. Not only does the overloading of the ordinary courts demand that judges and prosecutors allocate resources and time on the basis of some criteria, which might be rational, or rationally justified, but it still incorporates some degree of discretionary power into the court and prosecutor offices. Furthermore, the constitutional courts have gained progressive power, especially in those countries where the representative institutions suffered the lack or the withdrawal of political legitimacy. This happens in almost all new democracies and in all democracies where the overseeing institutions have absorbed the functions traditionally exercised by representative institutions. In short, and with some extent of approximation, one may say that the judicial branch has experienced and still is experiencing an expansion of power without a corresponding expansion of the mechanisms of accountability.

If this is so, scholars and policy makers, respectively engaged in two different, but related cognitive exercises—one consisting of explaining, the other consisting of designing, assessing, governing—are affected consistently. Let's start with the explanatory framework which seems to be more suited to the current status

6 Here we mean by "institutional" both written and unwritten rules.

of the rule of law. First of all, we committed ourselves to a paradigmatic move, one shifting from the explanation of the law on the books to the explanation of the law in action. Surely the rule of law covers an empirical field which goes beyond the mere judicial branch or the judicial function, but broadly speaking it can be considered as capable of exhausting the empirical domain of the concept of "rule of law." In this book we decided to narrow down the possible empirical field and to analyze only the part of the rule of law that is directly related to judicial institutions, both constitutional and ordinary. Therefore, the same methodological choice, consisting in limiting the field of analysis, holds if one focuses on the rule of law in action.

We also said, at the beginning of this volume, that the phenomenon we were concerned with was the rule of law in action as it comes from the countless actions of networking, all of them circumventing, if not dismantling, the boundaries that traditionally have confined the judicial function within the domestic territory of national States. Therefore, from the point of view of European citizens, what are the forces that enter into the game of creating the "rule of law in action" as it comes out in the EU across national borders? We adopted here a multi-level actor-centerd approach.

This means that judicial actors are situated into different and layered arenas and situations of action (Ostrom, 1990) where they allocate resources, gain resources, build legitimacy, take decisions, interact, build incrementally organizational practices, in the daily work life, and finally bridge among different levels of governance. The organizational context where these actors are located turns out as a key dimension of the puzzle this volume focuses on. Several factors are related to the organization and the institutional context as it is shaped at the meso level (at the level of the judicial office or at the level of the judicial school, as is discussed in the fourth chapter). Therefore, the uniformity of decisions is not assured ex ante. The legitimacy that came once upon a time from the guarantees of judicial independence and from the legal and institutional accountability of the judicial actors is necessary but it is not sufficient to ensure the legitimacy of the rule of law in action. In fact, today, the rule of law in action mirrors the forces and the inputs coming from a plural and diffuse pattern of legal and *quasi-legal* sources of norms and standards. For this reason, the rule of law in action, which resulted from the promotion of the rule of law and the quality of justice, is not regular and homogeneous ex ante. The regularity and the homogeneity are not given, they are built, meaning created thanks to an open process. If this is the case, the role played by the rule of law in European democracies, as demo-constitutional systems, is going to change. This holds in a two-fold manner.

The first way of changing refers to the increasing power gained by the judicial function, especially by entering into a dialogue through the judicial networks with other judicial institutions which belong to other political systems. In a way, the capacity of the domestic polity to hold accountable the judicial function decreases, if we consider exclusively the fact that part of the norms and ideas that enter into the judicial decision making—also from an organizational point of view—comes from abroad. This is partially balanced by the increasing importance allotted to public and the managerial accountability (Koppenjan and Klijn, 2004). Moreover, the expanding set of judicial reforms which touch upon the efficiency of the justice system is a matter of public debate and puts the judicial function under scrutiny, not as much from the legal point of view as from the managerial and organizational points of view.

The second way this is going to change the role played by the rule of law in our societies relates to the multi-level game which is to be played on different institutional levels, where the many sources of norms and standards are located. As we have underlined, the Commission of Venice is nowadays considered as a prominent source of norms. The check made by the European Union on domestic constitutional policies—such as in the case of Hungary and of Romania—is based on a supranational set of instruments and mechanisms, among which we have also detected the so-called mechanism of rule enforcement. Although it may be weak, it is true that respect of the rule of law in action is not only—and not any longer—in the exclusive hands of the national mechanisms of guarantees. It is shared among different levels of checks. This is not as effective as some may want it to be. We cannot take for granted that rights enforcement is ensured through this new pattern of checks and balance. However, the latter is the outcome of an interdependent system located across several levels of governance. The equilibrium is intricately made up of several elements, some of them situated at transnational levels. In this game the judicial networks play a dual role. As we have said, most of the time they work as amplifiers and create opportunities for mutual checks among individual judicial actors, who engaged in multiple and regular exchange of ideas and problem-solutions. This can be exploited as an external leverage of change in those systems where the domestic political élite is not capable of leading judicial reforms. The standards affirmed through the judicial networks can be borrowed, translated and made suitable for the country where they are to be applied (Agranoff, 2007). However, the judicial networks can also move on and reach a further step in their development. In some cases, in which the Commission of Venice seemed to us the most prominent and significant, they act as external change agents.

If then the rule of law in action is a goal and not a datum, how can we design a system of mechanisms where the judicial actors, situated in the multi-level and normatively pluralistic context as we have depicted it, can be held accountable? Law is part of the game. But we need more. An important part is now played by monitoring and assessing.[7] This innovative approach is worth being pursued because of two different reasons. Soft law exchanges and hybridizations are made

7 This point can be also argued by framing the same policy problem in a Foucauldian paradigm. The shift we are echoing here is that mentioned from the government to "governamentality." The center of the system does not perform the traditional function, which consisted in creating norms in a monopolistic setting. Rather it develops the techniques to measure and to assess. This entails different capacities, opportunities and

possible by mean of bilateral collaborations established (often on an informal basis) among local organizational units of national public institutions. Imitation and learning through isomorphism are in this respect taking place not by means of legal changes of national codes, but rather by means of experiments, organizational innovations and experiences that emerge within administrative units of the State.

As a matter of fact, courts seem to obey a larger and more variegated range of rules and values, many of which stem from extra-legal authorities, for instance from organizational and professional institutions. Judicial ethics, professional standards, organizational standards of efficiency, transparency and public accountability, are all norms that stem from extra-legal institutional orders. Despite being extra-legal, these values and rules maintain a sanguine relationship with the legality principle, as long as they are instrumental to its implementation. The assemblage of the mechanisms by means of which authority is exercised in the judicial field might be named "judicial governance". The system of judicial governance is to erase from the judicial field all personal motivations, preferences and inclinations. In a nutshell, it transforms individual judges and prosecutors into public roles. Much of the scholarship on judicial systems and judicial actions addresses the legitimacy of adjudication by unveiling and exploring the rationales of its governance: recruitment, appointment, evaluation and promotion, disciplinary control and ethical regulation are the most common aspects of judicial governance that enter into the focus of the analysis of social and political scholars. The injection of extra-legal norms into judicial governance creates a possible space for non-State-based actors in offering tools of governance within the judicial field. In recent times, the traditional configuration of judicial governance, which has been inherited from the modern age, has proved to be exceptionally lacking in addressing effectively the broader and differentiated demands of justice that have emerged today in democratic societies. The change in demands goes in parallel—even if not necessarily as a causal relationship—with the change of the external environment in which courts are located. National institutions are subjected to an increasingly depriving process of reallocation of resources and competences, some of which are key for the healthy functioning of judicial systems: law making, law enforcement, socialization of high ranked judges and prosecutors, many of these functions, which once were handled by national States, are nowadays spread among several actors and obey a large array of different rationales, cultural attitudes and perspectives.

The changes that affect the judicial field stand at the intersection between the reshape of judicial governance and three processes of rule making: trans-nationalization of law; the gain in legitimacy of extra-legal expertise in the judicial field (management, communicative skills, etc.); and standardization. It would be superficial and misleading to disregard and neglect these processes of standard setting due to the fact that they are apparently associated more with the

risks, for instance, the risk originating from the lack of cognitive capacity, i.e. the lack of reliable information (Kallinikos, 2006).

"ought" rather than with the "be." Instead, the European discourse developed on the quality of justice should be framed in a broader process of change, which touched and is going to touch in the very near future, not only on the way courts are governed, but also on the way courts interact with other sub-systems of modern societies.

These considerations create a new agenda for the analysis of scholars as well as for the decisions of the policy makers. This should relate to three points:

Territory and Courts

The creation and institutionalization of a system of courts is strictly related to the emergence and the arrival of constitutional government. In continental Europe, this is embodied in the processes of state building that took place in the sixteenth to the eighteenth centuries. Courts were developed in relationship with the centralization of power, which would later be handled by central agencies within the public sector under the aegis of the State.

> Historical sociologists have drawn our attention to diverse mechanisms of state formation: the imposition of a national language and a level of literacy, a common coinage, the fusing of a territory into a single time-space system through innovations in transportation, communication and temporality, the unification of legal codes and authorities. Key practices of rule were institutionalized within a central, more or less permanent body of offices and agencies, given a certain more or less explicit constitutional form, endowed with the capacity to raise funds in the form of taxes, and backed with the virtual monopoly of the legitimate use of force over a defined territory (Rose, 1993: 4).

Concerning this, the process of hollowing out that affected the modern State undermines the linearity of the association that for centuries linked the territorial control of the State with the law-making and enforcing function. Transnational and sub-national authorities are entitled to issue laws whereas soft law and quasi legal norms increasingly occupy the front stage of the political and social setting. The original system of law, which was bounded and isolated from the extra-domestic environment, has been penetrated by means of several and variegated mechanisms of legal transfer, legal imitation, and judicial cross fertilization. If at the very beginning this process took place mainly and foremost within the judicial field targeted by constitutional justice, later on the trans-nationalization of adjudication has become a distinctive mark of EU law and of the ways domestic courts interact horizontally (from one country to another) and vertically (from the European level to the level of the ordinary court).

Professional Expertise and Courts

Recent developments in politics and law did not leave unaltered the role that knowledge plays within the judicial field. Instead, as long as judicial actions are conceived as actions that belong to a multiple normative order, which is ruled by different types of standards, both legal and extra-legal, the knowledge that should be mastered by judicial actors turns out to be more variegated than before. Judges and prosecutors are expected to cope with norms of different origin and with different rationales, such as efficiency, public accountability, legality, as mentioned in the previous section. Professional accountability proves to be crucial. Supranational institutions become incrementally empowered because of the role they play in championing extra-legal values, judicial standards and legal ideologies.

Standards in Governing Courts

Whereas external actors—such as the EU and the Council of Europe—may deeply impact on judicial governance, despite being deprived of any binding authority in this field, their influence is not easily proved nor homogeneous or consistent in time and space, something that sounds, in the most optimistic view, contradictory toward the very idea of one unique European "rule of law." On the other hand, once again, the EU proves itself unresponsive and refractory to the "one-fits-all" recipe in policy making. Presumably we should resign ourselves and accept once forever that "one-fits-all solutions" do not fit at all the European pattern of governance, nor do they fit the judicial sector, which had for centuries been the realm of homogeneity and uniformity made possible through the law. If the rule of law in action depends on the way justice is administered, then it might be well possible that we have a range of models of "rule of law" which are different from one another as far as the five dimensions of accountability combine in different patterns of governance.

The three facets mentioned here as conclusive remarks of our long journey through networking and together with change agents and judicial networks leave open several possible – and still promising – research questions and research agendas. In a way this leads back to our three clusters of explaining and interpretative hypotheses, which stem from the following assumption: networking the rule of law is a process, where actors and rules seem to interplay in a new, interesting, innovative, and challenging manner. Inter-disciplinary approaches combining political science, sociology, legal studies, psychology, and history seem to be urgently needed and unescapably requested by all institutions and practitioners to reach a better understanding of this new phenomenon, which is also a way to govern better the changes that this phenomenon seems to entail, more or less intentionally.

Bibliography

Abbott, K. and Snidal, D. (2000), 'Hard and Soft Law in International Governance,' *International Organization* 54 (3), 421–41.

——— (2001), 'International Standards and International Governance,' *Journal of European Public Policy* 8 (3), 345–70.

Ackerman, B. (1997), 'The Rise of the World Constitutionalism,' *Virgin Law Review* 83, 771–97.

Agranoff, R. (2007), *Managing within Networks. Adding Value to Public Organizations*. Washington D.C.: George Town University Press.

Ahrne, G., Brunsson, N. and Garsten, C. (2000), 'Standardization through Organization,' in N. Brunsson and G. Jacobsson (eds), *A World of Standards*. Oxford: Oxford University Press, 50–68.

Ajani, G. (1996), *Il modello post-socialista*. Torino: Giappichelli.

Albers, P. (2007), 'Performance indicators and evaluation for judges and courts.' Available at http://www.coe.int/t/dghl/cooperation/cepej/events/OnEnParle/MoscowPA250507_en.pdf

——— (2008), 'Best Practices on the Prevention of the Unreasonable Length of Proceedings: Experiences of the CEPEJ,' Communication presented at the UniDem Campus Seminar, organized by the Venice Commission, Trieste, 25–28 February.

Alderson, K. (2001), 'Making Sense of State Socialization,' *Review of International Studies* 27 (3), 415–33.

Alexy, R. (1989), *Theory of Legal Argumentation: The Theory of Rational Discourse as a Theory of Legal Justification*. Oxford: Clarendon Press.

Allard, J. and Garapon, A. (2005), *Les juges dans la mondialisation: la nouvelle révolution du droit*. Paris: Seuil.

Alter, K.J. (2000), 'The European Union's Legal System and Domestic Policy: Spillover or Backlash,' *International Organization* 54 (3), 489–518.

Amato, R. (2014), 'La cooperazione giudiziaria in rete nello spazio di liberta, sicurezza e giustizia.' Unpublished PhD thesis in European Law, University of Bologna. Available at: http://amsdottorato.unibo.it/view/dottorati/DOT500/2014

Amato, R. and Dallara, C. (2012), 'Judicial and legal expert networks. New actors for a EU area of justice?' Paper presented at the conference 'National Courts vis-a-vis EU Law: New Issues, Theories and Methods,' 29–30 November 2012, European University Institute (Fiesole).

Ammannati L. (2008), 'Governance e regolazione attraverso reti,' in L. Ammannati and P. Bilancia (eds), *Governance dell'economia e integrazione europea. Governance multilivello regolazione reti*. Milano: Giuffrè.

Anderson, Benedict (1991), *Imagined Communities. Reflections on the Origin and Spread of Nationalism.* London: Verso.

Arnull, A. (1994), 'Refurbishing the Judicial Architecture of the European Community,' *International and Comparative Law Quarterly* 43 (2) 296–316.

Atkins, L. (2002), 'The Shifting of Judicial Reform: From Independence to Capacity.' Budapest: Open Society Institute, EU Accession Monitoring Program. Available at: http://www.eumap.org

Auby, J.B. (2008), 'Is Legal Globalization Regulated? Memling and the Business of Baking Camels,' *Utrecht Law Review* 4(3). Available at: http://www.utrechtlawreview.org

Barbuto, M. (2009), 'Per il miglioe servizio degli uffici del giudice civile,' in V. Lanteri and N.A. De Carlo (eds), *Giustizia al bivio.* Milano: Franco Angeli.

Bartolini, S. (2005), *Restructuring Europe: Centre Formation, System Building and Political Structuring Between the Nation-State and the European Union.* Oxford: Oxford University Press.

Baudenbacher, C. (2003), 'Judicial Globalization: New Development or Old Wine in New Bottles?' *Texas International Law Journal* 38.

Baum, L. (1998), *The Puzzle of Judicial Behavior.* Chicago: University of Michigan Press.

——— (2006), *Judges and Their Audience: A Perspective on Judicial Behavior.* Princeton: Princeton University Press.

Baxter, J. and Chua, F.W. (2009), 'Studying Accountability in Action: The Challenge of Engaging with Management Accounting Practice,' in C. Chapman, D. Cooper and P. Miller (eds), *Accounting, Organizations and Institutions.* Oxford: Oxford University Press, 65–84.

Bell, J. (2006), *Judiciaries within Europe: A Comparative Review.* Oxford: Oxford University Press, 13–24.

Bellamy, R. (2005), *Rethinking Liberalism (Continuum Studies in Political Thought).* London: Continuum.

Benda-Beckmann, F. von (2002), 'Who's Afraid of Legal Pluralism?,' *The Journal of Legal Pluralism and Unofficial Law* 34 (47), 37–82.

Benoit-Rohmer, F. and Klebes, H. (2005), *Le droit du Conseil de l'Europe: Vers un espace juridique européen.* Strasbourg: Le Conseil de l'Europe.

Benvenisti, E. and Downs, G.W. (2012), 'The Democratizing Effects of Transjudicial Coordination,' *Utrecht Law Review* 8 (2).

Benvenuti, Simone, 'Building a Common Judicial Culture in the European Union through Judicial Networks', Paper presented at the Interim Meeting on 'The Changing Nature of Judicial Power in Supranational, Federal, and Domestic systems,' IPSA Conference (RC09), 22–24 July 2013, Dublin.

Benz, A. (2004), 'Governance – Modebegriff oder nützliches sozialwissenschaftliches Konzept?' in A. Benz (ed.), *Governance – Regieren in komplexen Regelsystemen. Eine Einführung.* Wiesbaden: Verlag für Sozialwissenschaften, 13–32.

Berger, P.L. and Luckmann, T. (1966), *The Social Construction of Reality*. London: Penguin Books.

Bihari, M. (1986), 'The political system and the representation of interests,' in R. Andorka and L. Bertalan (eds) *Economy and Society in Hungary*. Budapest: Karl Marz University of Economic Sciences, 287–312.

Blokker, P. (2013a), 'Constitution-Making in Romania: From Reiterative Crises to Constitutional Moment?,' *Romanian Journal of Comparative Law* 3 (2), 187–204.

——— (2013b), *New Democracies in Crisis? A Comparative Constitutional Study of the Czech Republic, Hungary, Poland, Slovakia and Romania.* London: Routledge.

Bobek, M. (2007), 'Quantity or Quality? Re-Assessing the Role of Supreme Jurisdictions in Central Europe,' *EUI Law Working Papers*, no. 36, EUI: Florence, 1–28.

——— (2013), *Comparative Reasoning in European Supreme Courts.* Oxford: OUP.

Bode-Kirchhoff, L. (2014), 'Why the Road from Luxembourg to Strasbourg Leads through Venice – The Venice Commission as a Link between the EU and the ECHR,' in K. Dzehtsiarou et al. (eds), *Human Rights Law in Europe: The Influence, Overlaps and Contradictions of the EU and the ECHR*. London: Routledge.

Bogason, P. (2000), *Public Policy and Local Governance. Institutions in Post Modern Society*. Cheltenham: Edward Elgar.

Borras, S., Koutalakis, C. and Wendler F. (2007), 'European Agencies and Input Legitimacy: EFSA, EMEA and EPO in the Post-Delegation Phase,' *Journal of European Integration* 29 (5), 583–600.

Börzel, T. (1997), 'What's so special in policy network? An exploration of the concept and its usefulness in studying European governance,' *European Integration Online Papers (EIoP)* 1 (16).

——— (1998), 'Organizing Babylon: On the Different Conception of Policy Networks,' *Public Administration* 76 (2), 253–73.

——— (2002), 'Non-State Actors and the Provision of Common Goods. Compliance with International Institutions,' in A. Héritier (ed.) *Common Goods: Reinventing European and International Governance*. Lanham, MD: Rowman & Littlefield, 155–78.

Börzel, T. et al. (2003), 'Why Do States not Obey the Law?' Paper prepared for the EUSA Conference, Nashville, March 27–30.

Börzel, T., and Cichowski, R. (eds) (2003), *The State of the European Union, 6: Law, Politics, and Society.* Oxford University Press. Available at: http://www.oxfordscholarship.com/view/10.1093/019925740X.001.0001/acprof-9780199257409

Börzel, T. and Risse, T. (2005). 'Public-Private Partnerships: Effective and Legitimate Tools of Transnational Governance,' in Edgar Grande and Louis

W. Pauly (eds), *Complex Sovereignty: Reconstituting Political Authority in the Twenty-first Century*. Toronto: University of Toronto Press.

Bouckaert, G. (1993), 'Measurement and Meaningful Management,' *Public Productivity and Management Review* 17 (1), 31–43.

Boudon, R. (1993), 'Towards a Synthetic Theory of Rationality,' *International Studies in the Philosophy of Science* 7 (1), 5–19.

Bovens, M. (2006), 'Analysing and Assessing Public Accountability. A Conceptual Framework,' European Governance Papers C-06-01. Available at http://edoc.vifapol.de/opus/volltexte/2011/2459/pdf/egp_connex_C_06_01.pdf

Brubaker, Rogers, and Cooper Frederick (2000), 'Beyond Identity,' *Theory and Society* 29 (1), 1–47.

Bruter, Michael (2005), *Citizens of Europe? The Emergence of a Mass European Identity*. New York: Palgrave Macmillan.

Burchell, G., Colin Gordon and Peter Miller (eds) (1991), *The Foucault effect : studies in governmentality / with two lectures by and an interview with Michel Foucault*. London: Harvester Wheatsheaf.

Burgess, Peter (2002), 'What's European about the European Union? Legitimacy between Institutions and Identity,' *European Journal of Social Theory* 5 (4), 467–81.

Cadiet, L. (1997), *Decouvrir la justice*. Paris: Dalloz.

Caenegem, R.C. van (1987), *Judges, Legislators and Professors: Chapters in European Legal History*. Cambridge: Cambridge University Press.

——— (1991), *Legal History: A European Perspective*. London: Hambledon.

Caggiano, G. (1989), 'La Commissione per la Democrazia attraverso il Diritto,' *Rivista di Diritto Europeo* 417.

Camia, Valeria (2010), 'Normative Discussions on European Identity: A Puzzle for Social Science?' *Perspectives on European Politics and Society* 11 (1), 109–18.

Canepa, A. (2006), 'La progressiva "retificazione" dell'Unione europea: il caso del settore giustizia,' *Diritto Pubblico Comparato ed Europeo*.

——— (2010), *Reto europee in cammino. Regolazione dell'economia, informazione e tutela dei privati*. Napoli: Jovene.

Cappelletti M. (1988), *Giudici irresponsabili?: Studio comparativo sulla responsabilità dei giudici*. Milano: Giuffrè.

Carnevali, D. (2010), *Soggetti smarriti. Perché innovazione e giustizia non si incontrano quasi mai*. Milano : Franco Angeli.

Carothers, T. (2003), 'Promoting the Rule of Law Abroad. The Problem of Knowledge.' Available at http://carnegieendowment.org/files/wp34.pdf

Cassese, S. (2003), 'Le reti come figura organizzativa della collaborazione,' in S. Cassese (ed.), *Lo spazio giuridico globale*. Roma: Bari.

——— (2007), 'La funzione costituzionale dei giudici non statali. Dallo Spazio giuridico globale all'ordine giuridico globale,' *Rivista trimestrale di Diritto Pubblico* 3, 609–26.

——— (2009), *I Tribunali di Babele. I giudici alla ricerca di un nuovo ordine globale*. Roma: Donzelli.

Castelli, C. (2014), 'L'innovazione e la ricerca di risorse,' in C. Castelli et al. (eds), *Giustizia, territori e governo dell'innovazione*. Roma: Carocci editore.

Cavallini, D., Dallara, C., Guarnieri, C. and Piana, D. (2013), 'The Implementation of the ECtHR judgements,' Team paper for the Research Project on Implementation of Decisions by the Inter-American HH.RR. System University of Andes, Bogota-Colombia.

CEPEJ (2008), CEPEJ Guidelines on Judicial Statistics (GOJUST) adopted by the CEPEJ at its 12th plenary meeting (Strasbourg, 10–11 December 2008).

——— (2010), European judicial systems Edition 2010 (data 2008): Efficiency and quality of justice, available at http://www.coe.int/t/dghl/cooperation/cepej/evaluation/2010/JAReport2010_GB.pdf

——— (2012), European Judicial Systems – Edition 2012 (2010 data). Efficiency and Quality of Justice. CEPEJ Studies No. 18. Available at http://www.coe.int/t/dghl/cooperation/cepej/evaluation/2012/Presse_info_vienne_en.asp

Chalmers, D. (2000), 'The positioning of EU judicial politics within the United Kingdom,' *West European Politics* 23 (4).

Chapman, C., Cooper, D. and Miller, P. (2009), 'Linking Accounting, Organizations, and Institutions,' in C. Chapman and P. Miller (eds), *Accounting, Organizations and Institutions*. Oxford: Oxford University Press, 1–29.

Charnovitz, S. (2006), 'Nongovernmental Organizations and International Law,' *The American Journal of International Law* 100 (2), 348–72.

Checkel, J. (2001), 'Why Comply? Social Learning and European Identity Change,' *International Organization* 55(3), 553–88.

——— (2005), 'International Institutions and Socialization in Europe: Introduction and Framework,' *International Organization* 59 (4), 801–26.

Christensen, T. and Laegreid, P. (2001), *New Public Management: The Transformation of Ideas into Practice*. Aldershot: Ashgate.

Citi, M. and Rhodes, M. (2007), 'New Modes of Governance in the EU: Common Objectives versus National Preferences,' European Governance Papers, 07/01.

Claes, M. (2006), *The National Courts Mandate in the European Constitution*. Oxford: Hart Publishing.

Claes, M. and de Visser, M. (2012), 'Are you networked yet ? On dialogues in European Judicial Networks,' *Utrecht Law Review* 8 (2).

Coman, R. (2007), 'Media, Justice and Politics, or the Independence of the Judiciary Becomes an Issue on the Romanian Political Agenda,' in R. Coman and J.M. de Waefle (eds), *Judicial Reforms in Central and Eastern European Countries*. Bruges: Editions Vanden Broele.

——— (2009), *Réformer la justice dans un pays post-communiste. Le cas de la Roumanie*. Bruxelles: Editions de l'Université de Bruxelles.

——— (2014), 'Quo vadis judicial reforms? The quest for judicial independence in Central and Eastern Europe,' *Europe-Asia Studies* 66 (6).

Coman, R. and Dallara, C. (2010) (eds), *Handbook of Judicial Politics*. Iasi, Romania: Editura Institutul European.

Coman, R., Kostera, T. and Tomini L. (2014), *Europeanization and European Integration. From Incremental to Structural Change*. Basingstoke: Palgrave.
Communication from the Commission to the European Parliament and the Council of 22 November 2010 – The EU Internal Security Strategy in Action: Five steps towards a more secure Europe [COM(2010) 673 final].
Contini, F. (2001), 'Dynamics of ICT diffusion in European judicial systems,' in M. Fabri and F. Contini (eds), *Justice and Technology in Europe. How ICT is Changing the Judicial Business*. Amsterdam: Kluwer, 317–31.
Contini, F. and Fabri, M. (2003), 'Judicial Electronic Data Interchange in Europe,' in M. Fabri and F. Contini (eds), *Judicial Electronic Data Interchange in Europe: Applications, Policies and Trends*. Bologna: Lo Scarabeo, 1–28.
Contini, F. and Mohr, R. (2007), 'Reconciling Independence and Accountability in Judicial Systems,' *Utrecht Law Review* 3 (2), 26–43. Available at: http://www.utrechtlawreview.org/publish/articles/000053/article.pdf/
Costa Pinto, A. and Morlino, L. (eds) (2013), *Dealing with the Legacy of Authoritarianism: The 'Politics of the Past' in Southern European Democracies*. London: *Routledge*.
Costabile, A. (2009), *Legalità, manipolazione, democrazia*. Roma: Carocci.
Cotterrell, R. (1997), 'The Concept of Legal Culture,' in D. Nelken (ed.), *Comparing Legal Cultures*. Aldershot: Ashgate, 14–32.
——— (2006), *Law, Culture and Society: Legal Ideas in the Mirror of Social Theory*. Aldershot: Ashgate.
Coughlan, S. et al. (2011), 'Judicial training in the European Union member states – study', Directorate General for internal policies policy. Department C: Citizens' rights and constitutional affairs, legal affairs. Available at http://www.europarl.europa.eu/RegData/etudes/etudes/join/2011/453198/IPOL-JURI_ET(2011)453198_EN.pdf
Council of Europe (2005), *Council of Europe Law – Towards a pan-European legal area*. Official Publications Office.
Crozier, M. and Friedberg, E. (1977), *L'acteur et le système: Les contraintes de l'action collective*. Paris: Seuil.
Czarniawska, B. (2000), *Narrare l'organizzazione*. Torino: Edizioni Comunità.
Czarniawska, B. and Joerges, B. (1996), 'Travels of Ideas,' in B. Czarniawska and G. Sevon (eds), *Translating Organizational Change*. Berlin: de Gruyter, 13–48.
Dahl, R.A. (1969), *Who governs? Democracy and Power in an American city*. New Haven: Yale University Press.
Dahrendorf, R. (1980), *Life Chances: Approaches to Social and Political Theory*. Worthing: Littlehampton Book Services Ltd.
Dallara, C. (2010), *L'Unione Europea e la promozione della rule of law in Romania, Serbia e Ucraina. Le riforme dei sistemi giudiziari e le politiche anti-corruzione nei tre paesi*. [*The EU rule of law promotion in Romania, Serbia and Ukraine. The effects on judicial reforms and anticorruption policies*]. Bologna: Du Press editore.

——— (2012), 'The Definition of "Best Judicial Practices" by European Judicial Networks and Commissions,' in A. Vauchez (ed), *The Fabric of International Jurisprudence: An Interdisciplinary Encounter*. European University Institute: Robert Schuman Centre for Advanced Studies, 21–31.

——— (2013), 'Ten years of judicial reforms under the EU influence in the Balkans. Mixed results and challenging interactions,' *Southeastern Europe* (forthcoming).

——— (2014), *Democracy and Judicial reforms in Southeast Europe: Between the EU and legacies of the past*. Heidelberg: Springer.

Damaska, M.R. (1986), *The Faces of Justice and State Authority: A Comparative Approach to the Legal Process*. New Haven: Yale University Press.

——— (2003), *Evidence Law Adrift* (1997), trans. from Italian *Il diritto delle prove alla deriva*. Bologna: Il Mulino.

Davis, K., Kingsbury, B. and Merry, S. (2010), 'Indicators as Technology of Global Governance,' *Institute for International Law and Justice, Working Papers*, 2.

De Amicis, G. (2007), 'Cooperazione Giudiziaria e corruzione internazionale, Verso un sistema integrato di forme e strumenti di collaborazione tra le autorità giudiziarie,' *Quaderni di diritto penale comparato, internazionale ed europeo*.

De Bruïne, R.F. and Clarotti, G. (2001), Report of Working Group 'Networking people for a good governance in Europe,' (Group 4b), White Paper on Governance – Work area n. 4 'Coherence and Cooperation in a networked Europe,' p. 9.

De Visser, M. (2009), *Network-based Governance in EC Law. The Example of EC Competition Law and EC Communication Law*, Modern Studies on European Law Series. Oxford: Hart Publishing.

De Visser, M. and Claes, M. (2013), 'Courts United? On European Judicial Networks,' in B. de Witte and A. Vauchez (eds), *The European Legal Field*. Oxford: Hart Publishing.

De Vergottini, G. (2010), *Oltre il dialogo tra le Corti. Giudici, diritto straniero, comparazione*. Bologna: Il Mulino.

De Vervaele, J.A.E. (2004), 'Case notes on Gözutok and Brügge,' *Common Market Law Review* 41, 795–812.

Dehon P. (2005), 'State, Law and Politics in a Paradigmatic Transition. Elements for a Trans-Modern Social and Legal Theory,' paper presented at the Conference 'Innovations and Reproductions in Cultures and Societies' (IRICS) Vienna, 9–11 December.

Dehousse, R. (1997), 'Regulation by Networks in the European Community: The Role of European Agencies,' *Journal of European Public Policy* 4 (2), 246–61.

——— (1998), *La Cour de justice des Communautés européennes*. Paris: Montchrestien.

——— (1998), *The European Court of Justice : the politics of judicial integration*. Foreword by William E. Paterson. Basingstoke: Macmillan; New York: St. Martin's Press.

Dehousse, R. and Magnette, P. (2006), 'Institutional Change in the EU,' in J. Peterson and M. Shackleton (eds), *The Institutions of the European Union*. Oxford: Oxford University Press, 2nd edn.

Delmas-Marty, M. (2002), *Towards a Truly Common Law: Europe as a Laboratory for Legal Pluralism*. Cambridge: Cambridge University Press.

Demsorean, A., Parvulescu S. and Vetrici-Soimu B. (2009). 'Romania: Vetoed Reforms, Skewed Results,' in A. Magen and L. Morlino (eds), *International Actors, Democratization and the Rule of Law. Anchoring democracy*? London: Routledge.

Dezalay, Y. (2007) 'De la défense de l'environnement au développement durable, l'émergence d'un champ d'expertise des politiques européennes', *Actes de la recherche en science sociale* 1–2, 66–79.

Di Federico, G. (2012), 'Judicial Accountability and Conduct: an Overview,' in Anja Seibert-Fohr (ed.), *Judicial Independence in Transition*. New York: Springer.

Diamond, L. (1995), *Promoting Democracy in the 1990s: Actors and Instruments, Issues and Imperatives : A Report to the Carnegie Commission on Preventing Deadly Conflict*. New York: Carnegie Corporation of New York.

Dietrich, M. (2000), *Legal and Judicial Reform in Central Europe and the Former Soviet Union: Voices from Five Countries*. Washington, D.C.: World Bank, Legal Vice Presidency.

DiMaggio, P.J. and Powell, W. (1983), 'The Iron Cage Revisited: Institutional Isomorphism and Collective Rationality in Organizational Fields,' *American Sociological Review* 48 (2), 147–60.

Dimitrova, A. (2002), 'Enlargement, Institution-Building and the EU's Administrative Capacity Requirement,' *West European Politics* 25(4), 171–90.

Doise, W. (2001), *Droits de l'Homme et la Force des Idées*. Paris: PUF.

Dolowitz, D. and Marsh, D. (2000), 'Learning From Abroad: the Role of Policy Transfer in Contemporary Policy Making,' *Governance* 13 (1), 5–24.

Douglas, M. (1986), *How Institutions Think*. Syracuse: Syracuse University Press.

Draft Internal Security Strategy for the European Union (2010), 'Towards a European Security Model,' Brussels, 23 February 2010, 5842/2/10 REV 2.

DuGay, P. (2005), *The Values of Bureaucracy*. Oxford: Oxford University Press.

Easton, D. (1953), *The political system : an inquiry into the state of political science*. New York: Knopf.

EJTN (European Judicial Training Network) (2007), Report of website group activities, January–September 2006. Unpublished Working document.

ENCJ (European Network of Councils for the Judiciary) (2007), *Judicial Ethics: Principles, Values and Quality*. Bruxelles.

European Commission (1997), Report on PHARE HU97/IB-JH-02. COM (99) 234 final. [EU Commission – COM Document]

——— (1998), Communication on Democratisation, the Rule of Law, Respect for Human Rights and Good Governance: the Challenges of the Partnership between the European Union and the ACP States, COM (98) 146 final.

——— (1999), DG Enlargement, Accession Partnerships 1999 (final versions February 2000).
——— (2006), Communication from the Commission to the European Parliament and the Council of 29 June 2006 on judicial training in the European Union, COM(2006) 356 final.
——— (2012), Directorate B: Criminal justice. Open invitation to tender JUST/2012/JUTR/PR/0064/A4 – Implementation of the Pilot project – European judicial training.
European Council (2009), 'Presidency Conclusions.' Stockholm, Brussels: Office for Official Publications.
European Governance, White paper, Bruxelles, 5.8.2001- COM(2001) 428 def/2.
Eymeri-Douzans, J.M. (2005), 'La gouverne au miroir du néo-management public,' *Politique et Management Public* 23 (3), 1–18.
Fabri, M. (2005), 'Policies to Enhance the Quality of Justice in Europe,' in M. Fabri et al. (eds), *L'administration de la justice en Europe et l'évaluation de sa qualité*. Paris: Montchrestien, 68–83.
Fabri, M., Jean, J.-P., Langbroek, P. and Pauliat, H. (eds), (2005), *L'administration de la justice en Europe et l'évaluation de sa qualité*. Paris : Montchrestien.
Falkner, G. (2003), 'Comparing Europeanisation Effects: From Metaphor to Operationalisation,' *European Integration online Papers* (EIoP) 7 (13). Available at http://eiop.or.at/eiop/texte/2003-013a.htm
——— (ed.) (2011), *The EU's Decision Traps: Comparing Policies*. Oxford: Oxford University Press.
Featherstone, K. and Radaelli, C. (eds) (2003), *The Politics of Europeanization*. Oxford: Oxford University Press.
Ferrajoli, L. (1997), *La sovranità nel mondo moderno*. Roma-Bari: Laterza.
——— (2001), *Diritti fondamentali: un dibattito teorico*. Roma-Bari: Laterza.
Ferrarese, M.R. (2000), *Le istituzioni della globalizzazione*. Bologna: Il Mulino.
——— (2002), *Il diritto al presente*. Bologna: Il Mulino.
——— (2006), *Il diritto sconfinato. Inventiva giuridica e spazi del mondo globale*. Roma-Bari: Laterza.
——— (2009), 'When National actors become transnational: Transjudicial dialogue between democracy and constitutionalism,' *Global Jurists* 9 (1).
——— (2010), *La governance tra politica e diritto*. Bologna: Il Mulino.
Finnemore, M. and Sikkink, K. (1998), 'International Norm Dynamics and Political Change,' *International Organization* 52 (4), 887–917.
Franck, T. (1990), *The Power of Legitimacy Among Nations*. New York: Oxford University Press.
Friedman, L. (1969), 'Legal Culture and Social Development,' *Law and Society Review* 4 (1), 29–44.
——— (1975), *The Legal System: A Social Sciences Perspective*. New York: Sage Publishing.

——— (2006), 'Judging the Judges: Some Remarks on the Way Judges Think and the Way Judges Act,' in J.N. Drobak (ed.), *Norms and the Law.* New York: Cambridge University Press.

Frydman, B. (2007), 'L'évolution des critères et des modes de contrôle de la qualité des décisions de justice,' in *Working Papers Centre Perelman de philosophie du droit* 4. Available at : http://www.philodroit.be/IMG/pdf/WP-2007-4-BFrydman.pdf

——— (2011), *Le nouveau management de la justice et l'indépendence des juges.* Paris, Dalloz.

——— (2012), 'L'évolution des critères et des modes de contrôle de la qualité des décisions de justice,' *Série des Working Papers du Centre Perelman de philosophie du droit* (4).

Garapon, A. (1997), *Le Guardien des promesses.* Paris : Odile Jacob.

——— (2010), *La raison du moindre état. Le néolibéralisme et la justice.* Paris: Odile Jacob.

Gelter, M. and Siems, M. (2012), 'Networks, Dialogue or One-Way Traffic? An Empirical Analysis of Cross-Citations Between Ten of Europe's Highest Courts,' *Utrecht Law Review* 8 (2), 88–99.

Gibson, J.L. and Caldeira, G.A. (2011), 'Has Legal Realism Damaged the Legitimacy of the U.S. Supreme Court?' *Law and Society Review* 45 (1), 195–219.

Giddens, A. (1991), *Modernity and self-identity: self and society in the late modern age.* Cambridge: Polity press.

Gilardi, F. and Füglister, K. (2008), 'Empirical modeling of policy diffusion in federal states: the dyadic approach,' *Swiss Political Science Review* 14(3), 413–50.

Gilardi, F., Füglister, K. and Luyet, S. (2009), 'Learning from others the diffusion of hospital financing reforms in OECD countries,' *Comparative Political Studies* 42(4), 549–73.

Ginsburg, T. (2003), *Judicial Review in New Democracies: Constitutional Courts in Asian Cases.* Cambridge: Cambridge University Press.

Giuliani, M. (2004), 'Europeizzazione come istituzionalizzazione: questioni definitorie e di metodo,' *Rivista italiana di politiche pubbliche* 1, 141–61.

Goldstein, J., Kahler, M., Keohane, R.O. and Slaughter, A.-M. (2000), 'Legalization and World Politics,' *International Organization* 54 (3).

Goodwin-Gill, G.S. and Lambert, H. (2010), *The Limits of Transnational Law: Refugee Law, Policy Harmonization and Judicial Dialogue in the European Union* Cambridge: CUP.

Grabbe, H. (2002), 'European Union Conditionality and the Acquis Communautaire,' *International Political Science Review* 23 (3), 249–68.

——— (2006), *The EU's TransformativePower. Europeanization Through Conditionality in Central and Eastern Europe.* New York: Palgrave Macmillan.

Grabbe, H. and Hughes, K. (1998), 'Reform of the structural funds: Central and East European perspectives,' *European Planning Studies* 6 (6), 665–76.

Greenhill, B. (2010), 'The Company You Keep: International Socialization and the Diffusion of Human Rights Norms,' *Journal in International Studies Quarterly*, 54 (1), 127–45.

Groppi, T. (2012), 'Le recours aux précédents étrangers par les juges constitutionnels,' in F. Hourquebie and M.-C. Ponthoreau (eds), *La motivation des décisions des Cours suprêmes et des Cours constitutionnelles*. Bruxelles : Bruylant, 47–61.

Groppi, T. and Ponthoreau, M.-C. (eds) (2013), *The Use of Foreign Precedents by Constitutional Judges*. Oxford; Portland (OR): Hart Publishing.

Guarnieri, C. (2003), *Giustizia e politica: I nodi della Seconda Repubblica*. Bologna: Il Mulino.

——— (2004), 'Judicial Education as a Support to Judicial Independence and Major Justice Reform,' paper presented at the 2nd International Conference on Training of the Judiciary: Judicial Education in the World of Challenge and of Change, Ottawa, 31 Oct–5 Nov.

——— (2007), 'Courts and Marginalized Groups: Perspectives from Continental Europe,' *International Journal of Constitutional Law* 2, 187–210.

——— (2011), 'Reti giudiziarie europee e modelli di ordinamento giudiziario,' Le nuove competenze dell'Unione europea in materia di giustizia, TRENTO, Provincia autonoma di Trento, 2011, pp. 187–95.

Guarnieri, C. and Pederzoli, P. (2001), *The Power of Judges*. Oxford: Oxford University Press.

Guarnieri, C. and Piana, D. (2011), 'Judicial Independence and the Rule of Law: Exploring the European Experience,' in S. Shetreet and C. Forsyth (eds), *The Culture of Judicial Independence*. Leiden: Martinus Nijhoff, 113–24.

Guild E, and Geyer, F. (2008), *Security versus Justice? Police and Judicial Cooperation in the European Union*. Farnham: Ashgate Publishing.

Gyöngyi, P.M. (2012), 'Fundamental Principles of the European Union and Judicial Reforms in New Member States: Assessing Judicial Reforms in Hungary.' Thesis submitted to the Summer Academy of the European public law organization in partial fulfillment of the requirements for the degree of intensive international master of laws, Erasmus School of Law, Rotterdam.

Haas, P. (1992), 'Introduction: Epistemic communities and international policy coordination,' *International Organization* 46(1): 1–36.

——— (2000), 'Choosing to Comply: Theorizing from International Relations and Comparative Politics,' in Dinah Shelton (ed.), *Commitment and Compliance. The Role of Non-Binding Norms in the International Legal Systems*. Oxford: Oxford University Press.

Habermas, J. (1998), *Between facts and norms: contributions to a discourse theory of law and democracy* translated by William Rehg. - [Rist.]. Cambridge: Polity press.

Hayek, F.A. (1978), *The Road to Serfdom*. Chicago: University of Chicago Press.

Heinrich, C. (2002), 'Outcomes Based Performance Management in Public Sector,' *Public Administration Review* 62 (6) 712–25.

Héritier, A. (1999), *Policy Making and Diversity in Europe*. Cambridge, Cambridge University Press.

——— (2005) 'Europeanization Research East and West: A Comparative Assessment,' in Frank Schimmelfennig and Ulrich Sedelmeier (eds), *The Europeanization of Central and Eastern Europe*. Ithaca, NY: Cornell University Press, 199–209.

Héritier, A. and Rhodes, M. (eds) (2011), *New Modes of Governance in Europe: Governing in the Shadow of Hierarchy*. Basingstoke, Hampshire: Palgrave Macmillan.

Hillgenberg, H. (1999), 'A Fresh Look at Soft Law,' *European Journal International Law* 10, 499–515.

Hix, S. (1998), 'The Study of European Union II: The "New Governance" Agenda and its Rival,' *Journal of European Public Policy* 5.

Hood, C. (2007), 'Intellectual Obsolescence and Intellectual Makeovers: Reflections on the Tools of Government after Two Decades,' *Governance* 20 (1), 127–44.

Hughes, J., Sasse, G. and Gordon, C. (2004), 'Conditionality and Compliance in the EU's Eastward Enlargement: Regional Policy and the Reform of Sub-national Government,' *Journal of Common Market Studies* 42 (3), 523–51.

Jacob, S. (2000), 'La modernisation des administrations publiques fédérales. Révolution copernicienne ou quête du Graal ?' *Pyramides* 2, 135–58.

——— (2011), 'L'évaluation face aux défis de la professionnalisation et de l'éthique : Cahiers de la performance et de l'évaluation,' *PerfEval* 3.

Jean, J.-P. (2005). *L'administration de la justice en Europe et l'évaluation de sa qualité.* Paris: Dalloz.

Jean, J.-P. et al. (2012), 'Mieux administrer la justice en interne et dans les pays du Conseil de l'Europe pour mieux juger (MAJICE).' Research Report. Available at https://hal.archives-ouvertes.fr/hal-00974917

Jimeno-Bulnes, M. (2010), 'Towards common standards on rights of suspected and accused persons in criminal proceedings in the EU?', Center for European Policy Studies (CEPS) Policy Brief, February 2010.

Joerges, C. and Neyer J. (1997), 'From Intergovernmental Bargaining to Deliberative Political Processes: The Constitutionalization of Comitology,' *European Law Journal* 3, 273.

Johnsen, J.T. (2012), 'The European Commission for the Efficiency of Justice (CEPEJ) Reforming European Justice Systems – "Mission Impossible?"' Special Issue, 4 (3), 1–19. Available at: http://www.iacajournal.org/index.php/ijca/article/view/URN%3ANBN%3ANL%3AUI%3A10-1-115919/64

Jordan, A. and Schout, A. (eds) (2006), *The Coordination of the European Union. Exploring the Capacities of Networked Governance*. Oxford: Oxford University Press.

Juncker, J.C. (2006), 'Council of Europe – European Union: "A Sole Ambition for the European Continent".' Report by Jean-Claude Juncker, Prime Minister of the Grand Duchy of Luxembourg, to the attention of the Heads of State or

Government of the Member States of the Council of Europe, 11 April 2006. Available at: http://assembly.coe.int/Sessions/2006/speeches/20060411_report_JCJuncker_EN.pdf

Kallinikos, J. (2006), 'The institution of bureaucracy: administration, pluralism, democracy,' *Economy and Society* 35 (4), 611–27.

Kanterian, E. (2013), 'The Crisis of Democracy in Hungary and Romania – Learning from Weimar?,' Verfassungsblog. Available at: http://www.verfassungsblog.de/the-crisis-of-democracy-in-hungary-and-romania-learning-from-weimar

Kappen-Risse, T. (1995), *Bringing Transnational Relations Back In: Non-State Actors, Domestic Structures and International Institutions*. Cambridge: CUP.

Kelley, J. (2004), 'International Actors on the Domestic Scene,' *International Organization* 58 (3), 425–57.

Keohane, R. (2005), *After Hegemony: Cooperation and Discord in the World Political Economy.* Oxford and Princeton: Princeton University Press.

Kerwer, D. (2005), 'Rules that Many Use: Standards and Global Regulation,' *Governance* 18 (4), 611–32.

——— (2008), 'Watchdogs Beyond Control? The Accountability of Accounting Standard Organizations,' in M. Boström and C. Gastern (eds), *Organizing Transnational Accountability*. Cheltenham: Edward Elgar, 98–113.

Kickert, W. (1997), *Public Management and Administrative Reform in Western Europe*. Cheltenham: Edward Elgar.

Kingdon, J.W. (1995), *Agendas, Alternatives and Public Policies* (2nd edn). New York: Longman.

Knill, C. (2001), *The Europeanization of National Administration.* Cambridge: Cambridge University Press.

Kochenov, D. (2004), 'Behind the Copenhagen Façade. The meaning and structure of the Copenhagen political criterion of democracy and the rule of law,' European Integration online Papers (EIoP) 8 (10). Available at: http://eiop.or.at/eiop/texte/2004-010a.htm

Koppenjan, J. and Klijn, E.-H. (2004), *Managing Uncertainties in Networks: Public Private Controversies*. London: Routledge.

Kosar, D. (2010), 'Judicial Accountability and Democratic Transition: Visegrad Story,' Paper Presented at The 8th World Congress of Constitutional Law, December, Mexico City. Available at: http://www.juridicas.unam.mx/wccl/ponencias/16/288.pdf

Krygier, M. (ed.) (1999), *The Rule of Law After Communism: Problems and Prospects in East-Central Europe*. Aldershot: Ashgate.

Kubicek, P. (ed.) (2003), *The European Union and Democratization.* London: Routledge.

Kuhn, Z. (2004), 'Worlds Apart. Western and Central European Judicial Culture at the Onset of the European Enlargement,' *American Journal of Comparative Law* 3, 531–67.

Lane, R. (1996), 'The Fisherman's Tale: National Liability for Breaches of Community Law,' *Edinburgh Law Review* 1, 91–105.

Langbroek, P. and Fabri, M. (2000), *The Challenge of Change for Judicial Systems: Developing a Public Administration Perspective*. Amsterdam: Omsha.

Langbroek, P. (2005), 'Netherlands,' in M. Fabri, J.-P. Jean, P. Langbroek and H. Pauliat (eds), *L'administration de la justice en Europe et l'évaluation de sa qualité*. Paris: Montchrestien.

——— (ed.) (2010), 'Quality Management in courts and in the judicial organisations in 8 Council of Europe Member states.' CEPEJ, Council of Europe, Strasbourg.

Langer, M. (2004), 'From Legal Transplants to Legal Translation: The Globalization of Plea Bargaining and the Americanization Thesis in Criminal Procedure,' *Harvard International Law Journal* 45 (1), 1–64.

Lanzara, G. and Contini, F. (2009), *ICT and Innovation in the Public Sector: European Studies in the Making of e-Government*. Basingstoke: Palgrave Macmillan.

Law, D.S. and Chang, W.-C. (2011), 'The Limits of Global Judicial Dialogue,' *Washington Law Review* 86, Washington University in St. Louis Legal Studies Research Paper No. 11–04–02 APSA 2011 Annual Meeting Paper.

Leaf, M. and Alegre, S. (2004), 'Mutual Recognition in European Judicial Cooperation: A Step Too Far Too Soon? Case Study–the European Arrest Warrant,' *European Law Journal* 10 (2), 200–217.

Linz, J.J. and Stepan, A. (1996), *Problems of Democratic Transition and Consolidation: Southern Europe, South America and Post-Communist Europe*. Baltimore: Johns Hopkins University Press.

Littlepage, K., 'Transnational Judicial Dialogue and Evolving Jurisprudence in the Process of European Legal Integration,' paper presented at European Union Studies Association – Twelfth Biennial International Conference, 3–5 Mar 2011, Boston, Massachusetts.

Lundvall, B.-Å. and Tomlinson, M. (2002), 'International benchmarking as a policy learning tool,' in Rodrigues, M.J. (ed.) *The New Knowledge Economy in Europe*. Cheltenham: Edward Elgar Publishing.

Lynn, L. (2001), 'The Myth of the Bureaucratic Paradigm. What Traditional Public Administration Really Stood For,' *Public Administration Review* 61 (2), 144–60.

Lyotard, J.-F. (1979), *La Condition postmoderne: rapport sur le savoir*. Paris: Minuit.

MacCormick, N. (2007), *Institutions of Law*. Oxford: Oxford University Press.

McCrudden, C. (2000), 'A Common Law of Human Rights? Transnational Judicial Conversation on Constitutional Rights,' *Oxford Journal of Legal Studies* 20 (4), 499–532.

Madsen, M. and Vauchez, A. (2005), 'Euconstitutionalism at the Cradle. Law and Lawyers in the Construction of a European Political Order (1920–1960). Recht der Werkelikheid,' Special issue, *Lawyers' Networks and European Integration* 15–36.

Maduro, M. (2007), 'So Close and Yet so Far: The Paradoxes of Mutual Recognition,' *Journal of European Public Policy* 14 (5), 814–25.

Magen, A. and Morlino, L. (2009) (eds), *International Actors, Democratization and the Rule of Law: Anchoring Democracy?* Contemporary European Studies Series. London, New York: Routledge.

Magrassi, M. (2011), 'Reconsidering the Principle of Separation of Powers: Judicial Networking and Institutional Balance in the Process of European Integration,' *Contemporary Readings in Law and Social Justice* 3 (2), 159–80.

Majone, G. (1999), 'The Regulatory State and its Legitimacy Problems,' *West European Politics* 22 (1), 1–24.

——— (2000), 'The Credibility Crisis of Community Regulation,' *Journal of Common Market Studies* 38 (2), 273–302.

Marčeta, I. (2010), *EU Rule Promotion in Macedonia and Serbia on the Edge Between Security and Democratization.* Cevipol: Revue Transitions.

Markesinis, S.B., Fedtke, J. and Ackermann, L. (2006), 'Judicial Recourse to Foreign Law: A New Source of Inspiration?' *particolare* 5, 109–38.

Matteucci, N. (ed.) (1961), *Antologia degli scritti politici del Montesquieu.* Bologna : Il Mulino.

Mattina, L. (2004), 'La riforma delle istituzioni,' in L. Mattina (ed.), *La sfida dell'allargamento.* Bologna: Il Mulino, 85–129.

May, P.J. (2007), 'Regulatory Regimes and Accountability,' *Regulation & Governance* 1 (1), 8–26.

Mayntz, R. (1999), 'La teoria della governante: sfide e prospettive,' *Riv. It. Sc. Pol.*, 29 (1), 3.

Meij, A.W.H. (2010), 'Circles of Coherence: On Unity of Case-Law in the Context of Globalisation,' *European Constitutional Law Review* 6, 84–101.

Merryman, J.H. (1979), *Law and Social Change in Mediterranean Europe and Latin America.* Stanford California: Stanford Law School.

——— (1981), 'On the Convergence (and Divergence) of the Civil Law and the Common Law,' *Stanford Journal of International Law* 17(2), 357–88.

Merton, R. (1949), *Social Theory and Social Systems.* New York: Free Press.

Meyer, J.W. and Rowan, B. (1977), 'Institutional Organizations: Formal Structure as Myth and Ceremony,' *American Journal of Sociology* 83, 340–63.

Miller, P. (1990) 'On the Interrelations Between Accounting and the State,' *Accounting, Organizations and Society* 15 (4), 315–38.

——— (2001), 'Governing by Numbers: Why Calculative Practices Matter,' *Social Research* 68 (2), 379–396.

Miller, P. and O' Leavy, T. (1987), 'Accounting and the Construction of the Governable Person,' *Accounting, Organizations and Society* 12, 235–65.

Millett, J. (1954), *Management in the Public Service.* New York: McGraw Hill.

Mokrà, L. (2007), 'Rights of Foreigners: Slovakia,' *European Review of Public Law*, 19:1, 63.

Monar, J. (2006), 'New Modes of Governance. Specific factors, typology and development trends of modes of governance in the EU Justice and Home Affairs domain,' NewGov working paper, 1/D17.
Moore, A. and Chiavario, M. (2004), *Police and Judicial Co-operation in the European Union: FIDE 2004 National Reports*. Cambridge: Cambridge University Press.
Morlino, L. (2000), 'Architectures constitutionnelles et politiques démocratiques en Europe de l'Est,' *Revue Française de Science Politique* 50 (4–5), 679–711.
——— (2001), 'La consolidation de la démocratie: nouveaux questionnements,' *Revue Internationale de Politique Comparée* 8 (2), 245–67.
——— (2005), 'Anchors and Democratic Change,' *Comparative Political Studies* 38 (7), 743–70.
Morlino, L. and Magen, A. (eds) (2008), *International Actors, Democratization and the Rule of Law. Anchoring Democracy*. London: Routledge.
Morth, U. (2004), *Soft Law in the European Union*. Cheltenham: Edward Elgar.
Müller, J.W. (2013), 'Safeguarding Democracy inside the EU. Brussels and the Future of Liberal Order.' Transatlantic Academy Paper Series. Available at: http://www.transatlanticacademy.org/sites/default/files/publications/Muller_SafeguardingDemocracy_Feb13_web.pdf
Murphy, W. and Pritchett, H. (1961), *Courts, Judges, and Politics: An Introduction to the Judicial Process*. New York: Random House.
North, D. (1990), *Institutions, Institutional Changes, and Economic Performance*. Cambridge: Cambridge University Press.
Noutcheva, G. (2012), *European Foreign Policy and the Challenges of Balkan Accession: Conditionality, Legitimacy and Compliance*. London: Routledge.
Noutcheva, G. and Bechev, D. (2008), 'The Successful Laggards: Bulgaria and Romania's EU Accession,' *East European Politics & Societies* 22 (1), 114–44.
Nye, J.S. (2002), *Paradox of American Power: Why the World's Only Superpower Can't Go It Alone*. New York: Oxford University Press.
——— (2009), 'Get Smart: Combining Hard and Soft Power,' *Foreign Affairs*. Available at: http://www.foreignaffairs.com/articles/65163/joseph-s-nye-jr/get-smart?page=1.
Oberto, G. (2003), 'Recrutement et formation des magistrats en Europe. Etude comparative,' Council of Europe Publishing – Editions du Conseil de l'Europe, Strasbourg. Available at: http://www.coe.int/t/dghl/cooperation/lisbonnetwork/rapports/LivreOberto_fr.pdf
——— (2012), 'How to Identify New Judicial Training Needs? Suggestions and Experiences Drawn from National and International Training Programmes.' Available at: http://giacomooberto.com/Oberto_relazione_Bologna_30_marzo_2012.htm
O'Meara, N., 'The Role of Judicial Networks: Evolving Judicial Dialogue and Shaping EU Law?' paper presented at European Union Studies Association – Twelfth Biennial International Conference, 3–5 Mar 2011, Boston, Massachussets, p. 4.

Opinion no.10 (2007) of the Consultative Council of European Judges (CCJE) to the attention of the Committee of Ministers of the Council of Europe on the Council for the Judiciary at the service of society. This Opinion has been adopted by the CCJE at its 8th meeting (Strasbourg, 21–23 November 2007).

Ost, F. and Van de Kerchove, M. (2002), *De la pyramide au réseau? Pour une théorie dialectique du droit*. Brussels: Publications des Facultés universitaires Saint-Louis.

——— (n.d.), *Constructing the complexity of the law: towards a dialectic theory*, available from the website 'Droit de l'Homme et dialogue interculturelle.' Available at: http://www.dhdi.free.fr/recherches/theoriedroit/articles/ostvdk complex.pdf

Ostrom, B., Ostrom, C., Hanson, R. and Kleiman, M. (2007), *Trial Courts as Organizations*. Philadelphia: Temple University Press.

Ottaway, M. and Carothers, T. (eds) (2000), *Funding Virtue: Aid and Democracy Promotion*. Washington, DC: Carnegie Endowment for International Peace.

Palombella, G. (2009), 'The Rule of Law beyond the State: Failures, Promises, and Theory,' *International Journal of Constitutional Law* 7 (3), 442–67.

——— (2010), 'The Rule of Law,' *Comparative Sociology* 1 (4), 39.

Papadimitriou, D. and Phinnemore, D. (2004), 'Europeanisation, Conditionality and Domestic Change: the Twinning exercise and administrative reform in Romania,' *Journal of Common Market Studies* 42 (3), 619–39.

Parau, C. (2013), 'Explaining Judiciary Governance in Central and Eastern Europe: External Incentives, Transnational Elites and Parliament Inaction,' *Europe-Asia Studies* (forthcoming).

Pauliat, H. (2007), 'Le modèle française d'administration de la justice,' *Revue française d'administration publique* 125, 111–20.

Pech, L. (2009), 'The Rule of Law as a Constitutional Principle of the European Union,' *Jean Monnet Working Paper Series* No. 4/2009. Available at: http://ssrn.com/abstract=1463242.

Pederzoli, P.P. (2011), 'Judicial Governance,' in C.D.R. Coman (ed.), *The Handbook of Judicial Policies*. Cluje: Iasi.

Peters, B.G. (2005), 'Back to the Centre?: Rebuilding the State,' in A. Gamble and T. Wright (eds), 'Restating the State,' Special Issue, *The Political Quarterly* 130–41.

Peters, G. (1997), 'Policy Transfers Between Governments: The Case of Administrative Reforms,' *West European Politics* 20 (2), 22–36.

Piana, D. (2005), *Le istituzioni nella mente àncore di legittimità del potere politico*. Rubbettino: Soveria Mannelli.

——— (2006), 'Constitutional Cultures in New Member States. Between europeanization and national traditions,' in W. Sadurski and J. Ziller (eds) *Après Enlargement*. Fiesole: European University Institute.

——— (2007a), 'Judges and Legal Experts in the European Policy of Rule of Law Promotion,' in J.-M. De Waele and R. Coman (eds), *Judicial Reforms in Central and Eastern European Countries*, pp. 23–78.

——— (2007b), 'Judicial Policies and European Enlargement,' in F. Cerutti and S. Lucarelli (eds), *European Identity and Legitimacy*. London: Routledge.

——— (2007c), 'Unpacking Policy Transfer, Discovering Actors,' *French Politics* 3, 275–97.

——— (2009), 'The Power Knocks at the Courts' Back Door. Two Waves of Postcommunist Judicial Reforms,' *Comparative Political Studies* 42 (6), 816–40.

——— (2010), *Judicial Accountabilities in New Europe: From Rule of Law to Quality of Justice*. Farnham, UK: Ashgate.

——— (2011), 'Legal and Managerial Cultures in CEEC's Judicial Systems,' in W.S.A. Febbrajo (ed.), *New Meaning of the Rule of Law in CEECs*. Farnham: Ashgate.

——— (2012), 'New Legal Instruments in a Changing World: Legal, Political and Cultural Developments in EU Judicial Cooperation,' *International Spectator* 47 (1), 49–66.

——— (2013), 'Knowledge Transfer as a Leverage of Change: The Case of the Public Prosecutor Office of Naples,' *International Journal of Court Administration* 5 (2).

Piana, D. and Guarnieri, C. (2012), 'Bringing the Outside Inside. Macro and Micro Factors to Put the Dialogue among Highest Courts into its Right Context,' *Utrecht Law Review* 8 (2).

Piana, D., Langbroek, P., Berkmanas, T., Hammerslev, O. and Pacurari, O. (eds), *Legal Education and Judicial Training in Europe*. The Hague: Eleven International Publishing.

Piana, D. and Vauchez, A. (2012), *Il Consiglio superiore della magistratura*. Bologna: Il Mulino.

Piattoni, S. (2010), *The theory of multi-level governance : conceptual, empirical, and normative challenges*. Oxford : Oxford University Press.

——— (2012), 'Multilevel Governance,' in *The Oxford Companion to Comparative Politics*, Volume 1. Oxford: Oxford University Press, 116–20.

Pierson, P. (2000), 'Path Dependence, Increasing Returns, and the Study of Politics,' *American Political Science Review* 94 (2), 251–67.

Poggi, A. (2007), 'Soft law nell'ordinamento comunitario,' in *L'integrazione dei sistemi costituzionali europeo e nazionali* AIC, Annuario 2005, Padova, 2007, p. 369.

Poiares Maduro, M. (2002), *We, the Court*. Oxford: Oxford University Press.

——— (2003), 'Contrapunctual Law: Europe's Constitutional Pluralism in Action,' in N. Walker (ed.), *Sovereignty in Transition*. Oxford: Hart Publishing.

Preston, P. (1986), *The triumph of democracy in Spain*. London: Routledge.

Priban, J. (2007), *Legal Symbolism: On Law, Time and European Identity. Applied Legal Philosophy*. Farnham: Ashgate Publishing.

——— (2012), 'Constitutionalism as Fear of the Political? A comparative analysis of Teubner's Constitutional Fragments and Thornhill's *A Sociology of Constitutions*,' *Journal of Law and Society* 39 (3), 441–71.

Pridham, G. (2005), *Designing democracy: EU enlargement and regime change in post-communist Europe*. Basingstoke : Palgrave MacMillan.

——— (2007), 'The Effects of the European Union's Democratic Conditionality: The Case of Romania during Accession,' *Journal of Communist Studies and Transition Politics* 23 (2), 233–58.

Radaelli, C.M. (2005), 'Diffusion without Convergence: How Political Context Shapes the Adoption of Regulatory Impact Assessment,' *Journal of European Public Policy* 12 (5), 924–43.

Radaelli, C.M. and Vivien A. Schmidt (eds) (2005), *Policy change and discourse in Europe*. London: New York: Routledge.

Raustiala, K. (2005), 'Form and Substance in International Agreements,' *American Journal of International Law* 99 (3), 581–614.

Recommendation CM/Rec(2010)12 of the Committee of Ministers to member states on judges: independence, efficiency and responsibilities (Adopted by the Committee of Ministers on 17 November 2010 at the 1098th meeting of the Ministers' Deputies).

Rhodes, R. (1997), *Understanding Governance: Policy Networks, Governance, Reflexivity and Accountability*. Buckingham: Open University Press.

Ricoeur, P. (1995), 'Reflections on a New Ethos for Europe,' *Philosophy and Social Criticism* 21 (5).

Risse, T. (2000), 'Let's Argue! Persuasion and Deliberation in International Relations,' *International Organization* 54 (1), 1–39.

——— (2004), 'Global Governance and Communicative Action,' *Government and Opposition* 39 (2), 288–313.

Risse, T. and Sikkink, K. (1999), 'The Socialization of International Human Rights Norms into Domestic Practices: Introduction,' in Thomas Risse et al. (eds), *The Power of Human Rights: International Norms & Domestic Change*. Cambridge: Cambridge University Press.

Rogowski, R. (2007) 'Flexicurity and Reflexive Coordination of European Social and Employment Policies,' in H. Jørgensen and P.K. Madsen (eds), *Flexicurity and Beyond. Finding a new agenda for the European Social Model*. Copenhagen: DJØF Publishing, 132–53.

Rosas, A. (2007), 'The European Court of Justice in Context: Forms and Patterns of Judicial Dialogue,' *European Journal of Law Studies* 2.

Rose, R. (1993), *Lesson-Drawing in Public Policy*. London: Chatham House.

Rosenbloom, D. (1998), *Understanding Management, Politics, and Law in the Public Sector*. New York: McGraw Hill.

Russell, P. (2001), 'Toward a General Theory of Judicial Independence,' in Peter Russell and David O'Brien (eds), *Judicial Independence in the Age of Democracy*, London: University Press of Virginia, 1–24.

Russell, P.H. and D.M. O'Brien (eds) (2001), *Judicial independence in the age of democracy: critical perspectives from around the world*. Charlottesville; London: University press of Virginia.

Sadurski, W. (2003), 'Constitutional Courts, Individual Rights and the Problem of Judicial Activism in Postcommunist Central Europe,' in J. Priban, P. Roberts and J. Young (eds), *Systems of Justice in Transition: Central European Experiences since 1989*. Farnham: Ashgate, 13–28..

——— (2004), 'Accession's democracy dividend: The impact of the EU enlargement upon democracy in the new member states of Central and Eastern Europe,' *European Law Review* 10, 371–401.

Sajo, A. (2006) *Abuse: The Dark Side of Fundamental Rights*. Utrecht: Eleven International Publishing.

Salas, D. (2000), *Le Tiers Pouvoir, vers une autre justice*. Paris: Hachette.

Salas, D. and Epineuse, H. (2004), *L'*éthique du juge: Une approche éuropéenne. Paris: Dalloz.

Santos, Boaventura de Sousa (2005), 'Beyond Neoliberal Governance: The World Social Forum as Subaltern Cosmopolitan Politics and Legality,' in Boaventura de Sousa Santos and César Rodríguez-Garavito (eds), *Law and Globalization from Below. Towards a Cosmopolitan Legality*. Cambridge: Cambridge University Press.

Santos, Boaventura de Sousa, Marques, M.M.L., Pedroso, J. and Ferreira, P.L. (1996), *Os Tribunais nas Sociedades Contemporâneas –O caso português*. Porto: Edições Afrontamento, 2nd edition.

Sarat, A. and Scheingold, S. (2005), *Something to Believe In: Politics, Professionalism, and Cause Lawyering*. Stanford, CA.: Stanford University Press.

Sarkin, J. and Binchy, J. (2004), *The Administration of Justice: Current Themes in Comparative Perspective*. Dublin: Four Court Press.

Sasse, G. (2005), 'Securitization or Securing Rights? Exploring the Conceptual Foundations of Policies towards Minorities and Migrants in Europe,' *JCMS: Journal of Common Market Studies* 43 (4), 673–93.

Scharpf, Fritz W. (1990), 'Games real actors could play: The problem of connectedness.' MPIfG Discussion Paper, 90/8. Available at: http://hdl.handle.net/11858/00-001M-0000-0012-5B12-A

Schedler, A., Diamond, L. and Plattner M. (eds) (1999), *The Self-Restraining State. Power and Accountability in New Democracies*. Boulder, CO: Lynne Rienner Publishers.

Scheeck, L. (2009), 'La diplomatie commune des cours européennes,' in P. Mbongo and A. Vauchez (eds), *Dans la fabrique du droit européen, Scènes, acteurs et publics de la Cour de justice des Communautés européennes*. Bruxelles: Ed. Bruylant.

Schimmelfenning, F. (2000), 'International Socialization in the New Europe. Rational Action in an Institutional Environment,' *European Journal of International Relations* 6 (1), 109–39.

Schimmelfennig, F. and Sedelmeier, U. (2004), 'Governance by conditionality: EU rule transfer to the candidate countries of Central and Eastern Europe,' *Journal of European Public Policies* 11, 669–87.

Schwellnus, G. (2005), 'Adoption of Non-Discrimination and Minority Protection Rules in Romania, Hungary and Poland,' in F. Schimmelfennig and U. Sedelmeier (eds), *The Europeanization of Central and Eastern Europe*. Ithaca, NY: Cornell University Press, 51–70.

Scott, J. and Trubek, D. (2002), 'Mind the Gap: Law and New Approaches to Governance in the European Union,' *European Law Journal* 8 (1), 1–18.

Scott, R. (2007), *Institutions and Organizations: Ideas and Interests*. London: Sage.

Selznick, P. (1949), *TVA and the Grass Roots: A Study in the Sociology of Formal Organization*. Berkeley: University of California Press.

Senden, L. (2004), *Soft Law in European Community Law*. Portland: Hart Publishing.

Serzysko, A. (2011), Eurojust and the European Judicial network on a New Legal Basis. *ERA Forum* 11, 585–600.

Shany, Y. (2007), *Regulating Jurisdictional Relations Between National and International Courts*. Oxford: Oxford University Press.

Shapiro, M. (1981), *Courts. A Comparative and Political Analysis*. Chicago: University of Chicago Press.

Shugart, M.S. and Carey, J.M. (1992), *Presidents and Assemblies: Constitutional Design and Electoral Dynamics*. Cambridge and New York: Cambridge University Press.

Simmel, G. (1917), *Grundfragen der Soziologie*. Berlin: Göschen.

Simmons, B. and Elkins, Z. (2004), 'The Globalization of Liberalization: Policy Diffusion in the International Political Economy,' *American Political Science Review* 98 (1), 171–89.

Slaughter, A.M. (2001), 'The Accountability of Government Networks,' *Indiana Journal of Global Legal Studies* 8, 347–81.

——— (2004), *A New World Order*. Princeton: Princeton University Press.

Slaughter, A.M., Stone Sweet, A. and Weiler, J.H.H. (eds) (1998), *The European Courts and National Courts: Doctrine and Jurisprudence*. Oxford: Hart Publishing.

Smith, A. (1796), *The Wealth of Nations*. Chicago: University of Chicago Press.

Smolej, M. (with T. Johnsen) (2012), 'Time management of justice systems: a Northern Europe study.' Report of the European Commission for the Efficiency of Justice (CEPEJ). Available at http://www.coe.int/t/dghl/cooperation/cepej/Delais/GestionTemps_en.pdf

Smulovitz, E. and Peruzzotti, C. (2000), 'Societal Accountability in Latin America,' *Journal of Democracy* 11 (4), 147–58.

Sólyom, L. (2003), 'The role of constitutional courts in the transition to democracy,' *International Sociology* 18, 133–61.

Stanciulescu, A. (2010), 'Romania: A Personalistic Approach to Accountability,' in W. Sadurski and L. Morlino (eds), *Democratization and the European Union. London, New York: Routledge.*

Stockholm Programme (2010) – An Open And Secure Europe Serving And Protecting Citizens (2010/C 115/01).

Stone Sweet, A. (2000), *Governing with Judges: constitutional politics in Europe*. Oxford: Oxford University Press.

——— (2002), 'Judicialization and the Construction of Governance,' in M. Shapiro and A. Stone-Sweet (eds), *On Law, Politics, Judicialization*. Oxford: Oxford University Press.

Stone Sweet, A. and Sandholtz, W. (1997), 'European Integration and Supranational Governance,' *Journal of European Public Policy* 4.

Stone Sweet, A., Sandholtz, W. and Fligstein, N. (2001), *The Institutionalization of Europe*. Oxford University Press, Oxford.

Tarfusser, C. (2008), 'Progetto di riorganizzazione della procura di Bolzano.' Available at: http://noisefromamerika.org/articolo/progetto-riorganizzazione-procura-bolzano

Teubner, G. (1989), 'How the Law Thinks: Toward a Constructivist Epistemology of Law,' *Law and Society Review* 23, 727–57.

The Budapest Times (2013), 'Controversial judicial reform to be scrapped,' June 16. Available at: http://www.budapesttimes.hu/2013/06/16/controversial-judicial-reform-to-be-scrapped/.

Thomas C. (2006), 'Judicial Diversity and the Appointment of Deputy District Judges,' Unpublished Report, London.

Tolbert, P.S. and Zucker, L.G. (1983), 'Institutional Sources of Change in the Formal Structure of Organizations: The Diffusion of Civil Service Reform, 1880–1935,' *American Sociological Quarterly* 28, 22–39.

Toniatti, R. (2011), 'Il sistema delle reti giudiziarie nel contesto dello Spazio di libertà, sicurezza e giustizia (SLSG) dell'Unione europea,' in R. Toniatti, M. Magrassi and M. Zenatti (eds), *Le nuove competenze dell'Unione europea in materia di giustizia*. Trento: Centro di Documentazione Europea.

Toniatti, R. and Magrassi, M. (eds) (2011), *Magistratura, giurisdizione ed equilibri istituzionali. Dinamiche e confronti europei e comparati*. Dipartimento di Scienze Giuridiche Università di Trento XCV.

Toniatti, R., Magrassi, M. and Zenatti, M. (2010), *Le nuove competenze dell'Unione in materia di giustizia*. Trento: Provincia Autonoma di Trento.

Tribulane di Milano (2013), *Social Budget Report of the Court of Milan* (Bilancio di responsabilità sociale del Tribunale di Milano). Available at: https://www.tribunale.milano.it/files/BRS%20Tribunale%20Milano%202013.pdf

Trubek, D.M. (2004), 'The Rule of Law in Development Assistance: Past, Present, and Future,' Occasional Papers, University of Wisconsin, September.

True, J. and Mintrom, M. (2001), 'Transnational Networks and Policy Diffusion: The Case of Gender Mainstreaming,' *International Studies Quarterly* 45 (1), 27–57.

Tyler, T.R. (2003), 'Procedural Justice, Legitimacy, and the Effective Rule of Law,' *Crime and Justice* 30, 283–357.

Vachudova, M.A. (2007), 'Historical institutionalism and the EU's eastern enlargement,' in K. McNamara and S. Meunier (eds), *Making History:*

European Integration and Institutional Change at Fifty. Oxford: Oxford University Press, 105–22.

Van Harten, H. (2012), 'Who's Afraid of a True European Judicial Culture? On judicial training, pluralism and national autonomy.' Working Paper presented at the Second REALaw Research Forum: 'Pluralism in European Administrative Law' Groningen. Available at: http://www.rug.nl/Rechten/faculteit/vakgroepen/

Vauchez, A. (2007), 'Embedded Law: Political Sociology of the European Community Law,' Fiesole, EUI Working papers, RSCAS 2007/23.

——— (2008), 'The Force of a Weak Field. Law and Lawyers in the Government of Europe,' *International Political Sociology* 2, 128–144.

Vauchez, A. and de Witte, B. (2013), *Lawyering Europe. European Law as a Transnational Social Field*. Oxford: Hart Publishing.

Vecchi, G. (2013), 'Studying Good Practices to Lesson-Drawing and Transfer: Introduction to the Causal Mechanisms Approach. A proposal for Exchanges Among European Networks on Time- oriented Policies,' in D. Henkel et al., *Space-Design of the Public City*. Berlin: Springer, 255–88.

Voermans, W. (2007), 'Judicial Transparency Furthering Public Accountability for New Judiciary,' *Utrecht Law Review* 3 (1), 148–59.

Voigt, S. (2005), 'The Economic Effects of Judicial Accountability. Some Preliminary Insights.' ICER Working Papers Series, No.19, Turin: ICER.

Walker, N. (2003), *Sovereignty in Transition*. Oxford: Hart Publishing.

Wallace, H. and Wallace, W. (2000), *Policy-making in the European Union*. Oxford: Oxford University Press.

Wedel, J. (2009), *Shadow Elite: How the World's New Power Brokers Undermine Democracy, Government, and the Free Market*. New York: Basic Books.

Weick, K. (1976), 'Educational Organizations as Loosely Coupled Systems,' *Administrative Science Quarterly*, 21 (1), 1–19.

——— (2000), *Making Sense of the Organization*. New York: Wiley.

Wessels, W. (1998), 'Comitology: Fusion in Action – Politico-Administrative Trends in the EU System,' *Journal of European Public Policy* 5, 209.

Whitehead, L. (ed.) (2001), *The international dimensions of democratization: Europe and the Americas*. Oxford: Oxford University Press.

Whytock, C.A. (2009), 'Domestic Courts and Global Governance,' *Tulane Law Review* 84 (67).

——— (2012), 'Transnational Judicial Governance,' Legal Studies Research Paper Series No. 2012–39.

Wouters, J. and Naerts, F. (2004), 'Of Arrest Warrant, Terrorist Offences and Extradition Deals: An Appraisal of the EU's Main Criminal Law Measures Against Terrorism After 11 September,' *Common Market Law Review* 41, 909–35.

Xilo, G. (2010), 'Il piano strategico della giustizia nella città di Milano,' *Quaderni di Giustizia ed organizzazione* 6.

Youngs, R. (2001), 'European Union Democracy Promotion Policies: Ten Years On,' *European Foreign Affairs Review* 6 (3), 355–73.

Zan, S. (2011), *Le organizzazioni complesse. Logiche di azione dei sistemi a legame debole*. Roma: Carocci.

Zemanek J. (2003), 'Making of The European Constitution: The Czech View,' Ingolf Pernice and Roberto Miccù (eds), *The European Constitution in the Making*. Rome: Nomos Editions.

Zielonka, J. and Pravda, A. (eds) (2001), *International and transnational factors*. Oxford: Oxford University Press.

Zürn, M. (2000), 'Democratic Governance Beyond the Nation-State,' *European Journal of International Relations* 6 (2), 183–221.

Index

For Product Safety Concerns and Information please contact our EU representative GPSR@taylorandfrancis.com Taylor & Francis Verlag GmbH, Kaufingerstraße 24, 80331 München, Germany